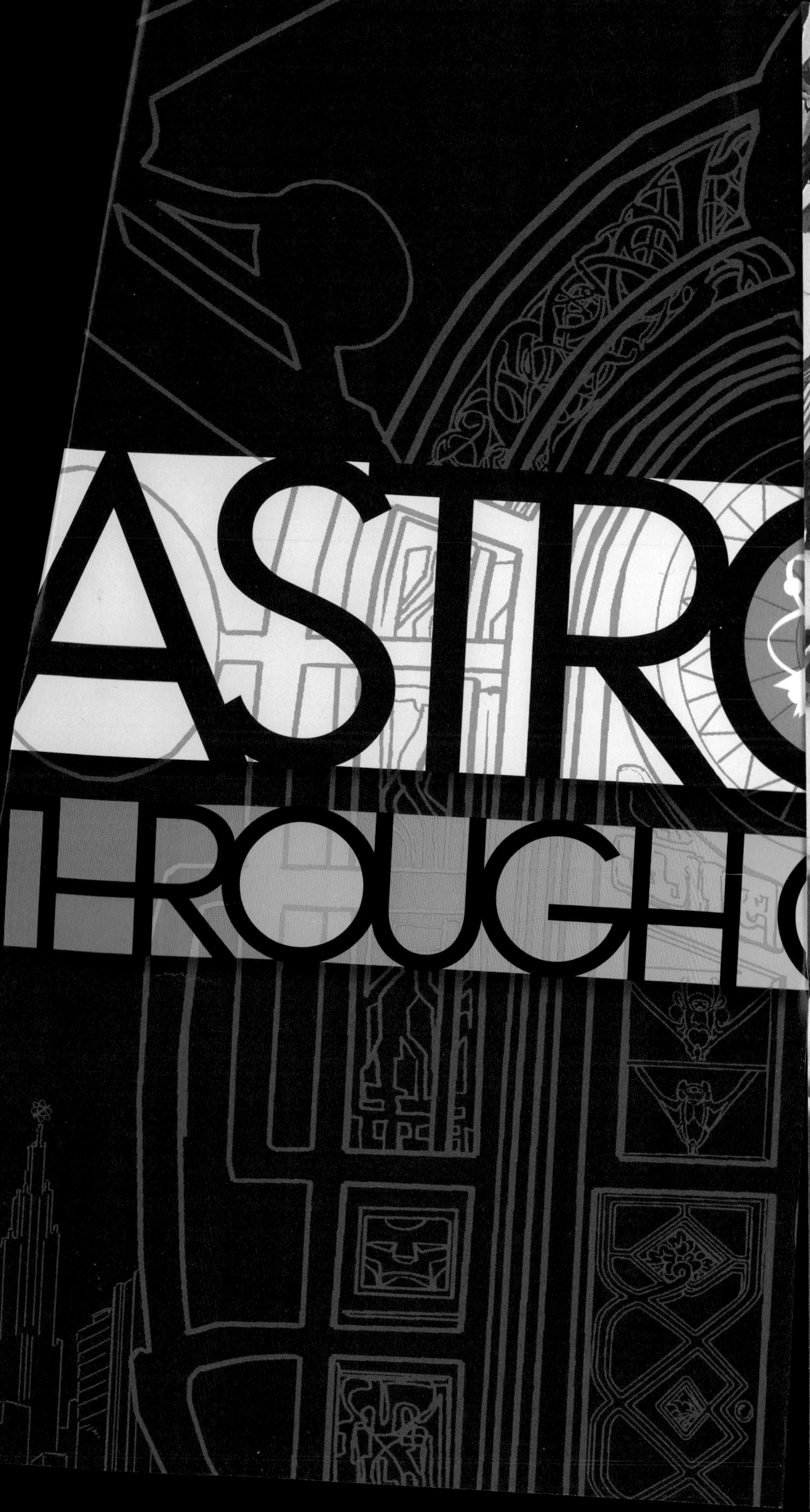
ASTR
ROUGH
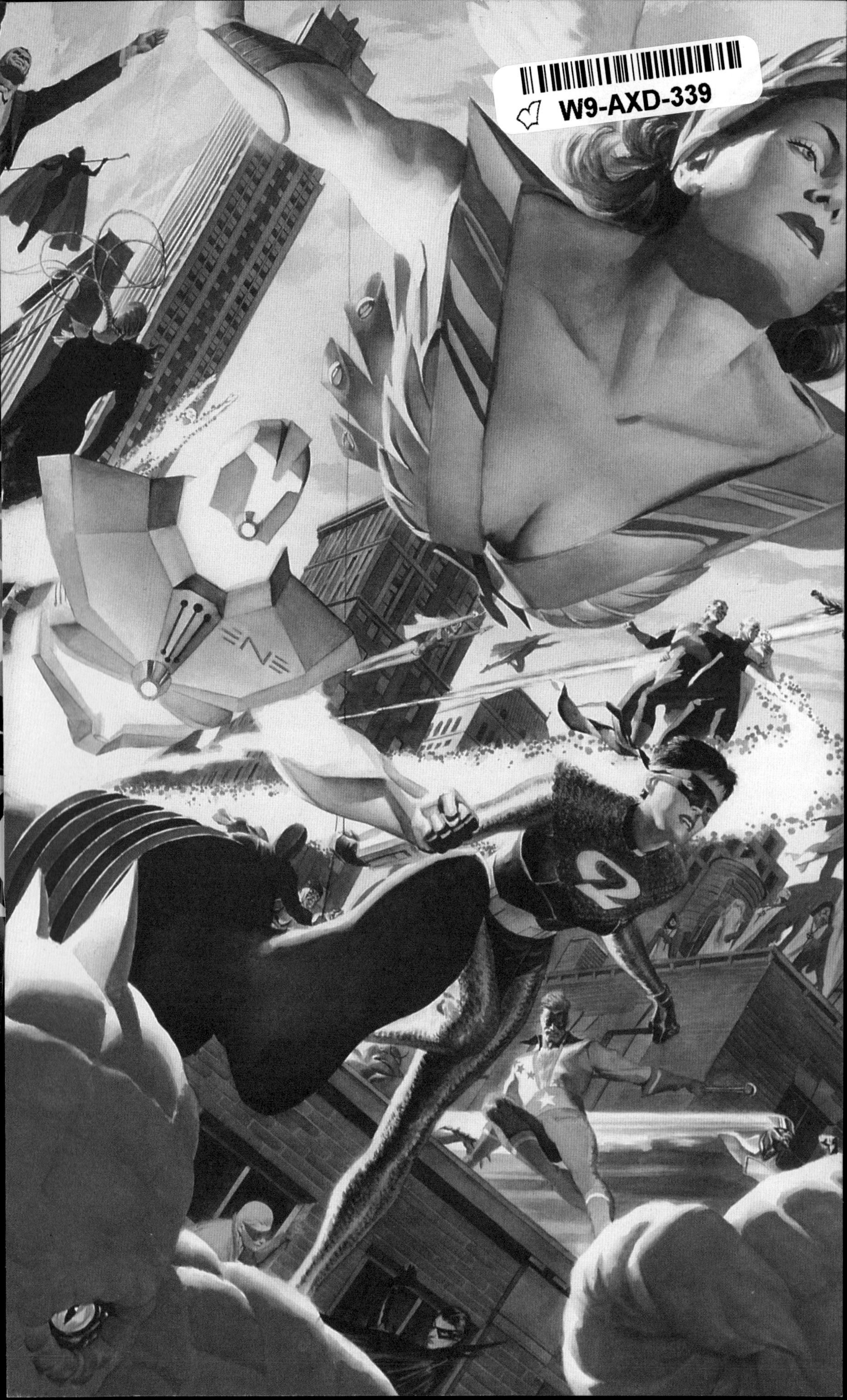

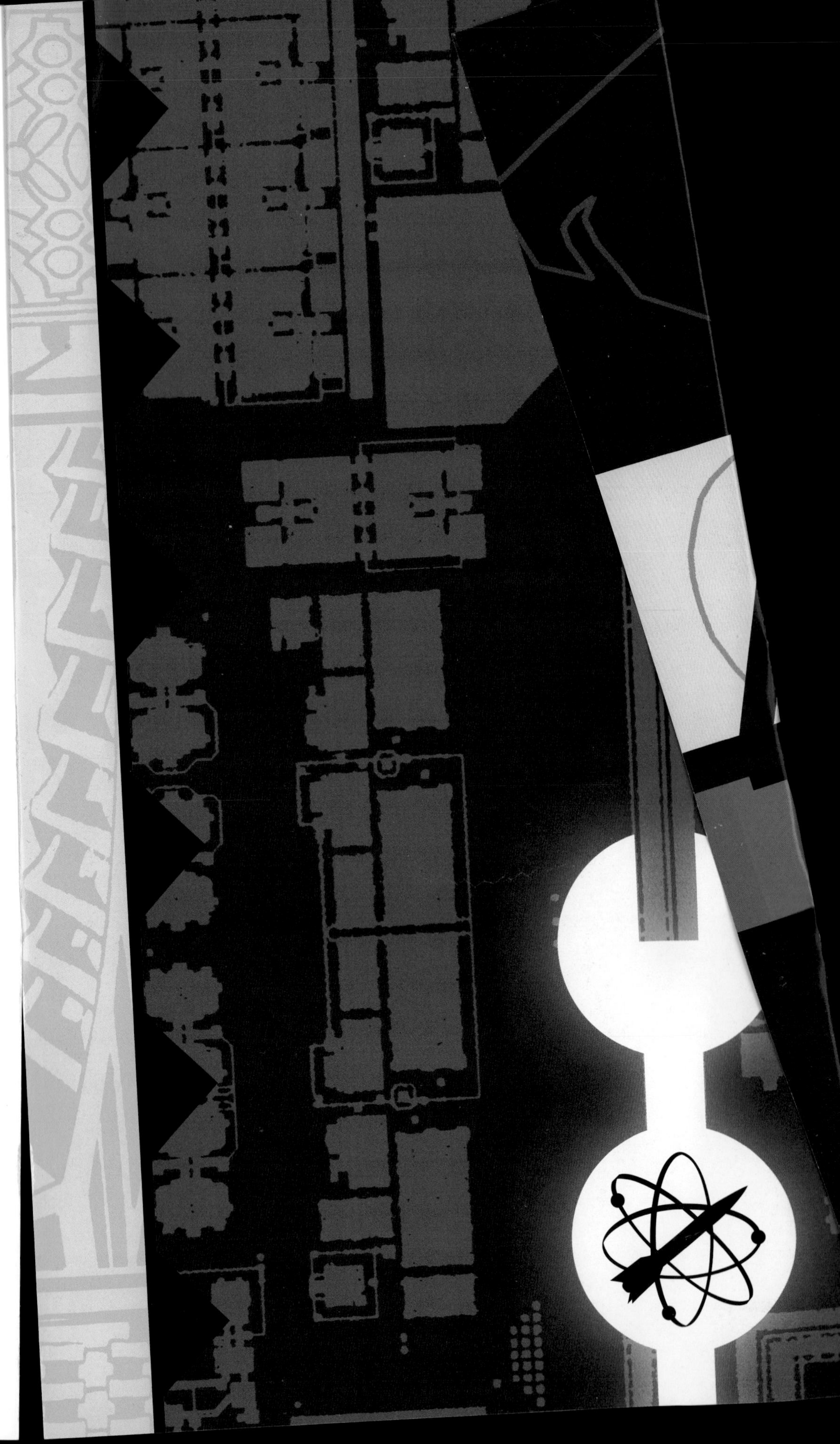

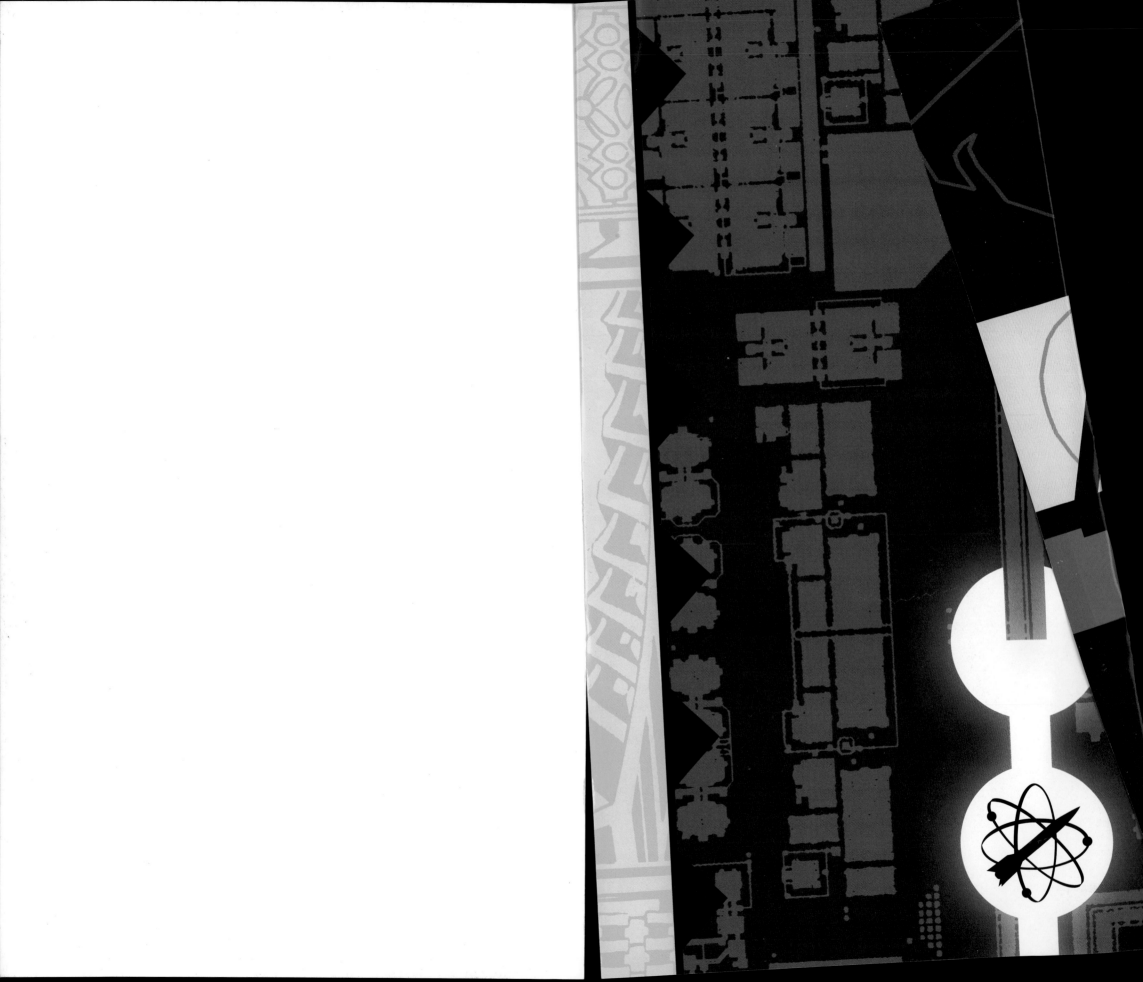

O CITY
OPEN DOORS

KURT BUSIEK
WRITER

BRENT ERIC ANDERSON
ARTIST

ALEX ROSS
COVERS

ALEX SINCLAIR &
WENDY BROOME
COLORS

JG ROSHELL & COMICRAFT'S
JIMMY BETANCOURT
LETTERING & DESIGN

ASTRO CITY
CREATED BY BUSIEK,
ANDERSON & ROSS

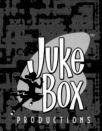

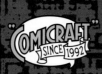

RICHARD STARKINGS
Art Director

ART NICHOLS Endpapers

Kristy Quinn	Editor
Jessica Chen	Assistant Editor
Robbin Brosterman	Design Director – Books
Shelly Bond	Executive Editor – Vertigo
Hank Kanalz	Senior VP – Vertigo & Integrated Publishing
Diane Nelson	President
Dan DiDio and Jim Lee	Co-Publishers
Geoff Johns	Chief Creative Officer
John Rood	Executive VP – Sales, Marketing & Business Development
Amy Genkins	Senior VP–Business & Legal Affairs
Nairi Gardiner	Senior VP – Finance
Jeff Boison	VP – Publishing Planning
Mark Chiarello	VP – Art Direction & Design
John Cunningham	VP – Marketing
Terri Cunningham	VP – Editorial Administration
Alison Gill	Senior VP – Manufacturing & Operations
Jay Kogan	VP – Business & Legal Affairs, Publishing
Jack Mahan	VP – Business Affairs, Talent
Nick Napolitano	VP – Manufacturing Administration
Sue Pohja	VP – Book Sales
Courtney Simmons	Senior VP – Publicity
Bob Wayne	Senior VP – Sales

SUSTAINABLE FORESTRY INITIATIVE
Certified Chain of Custody
At Least 20% Certified Forest Content
www.sfiprogram.org
SFI-01042

Fiber used in this product line meets the sourcing requirements of the SFI program.
www.sfiprogram.org
SGS-SFICOC-0130

Printed by RR Donnelley, Salem, VA. 3/7/2014.

DC Comics, a Warner Bros. Entertainment Company.

ISBN: 978-1-4012-4752-2

ASTRO CITY: THROUGH OPEN DOORS collects material originally published in ASTRO CITY #1-6.

CONTENTS

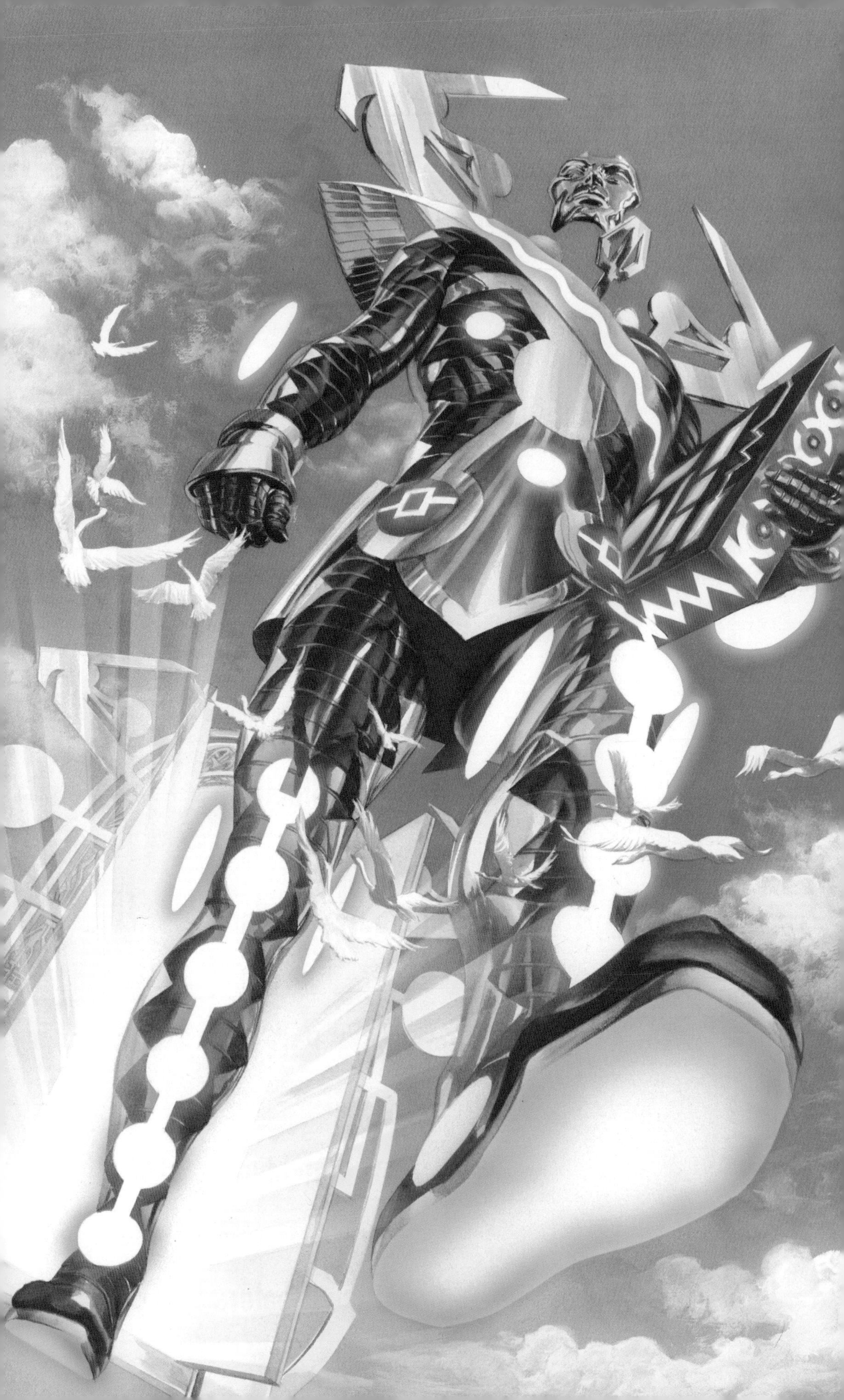

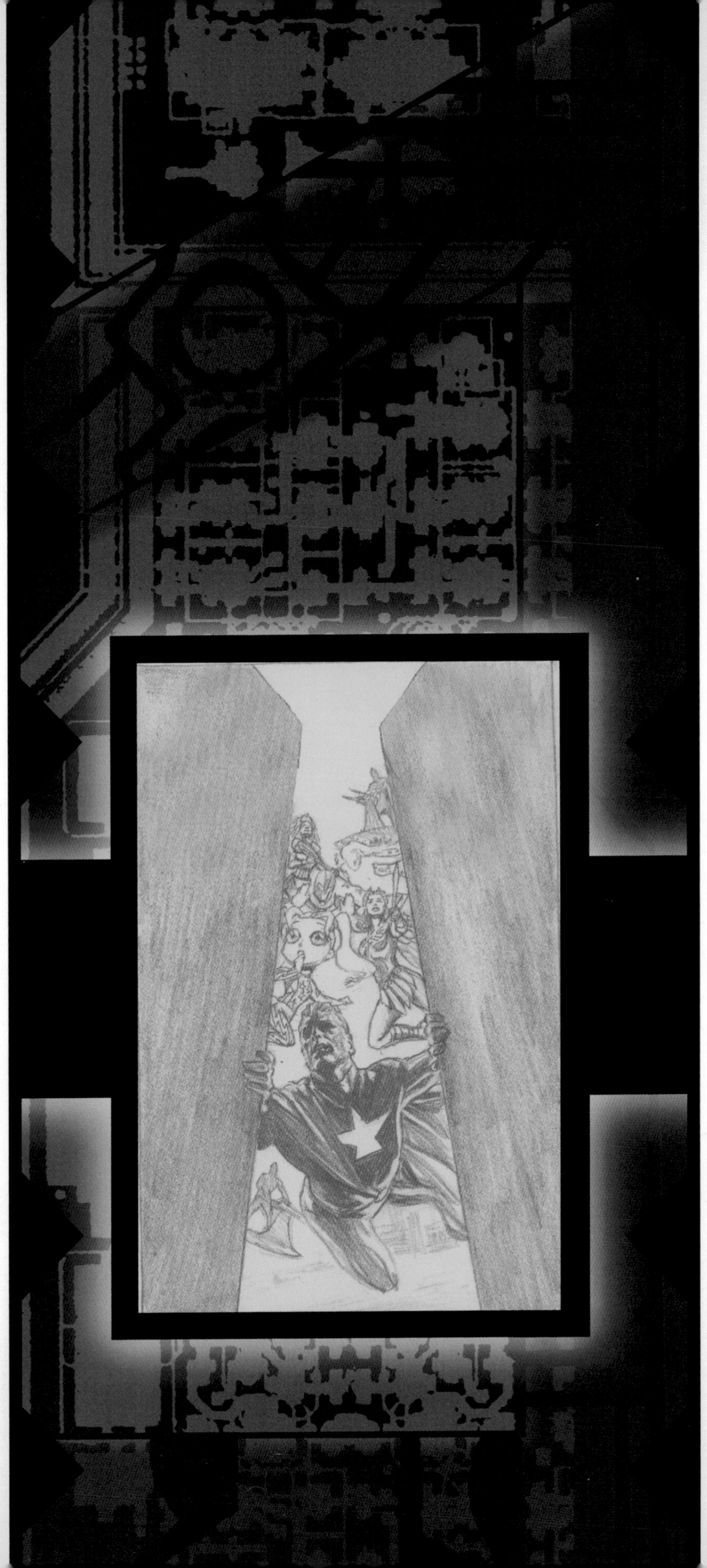

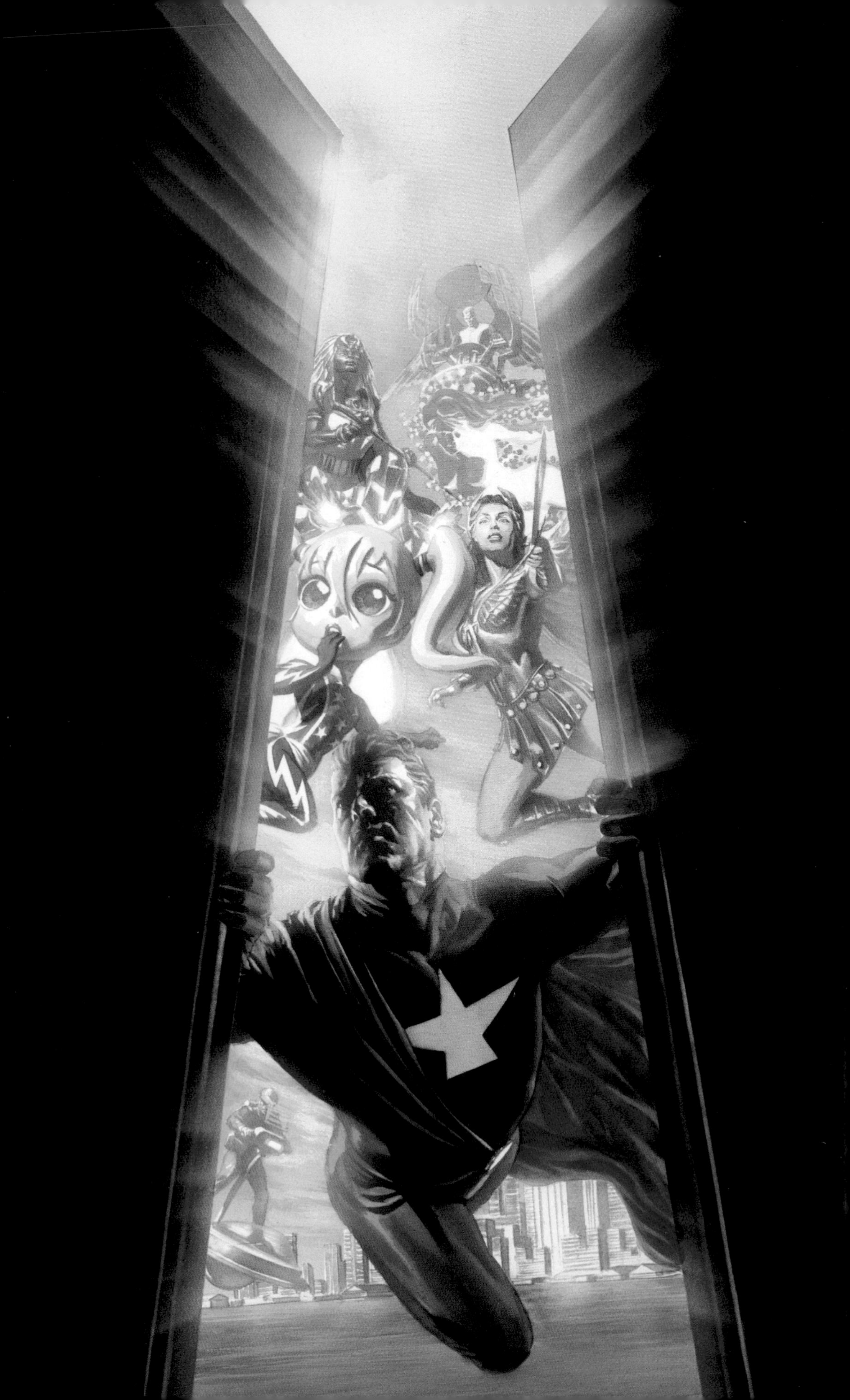

IT'S ALL TIED **TOGETHER**, SEE? DAME PROGRESS AND **JAZZBABY** IN '19, WHAT HAPPENED TO THE **BLASPHEMY AGENCY**, THE TREMORS FROM THE **HOLLOW BLOCKS** --

IT'S THE **OUBOR**, BEHIND IT ALL. AND EVERY DAY, ITS SHADOW **GROWS**. EVEN **NOW**, IT MIGHT BE TOO LATE, BUT WE HAVE TO --

WHAT?

LOOK, I CAN'T EXPLAIN EVERYTHING **ALL AT ONCE** -- WE'D BE HERE FOR LIKE A **DOZEN ISSUES** AND YOUR EYES WOULD GLAZE OVER!

AND IT **WOULD NOTICE US!**

BUT THE **OUBOR** -- IT LISTENS TO THE COMMUNICATIONS BANDS. RADIO, VIDEO, THE **NEWS**, A LOT OF THE INTERNET -- EVEN **FACE-TO-FACE**, WITH THE BIGGER NAMES.

AND I'VE **GOT** TO HAVE A **NETWORK**. A WAY TO REACH OUT, THAT IT CAN'T DETECT.

THAT'S **YOU.**

THAT'S **ALL** OF YOU.

HERE. I'LL SHOW YOU HOW IT **WORKS.**

DOWNTOWN **ASTRO CITY.** RIGHT NOW. THE **IRON LEGION** ARE MAKING A COMMANDO STRIKE ON THE ELLSWORTH MUSEUM --

ASTRO CITY ROCKET

HARLOW BLOCKS EVACUATED
AFTER WARPITRON

PIKE'S PEAK EXPRESS CO.
FROM ST. JOSEPH

The Romeny
Democrat-American

OTHER DARING
CIETY ROBBERY:
JOHNNY RAGTIME?

Seattle Post-Intelligencer

TELLS OF 54-HOUR

Miner Saved After 54 Hrs.
Of Torture In Living Tomb

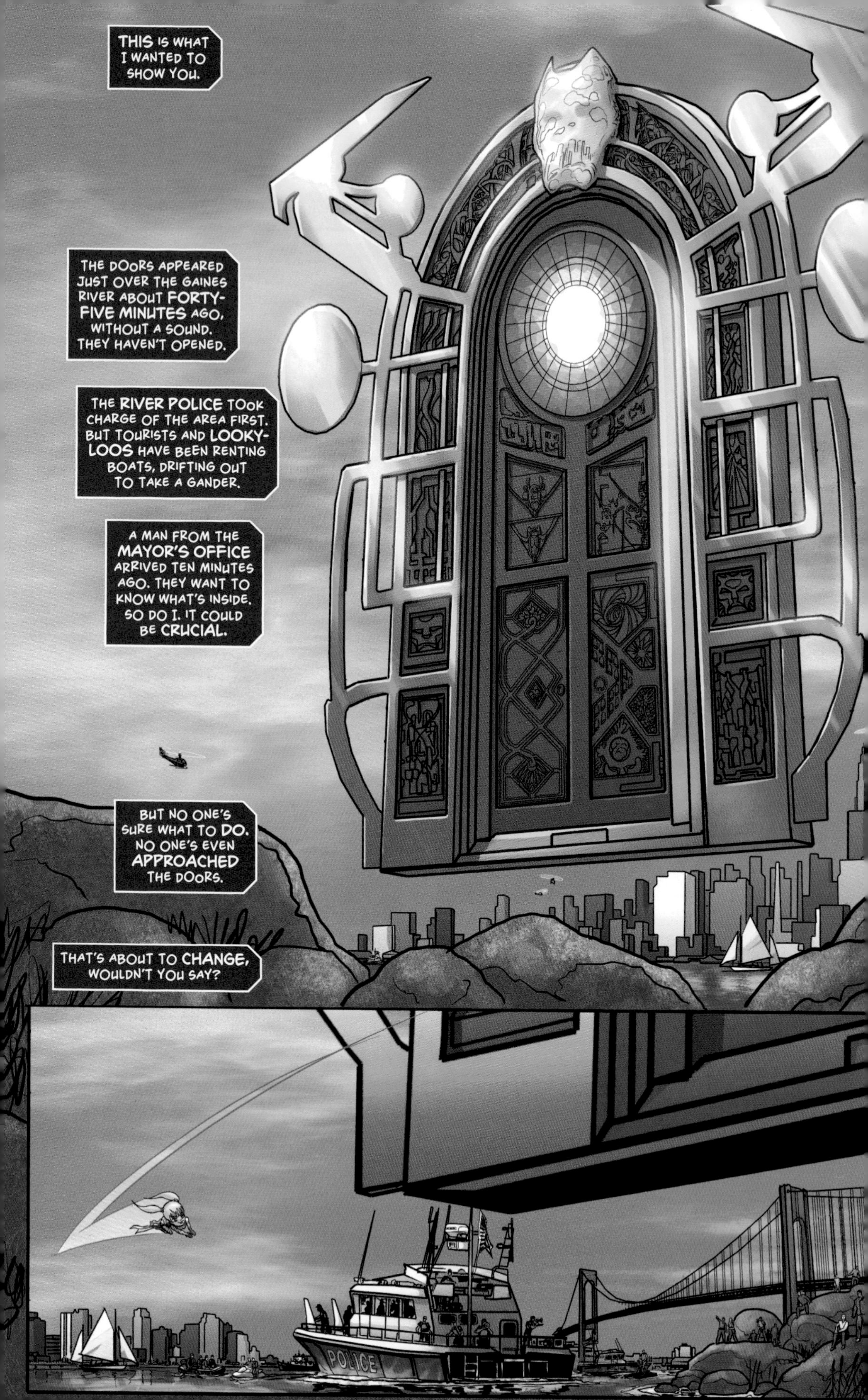
THIS IS WHAT I WANTED TO SHOW YOU.
THE DOORS APPEARED JUST OVER THE GAINES RIVER ABOUT FORTY-FIVE MINUTES AGO, WITHOUT A SOUND. THEY HAVEN'T OPENED.
THE RIVER POLICE TOOK CHARGE OF THE AREA FIRST. BUT TOURISTS AND LOOKY-LOOS HAVE BEEN RENTING BOATS, DRIFTING OUT TO TAKE A GANDER.
A MAN FROM THE MAYOR'S OFFICE ARRIVED TEN MINUTES AGO. THEY WANT TO KNOW WHAT'S INSIDE. SO DO I. IT COULD BE CRUCIAL.
BUT NO ONE'S SURE WHAT TO DO. NO ONE'S EVEN APPROACHED THE DOORS.
THAT'S ABOUT TO CHANGE, WOULDN'T YOU SAY?
POLICE

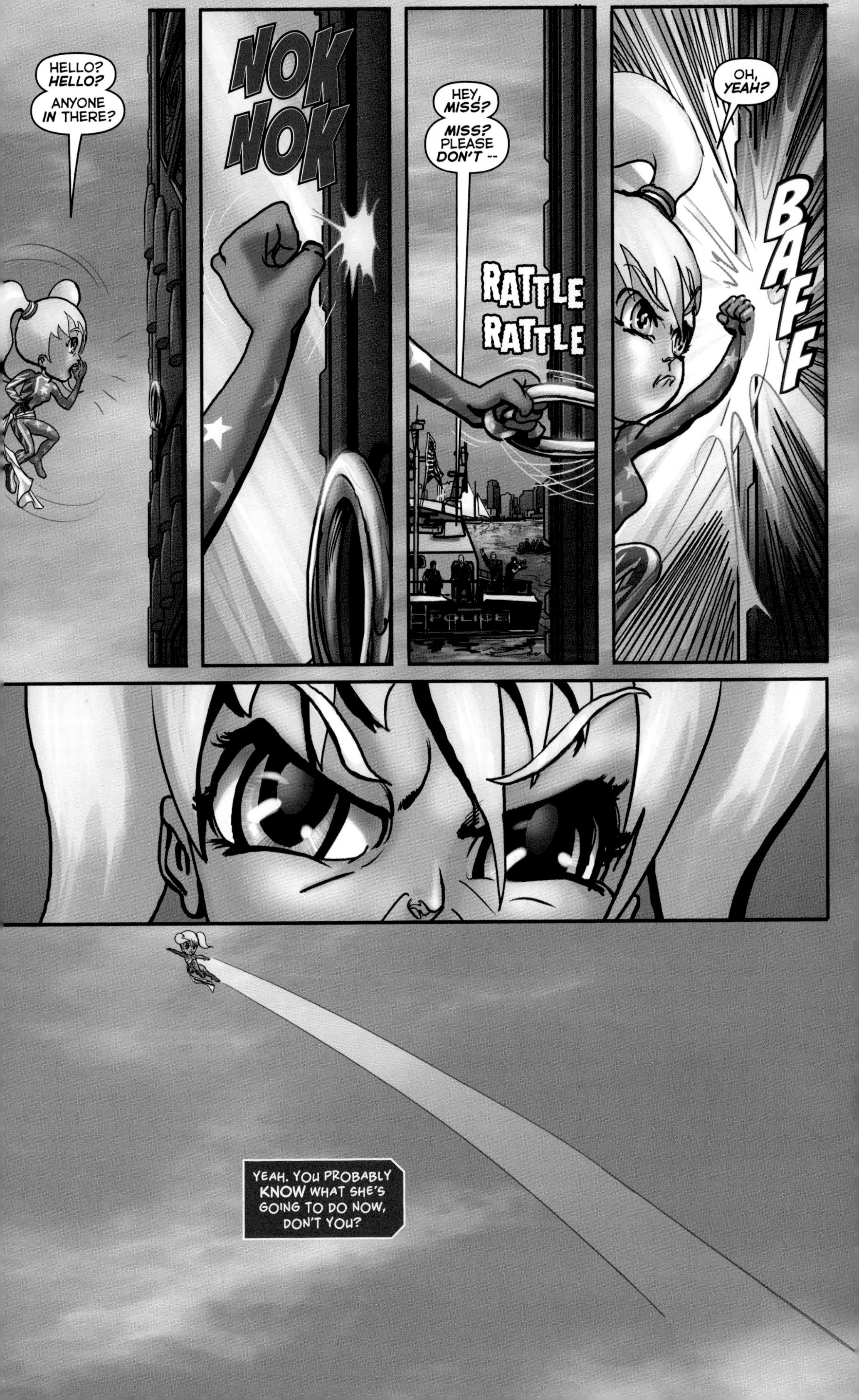
HELLO? HELLO? ANYONE IN THERE?
NOK NOK
HEY, MISS? MISS? PLEASE DON'T --
RATTLE RATTLE
OH, YEAH?
BAFF
YEAH. YOU PROBABLY KNOW WHAT SHE'S GOING TO DO NOW, DON'T YOU?

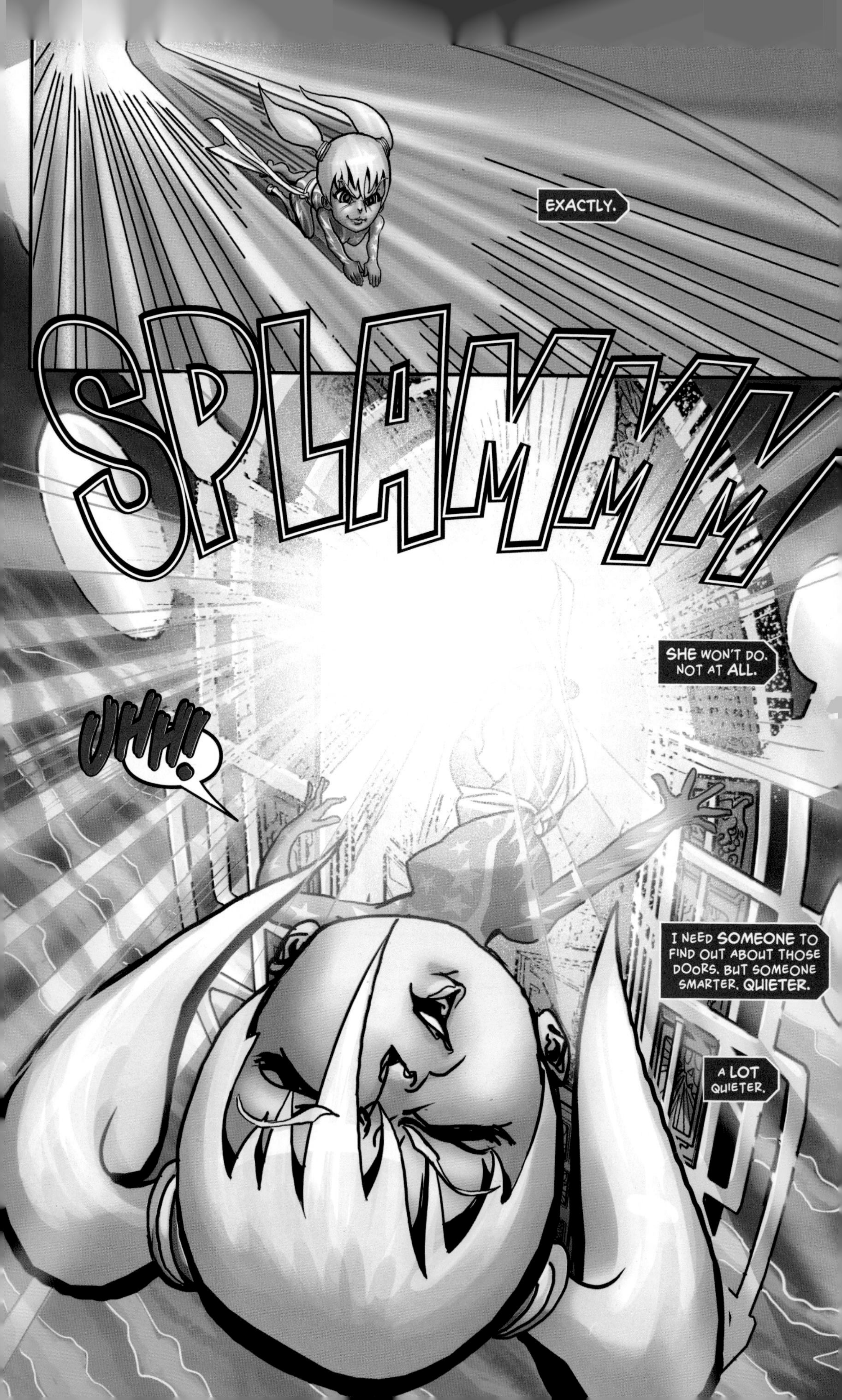
EXACTLY.
SPLAMMMM
SHE WON'T DO. NOT AT ALL.
UHH!
I NEED SOMEONE TO FIND OUT ABOUT THOSE DOORS. BUT SOMEONE SMARTER. QUIETER.
A LOT QUIETER.

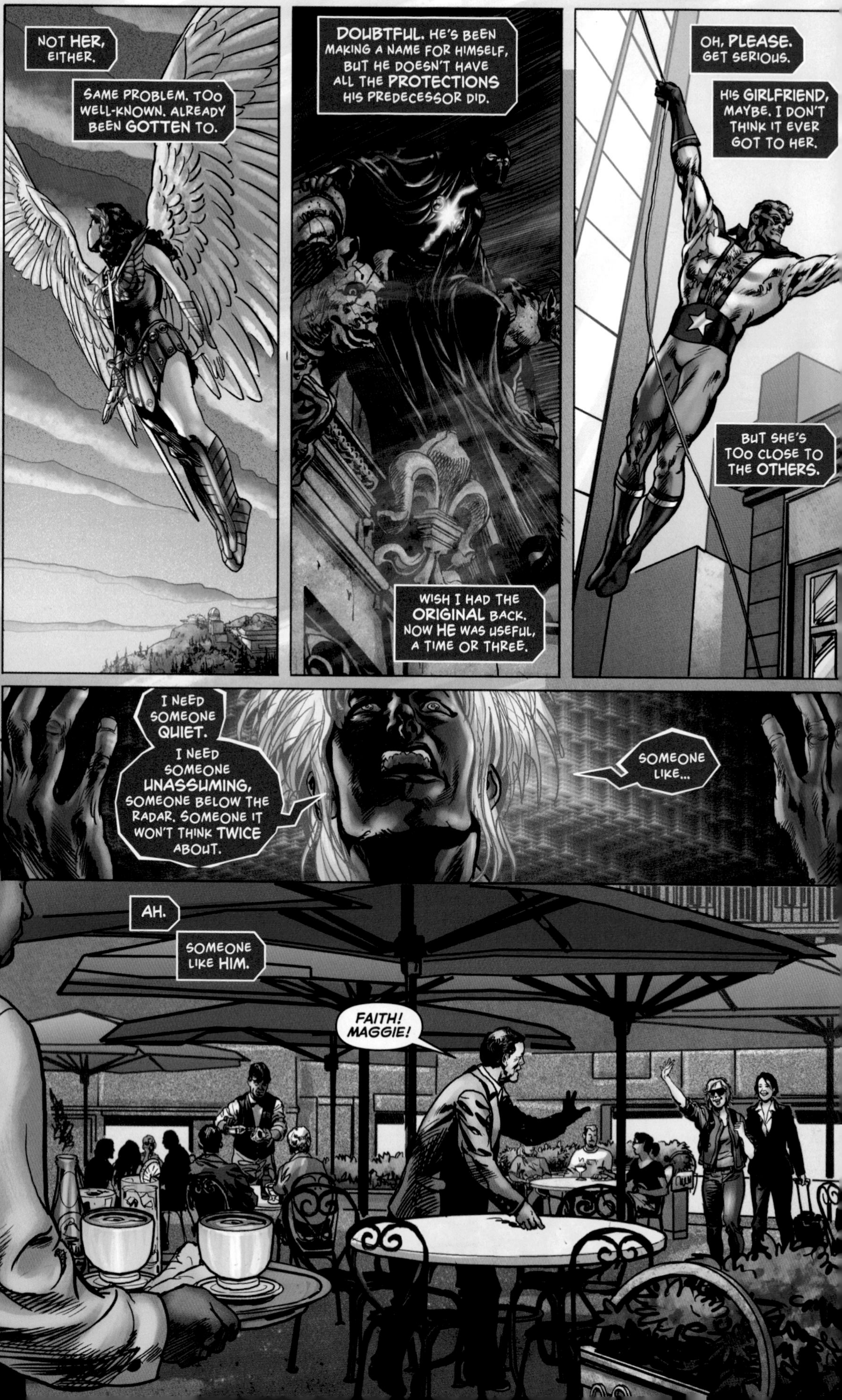
NOT HER, EITHER.
SAME PROBLEM. TOO WELL-KNOWN. ALREADY BEEN GOTTEN TO.
DOUBTFUL. HE'S BEEN MAKING A NAME FOR HIMSELF, BUT HE DOESN'T HAVE ALL THE PROTECTIONS HIS PREDECESSOR DID.
WISH I HAD THE ORIGINAL BACK. NOW HE WAS USEFUL, A TIME OR THREE.
OH, PLEASE. GET SERIOUS.
HIS GIRLFRIEND, MAYBE. I DON'T THINK IT EVER GOT TO HER.
BUT SHE'S TOO CLOSE TO THE OTHERS.
I NEED SOMEONE QUIET.
I NEED SOMEONE UNASSUMING, SOMEONE BELOW THE RADAR. SOMEONE IT WON'T THINK TWICE ABOUT.
SOMEONE LIKE...
AH.
SOMEONE LIKE HIM.
FAITH! MAGGIE!

HE'S BEEN AN INFORMATION SERVICES MANAGER FOR **HEMISPHERE** INSURANCE, KEEPING THEIR COMPUTERS RUNNING. HE TOOK **PRIDE** IN IT, AND IT KEPT THE GIRLS FED.

THERE WERE WOMEN -- **SOME** -- BUT NO ONE TO REPLACE THEIR MOTHER, NOT FOR VERY LONG.

SO WHAT **NOW?**

THE GIRLS ARE FINE. HE'LL **WORRY** ABOUT THEM, SURE, BUT HE KNOWS HE DOESN'T NEED TO.

WHAT HE WAS WORKING TO **DO,** HE'S DONE. AND WELL.

HE WROTE AN **APP,** FOR SMARTPHONES -- IT CORRELATES TRAFFIC AND NEWS REPORTS TO TELL YOU THE BEST **ROUTE** TO TAKE TO AVOID ANY **SUPERHERO TROUBLE** IN TOWN.

OR TO **FIND** IT -- HE WROTE THE APP TO GET HIMSELF TO **WORK** FASTER, BUT **TOURISTS** SNAPPED IT UP LEFT AND RIGHT.

-- BOULEVARD BURGER --

Boyer's Boutique

BUT **RETIREMENT?** THAT'S TOO FAR OFF.

IT MADE **GOOD MONEY.**

HE'S WRITTEN A FEW MORE, WHICH DID **OKAY.** HE COULD PROBABLY SUPPORT HIMSELF JUST DOING THAT, WORKING **FEWER HOURS.**

BUT WHAT **THEN?** HE WOULDN'T EVEN HAVE TO LEAVE THE APARTMENT.

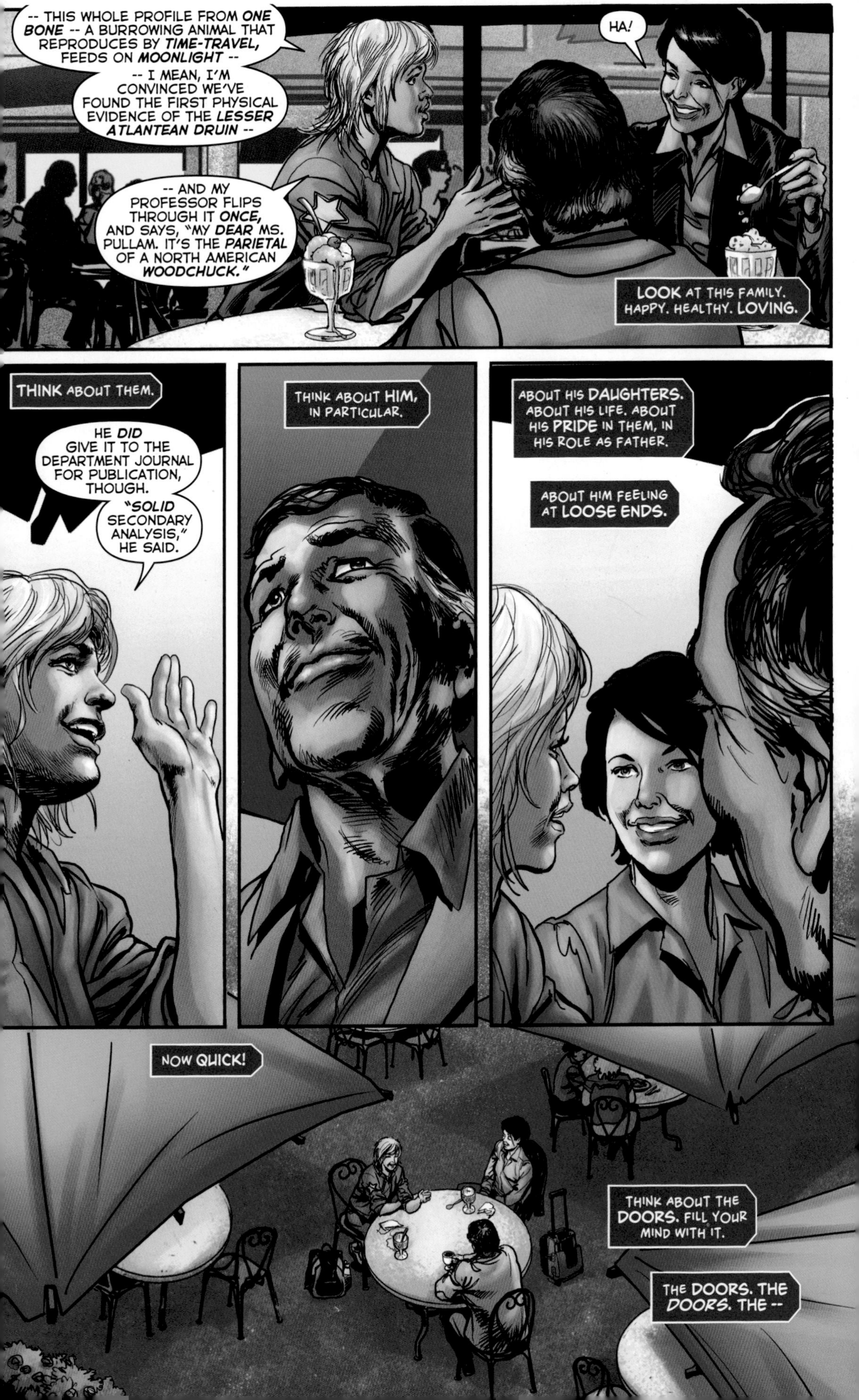

-- THIS WHOLE PROFILE FROM ONE BONE -- A BURROWING ANIMAL THAT REPRODUCES BY TIME-TRAVEL, FEEDS ON MOONLIGHT --
-- I MEAN, I'M CONVINCED WE'VE FOUND THE FIRST PHYSICAL EVIDENCE OF THE LESSER ATLANTEAN DRUIN --
HA!
-- AND MY PROFESSOR FLIPS THROUGH IT ONCE, AND SAYS, "MY DEAR MS. PULLAM. IT'S THE PARIETAL OF A NORTH AMERICAN WOODCHUCK."
LOOK AT THIS FAMILY. HAPPY. HEALTHY. LOVING.
THINK ABOUT THEM.
HE DID GIVE IT TO THE DEPARTMENT JOURNAL FOR PUBLICATION, THOUGH. "SOLID SECONDARY ANALYSIS," HE SAID.
THINK ABOUT HIM, IN PARTICULAR.
ABOUT HIS DAUGHTERS. ABOUT HIS LIFE. ABOUT HIS PRIDE IN THEM, IN HIS ROLE AS FATHER.
ABOUT HIM FEELING AT LOOSE ENDS.
NOW QUICK!
THINK ABOUT THE DOORS. FILL YOUR MIND WITH IT.
THE DOORS. THE DOORS. THE --

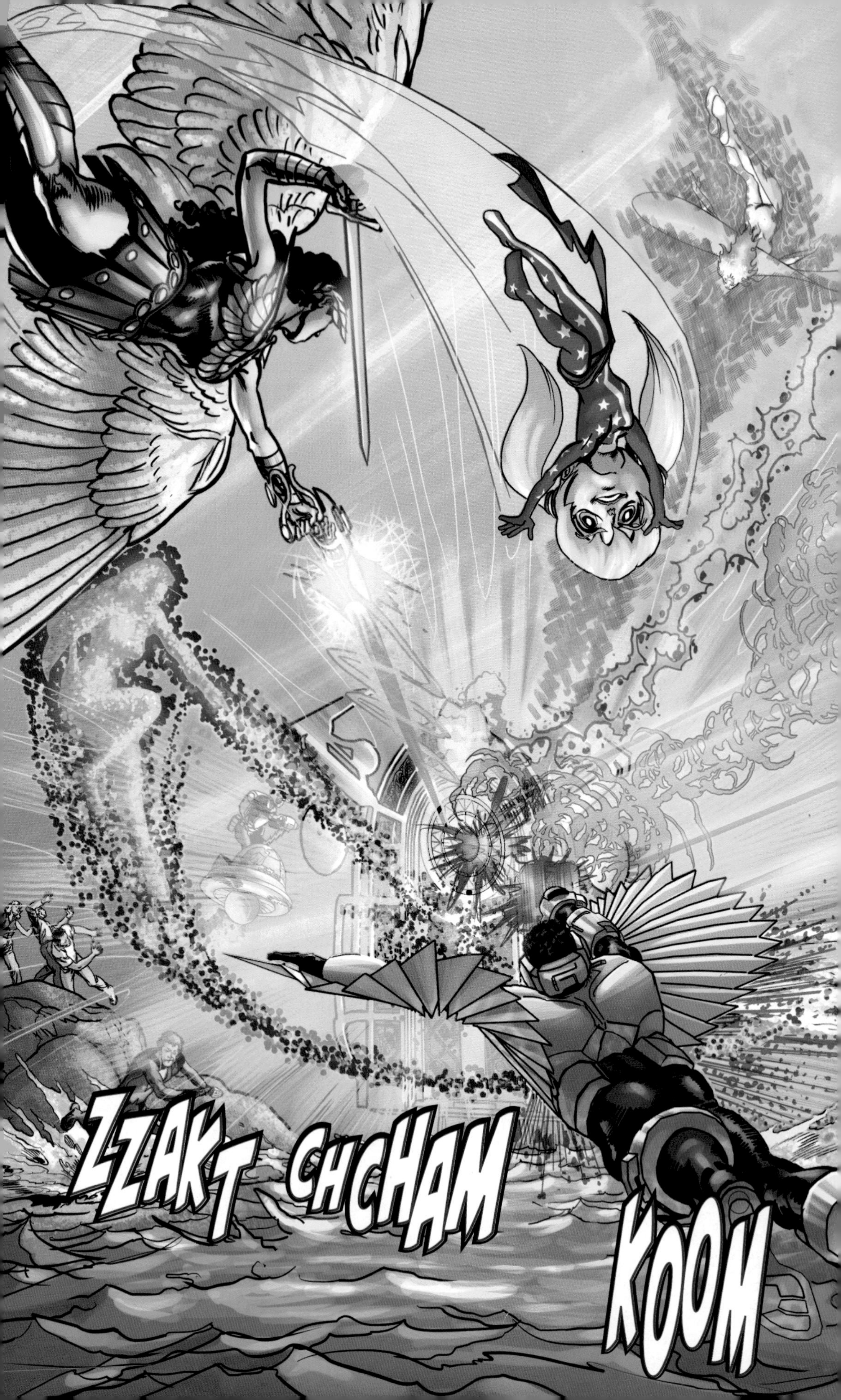
ZZAKT
CHCHAM
KOOM

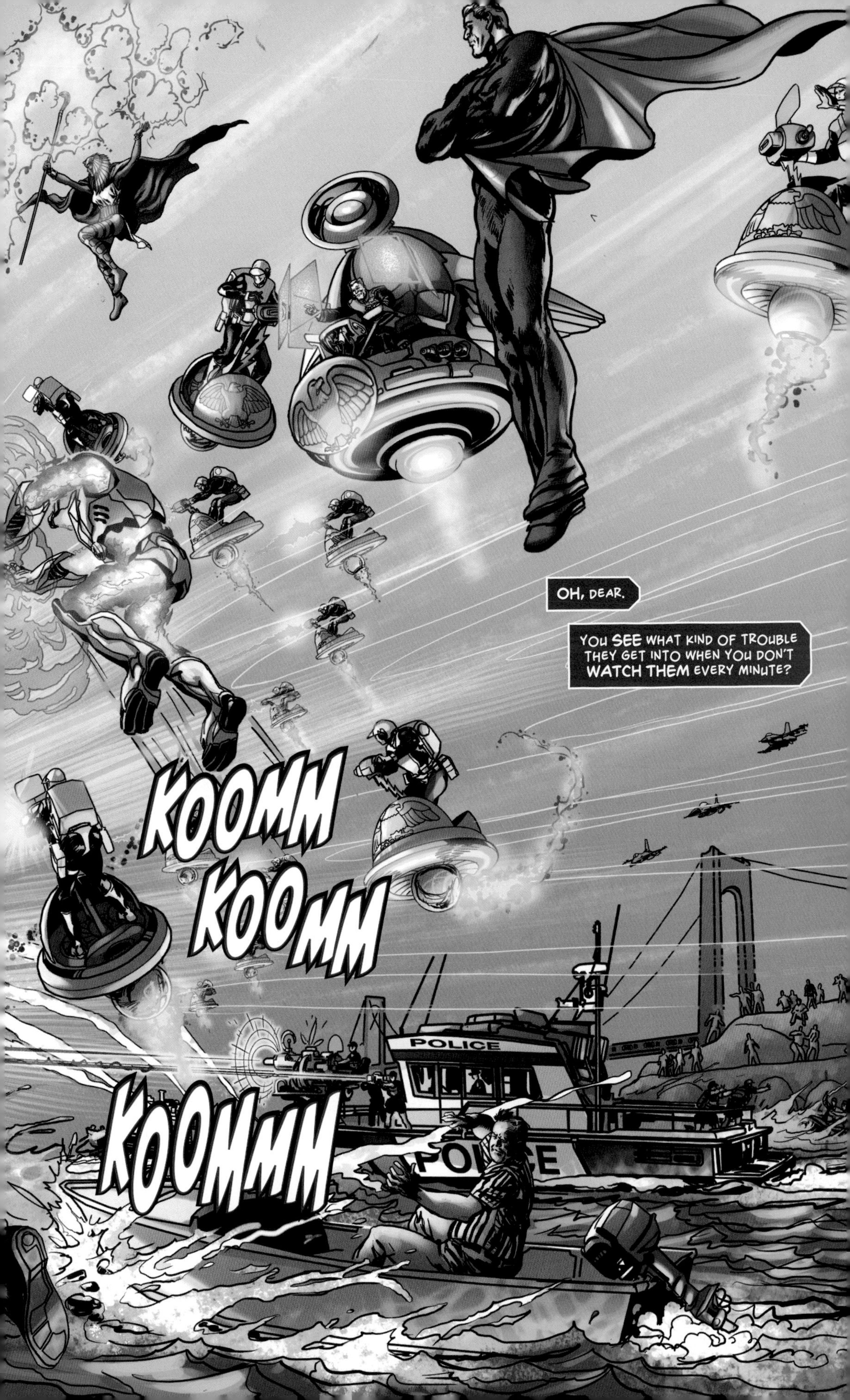
OH, DEAR.
YOU SEE WHAT KIND OF TROUBLE THEY GET INTO WHEN YOU DON'T WATCH THEM EVERY MINUTE?
KOOMM
KOOMM
KOOMMM
POLICE
POLICE

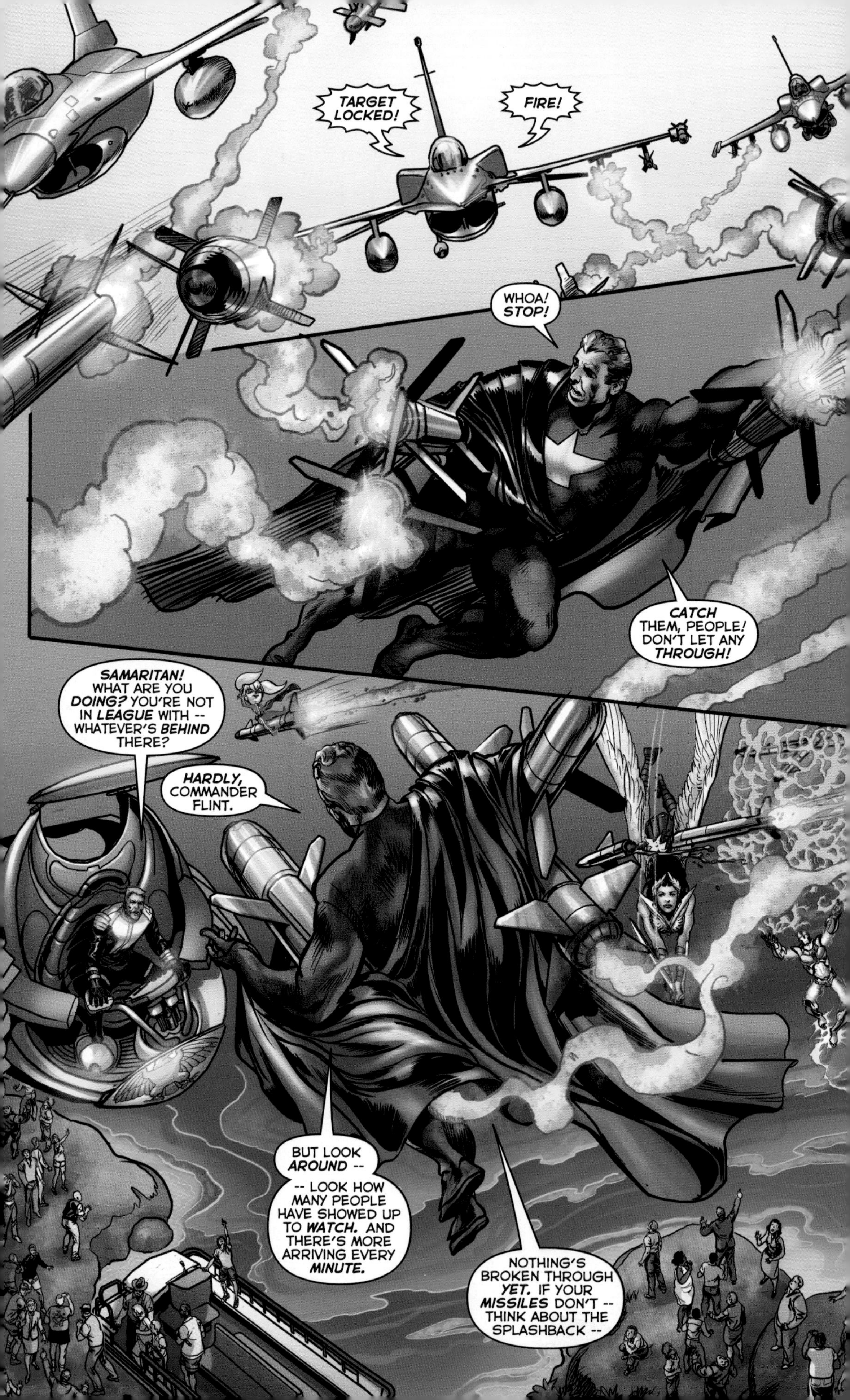
TARGET LOCKED!
FIRE!
WHOA! STOP!
CATCH THEM, PEOPLE! DON'T LET ANY THROUGH!
SAMARITAN! WHAT ARE YOU DOING? YOU'RE NOT IN LEAGUE WITH -- WHATEVER'S BEHIND THERE?
HARDLY, COMMANDER FLINT.
BUT LOOK AROUND --
-- LOOK HOW MANY PEOPLE HAVE SHOWED UP TO WATCH. AND THERE'S MORE ARRIVING EVERY MINUTE.
NOTHING'S BROKEN THROUGH YET. IF YOUR MISSILES DON'T -- THINK ABOUT THE SPLASHBACK --

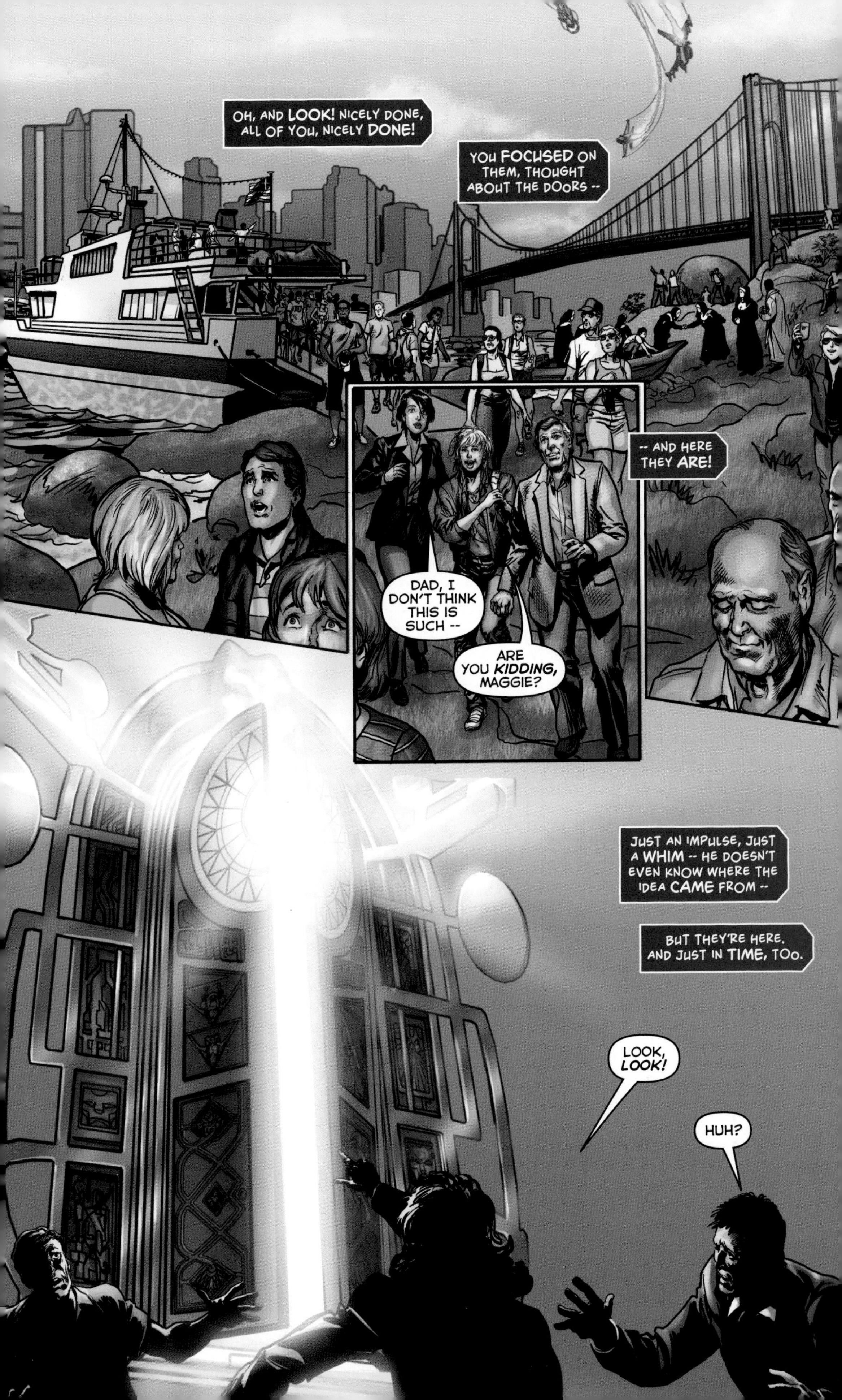
OH, AND LOOK! NICELY DONE, ALL OF YOU, NICELY DONE!
YOU FOCUSED ON THEM, THOUGHT ABOUT THE DOORS --
-- AND HERE THEY ARE!
DAD, I DON'T THINK THIS IS SUCH --
ARE YOU KIDDING, MAGGIE?
JUST AN IMPULSE, JUST A WHIM -- HE DOESN'T EVEN KNOW WHERE THE IDEA CAME FROM --
BUT THEY'RE HERE. AND JUST IN TIME, TOO.
LOOK, LOOK!
HUH?

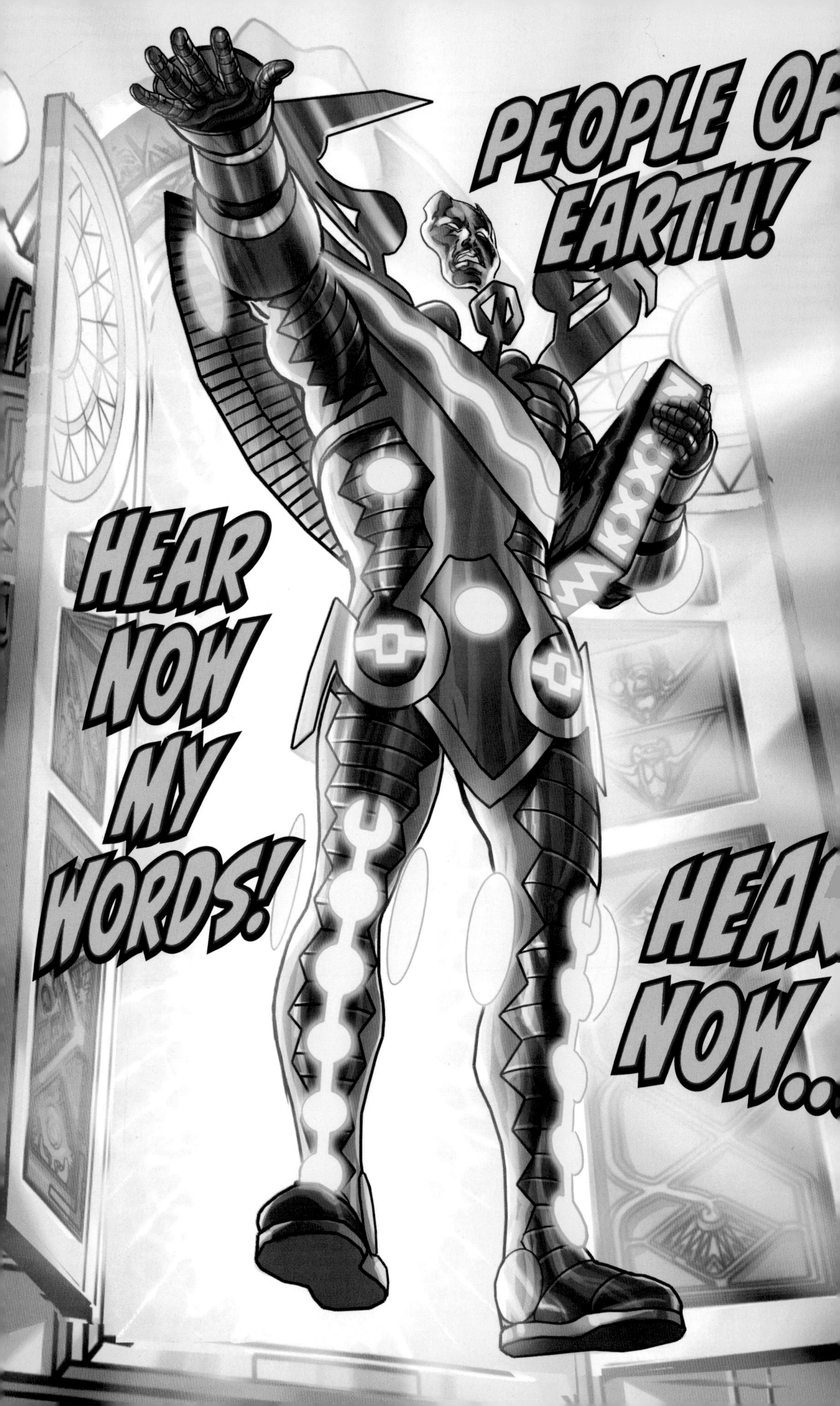
PEOPLE OF EARTH!
HEAR NOW MY WORDS!
HEAR NOW...

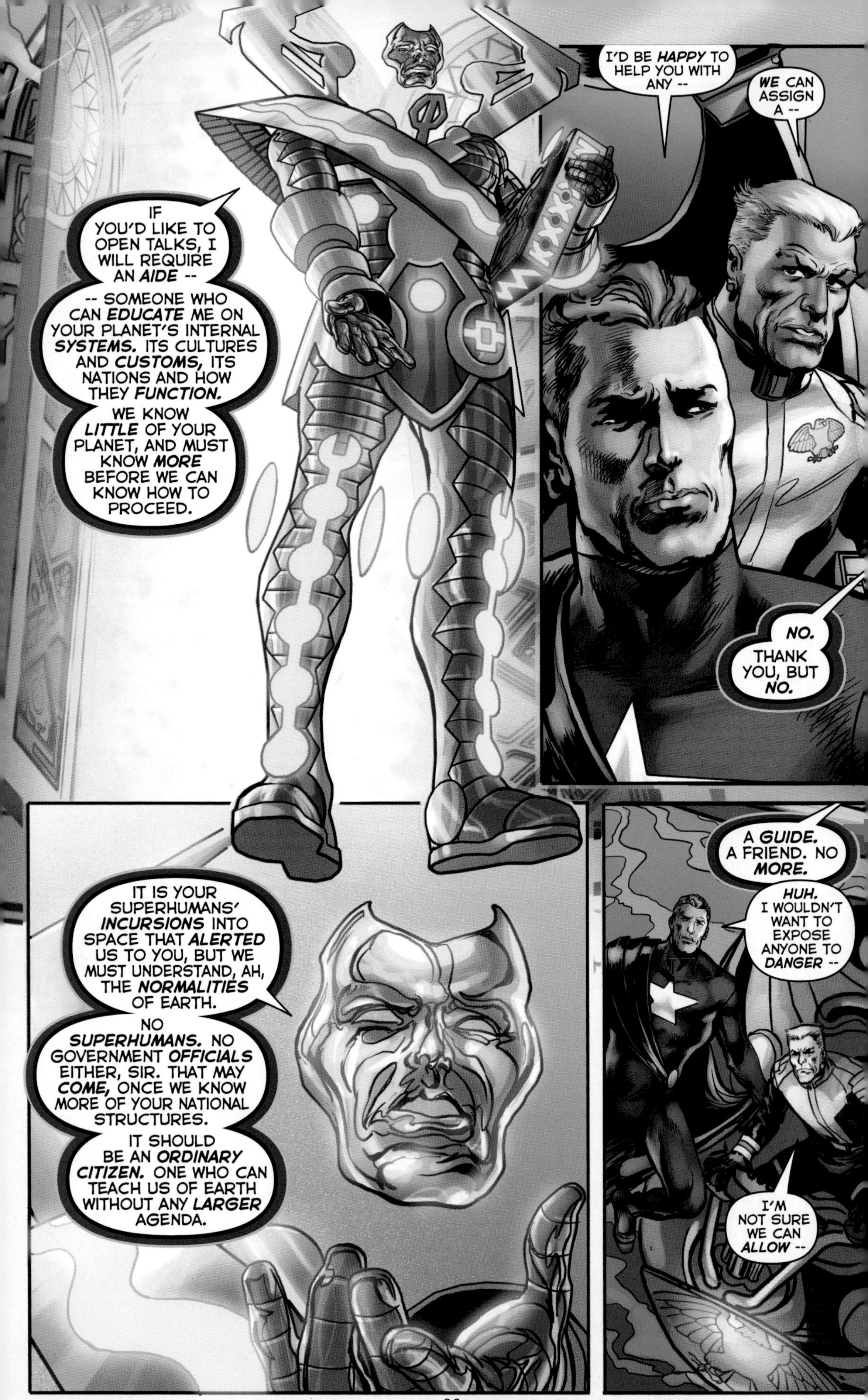
IF YOU'D LIKE TO OPEN TALKS, I WILL REQUIRE AN AIDE --
-- SOMEONE WHO CAN EDUCATE ME ON YOUR PLANET'S INTERNAL SYSTEMS. ITS CULTURES AND CUSTOMS, ITS NATIONS AND HOW THEY FUNCTION.
WE KNOW LITTLE OF YOUR PLANET, AND MUST KNOW MORE BEFORE WE CAN KNOW HOW TO PROCEED.
I'D BE HAPPY TO HELP YOU WITH ANY --
WE CAN ASSIGN A --
NO. THANK YOU, BUT NO.
IT IS YOUR SUPERHUMANS' INCURSIONS INTO SPACE THAT ALERTED US TO YOU, BUT WE MUST UNDERSTAND, AH, THE NORMALITIES OF EARTH.
NO SUPERHUMANS. NO GOVERNMENT OFFICIALS EITHER, SIR. THAT MAY COME, ONCE WE KNOW MORE OF YOUR NATIONAL STRUCTURES.
IT SHOULD BE AN ORDINARY CITIZEN. ONE WHO CAN TEACH US OF EARTH WITHOUT ANY LARGER AGENDA.
A GUIDE. A FRIEND. NO MORE.
HUH. I WOULDN'T WANT TO EXPOSE ANYONE TO DANGER --
I'M NOT SURE WE CAN ALLOW --

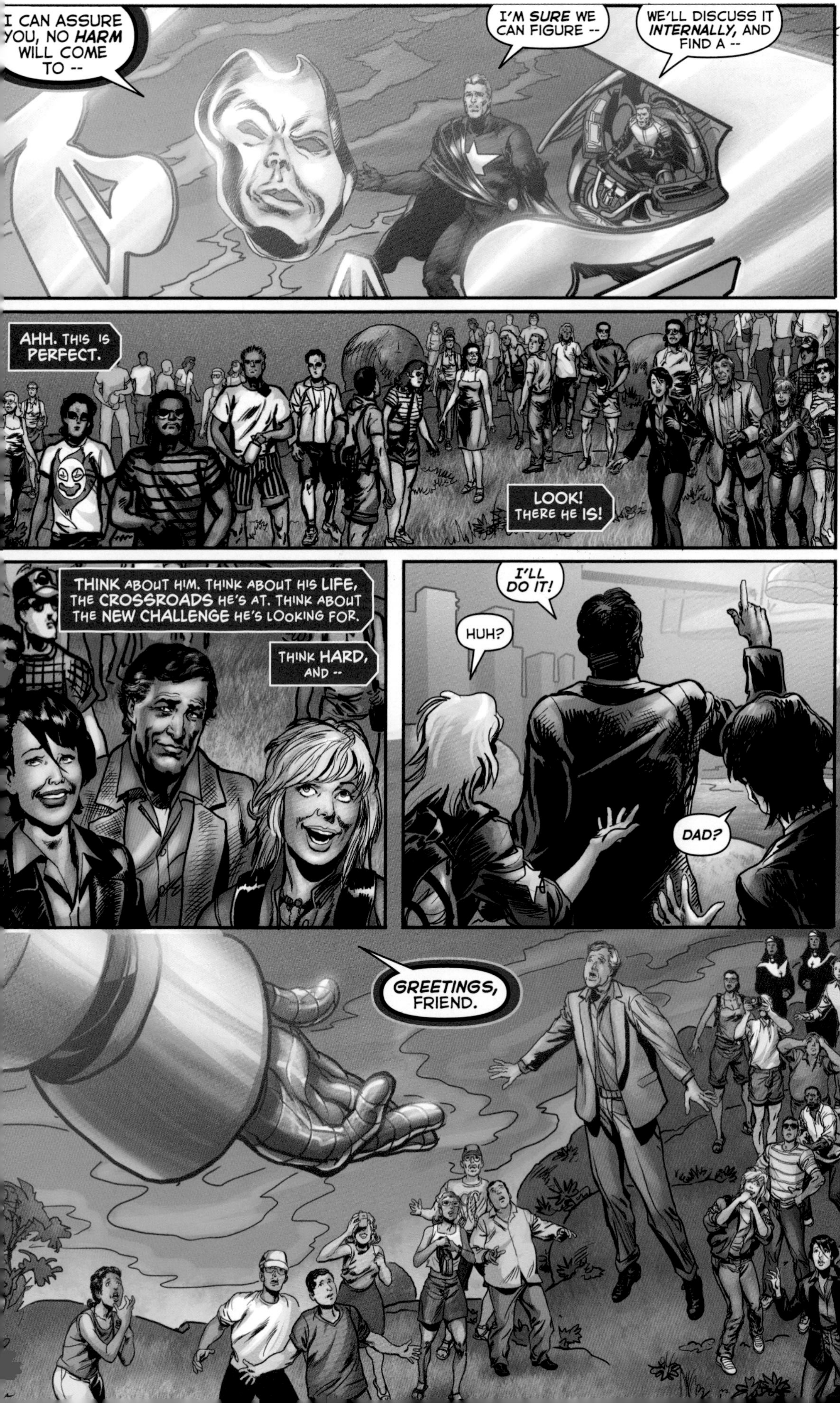
I CAN ASSURE YOU, NO HARM WILL COME TO --
I'M SURE WE CAN FIGURE --
WE'LL DISCUSS IT INTERNALLY, AND FIND A --
AHH. THIS IS PERFECT.
LOOK! THERE HE IS!
THINK ABOUT HIM. THINK ABOUT HIS LIFE, THE CROSSROADS HE'S AT. THINK ABOUT THE NEW CHALLENGE HE'S LOOKING FOR.
THINK HARD, AND --
I'LL DO IT!
HUH?
DAD?
GREETINGS, FRIEND.

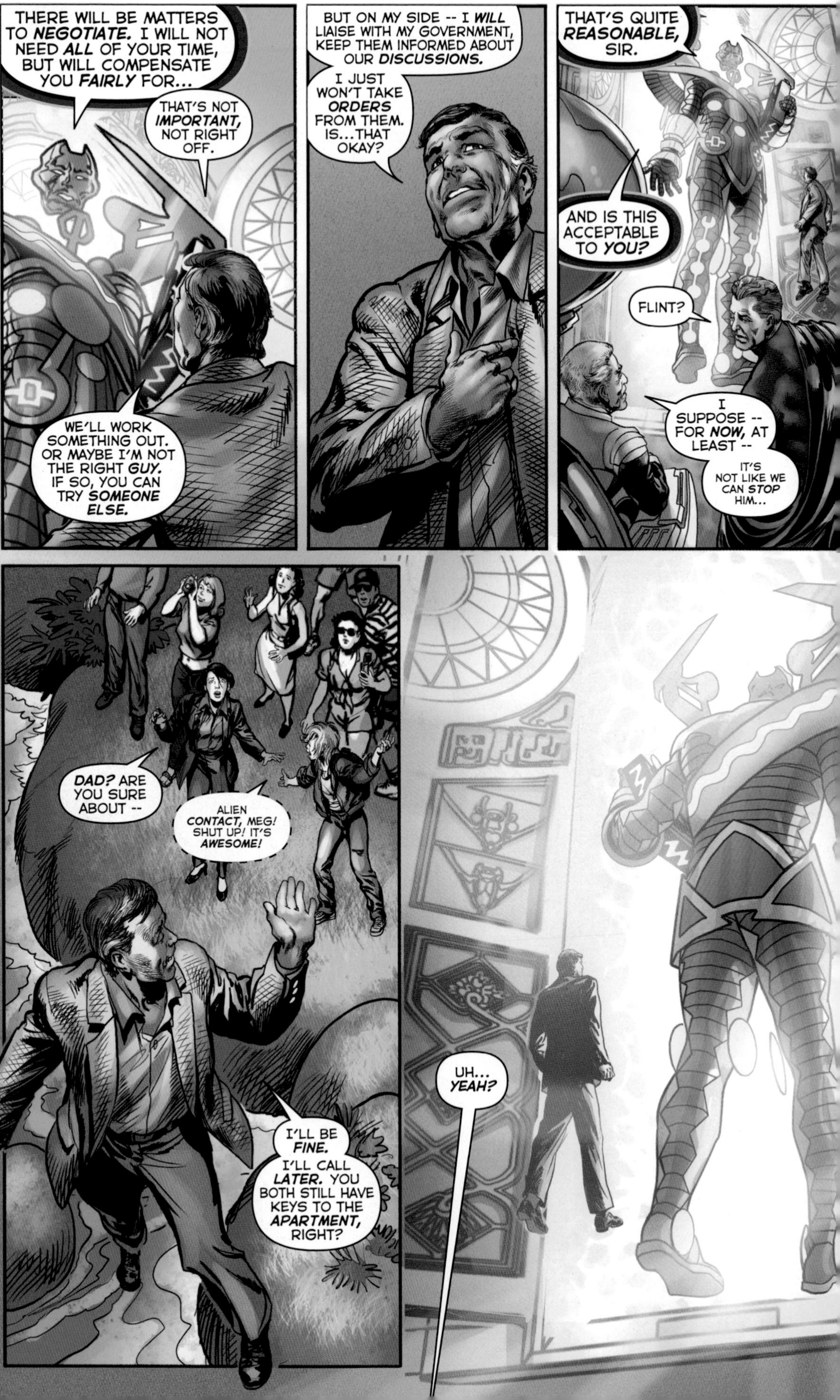
THERE WILL BE MATTERS TO NEGOTIATE. I WILL NOT NEED ALL OF YOUR TIME, BUT WILL COMPENSATE YOU FAIRLY FOR...
THAT'S NOT IMPORTANT, NOT RIGHT OFF.
WE'LL WORK SOMETHING OUT. OR MAYBE I'M NOT THE RIGHT GUY. IF SO, YOU CAN TRY SOMEONE ELSE.
BUT ON MY SIDE -- I WILL LIAISE WITH MY GOVERNMENT, KEEP THEM INFORMED ABOUT OUR DISCUSSIONS.
I JUST WON'T TAKE ORDERS FROM THEM. IS...THAT OKAY?
THAT'S QUITE REASONABLE, SIR.
AND IS THIS ACCEPTABLE TO YOU?
FLINT?
I SUPPOSE -- FOR NOW, AT LEAST --
IT'S NOT LIKE WE CAN STOP HIM...
DAD? ARE YOU SURE ABOUT --
ALIEN CONTACT, MEG! SHUT UP! IT'S AWESOME!
I'LL BE FINE. I'LL CALL LATER. YOU BOTH STILL HAVE KEYS TO THE APARTMENT, RIGHT?
UH... YEAH?

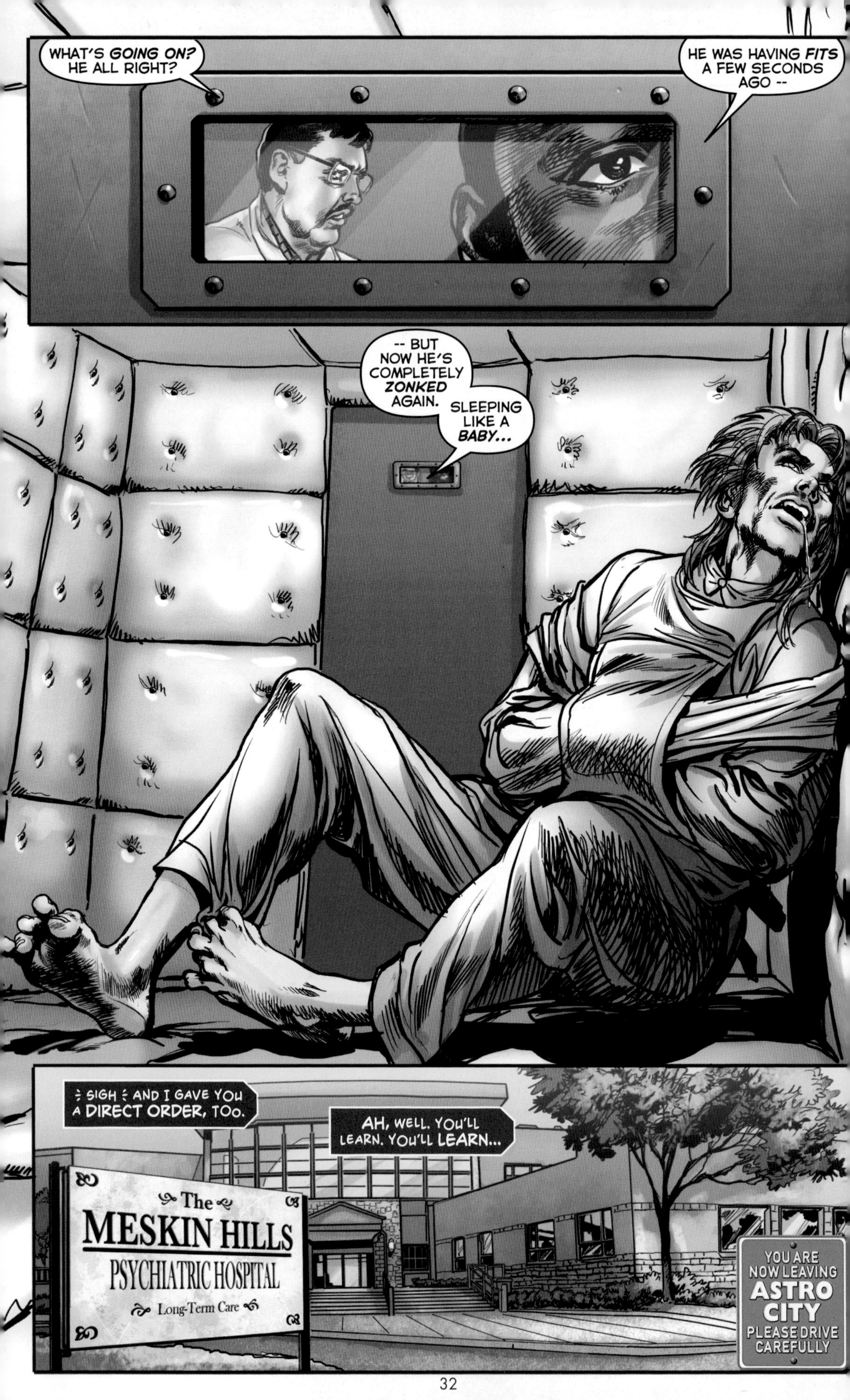
WHAT'S GOING ON? HE ALL RIGHT?
HE WAS HAVING FITS A FEW SECONDS AGO --
-- BUT NOW HE'S COMPLETELY ZONKED AGAIN.
SLEEPING LIKE A BABY...
⁝ SIGH ⁝ AND I GAVE YOU A DIRECT ORDER, TOO.
AH, WELL. YOU'LL LEARN. YOU'LL LEARN...
The MESKIN HILLS PSYCHIATRIC HOSPITAL
Long-Term Care
YOU ARE NOW LEAVING ASTRO CITY PLEASE DRIVE CAREFULLY

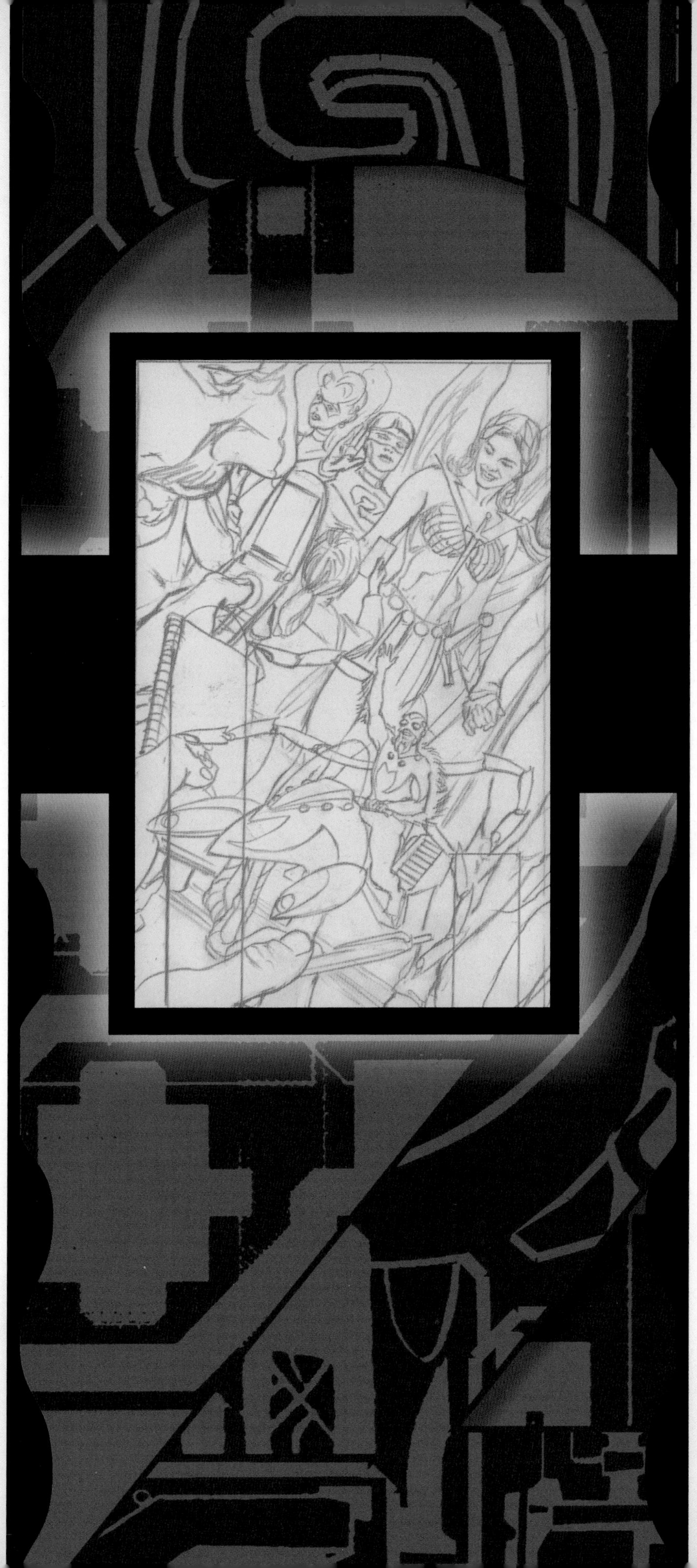

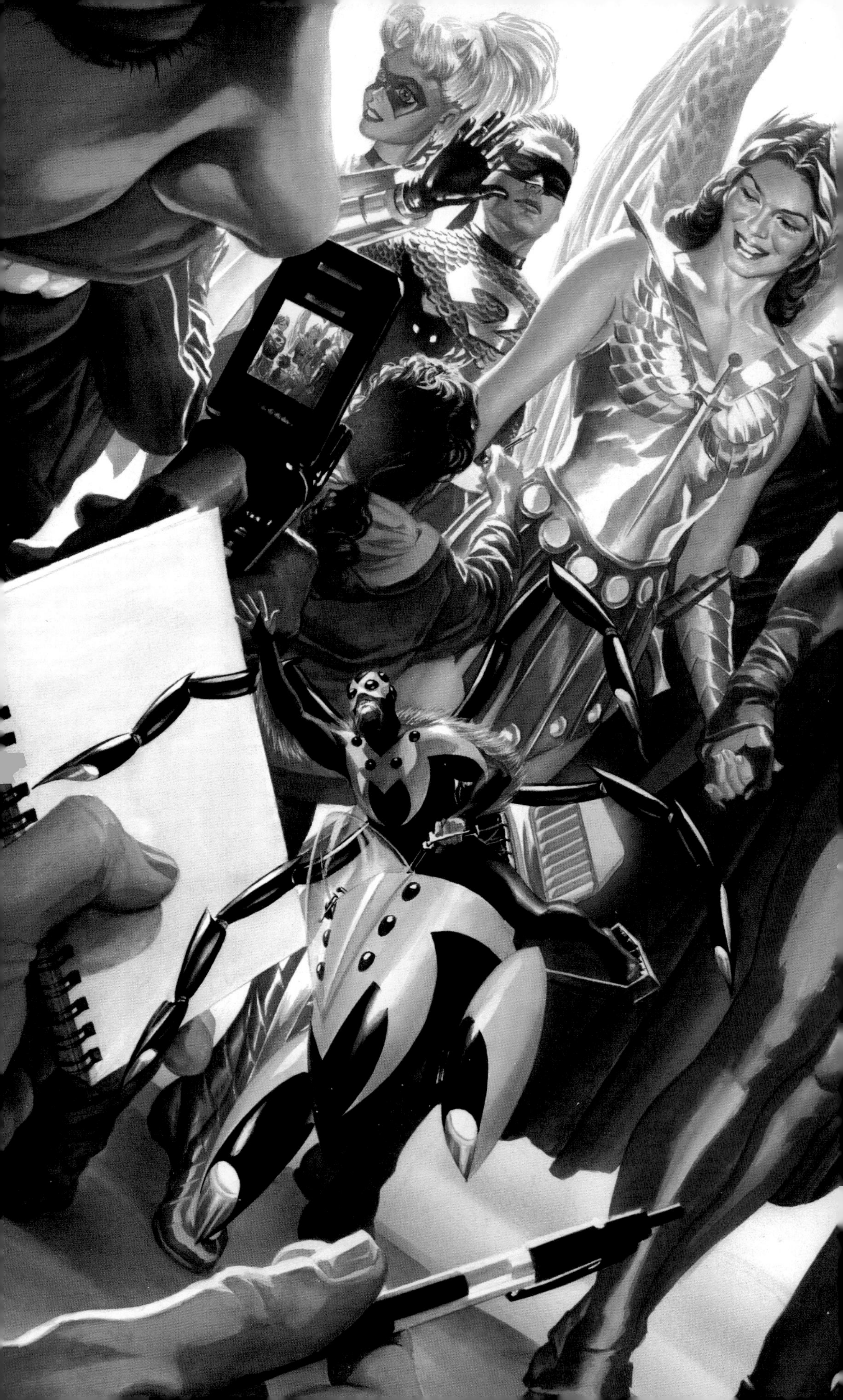

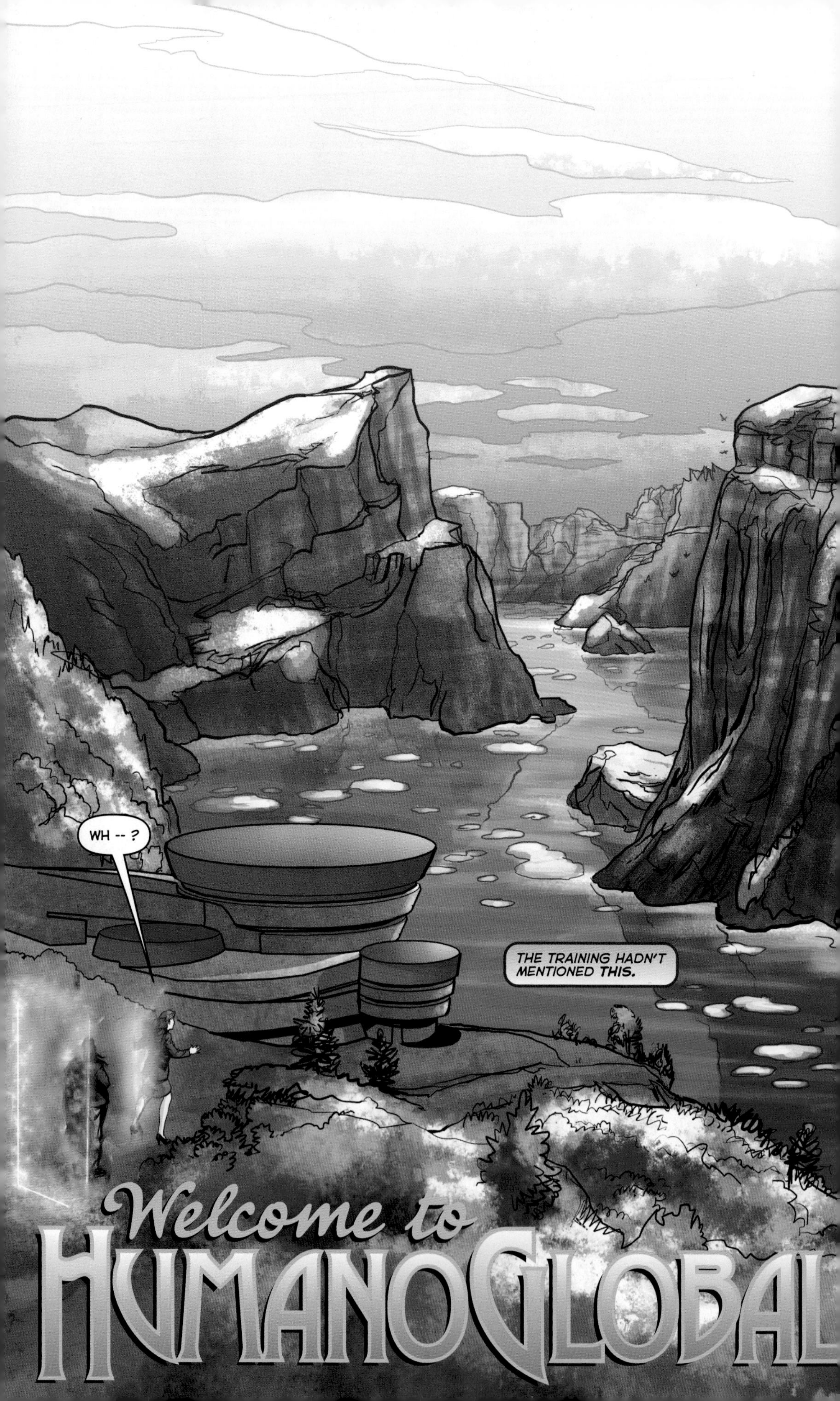
WH -- ?
THE TRAINING HADN'T MENTIONED THIS.
Welcome to HUMANOGLOBAL

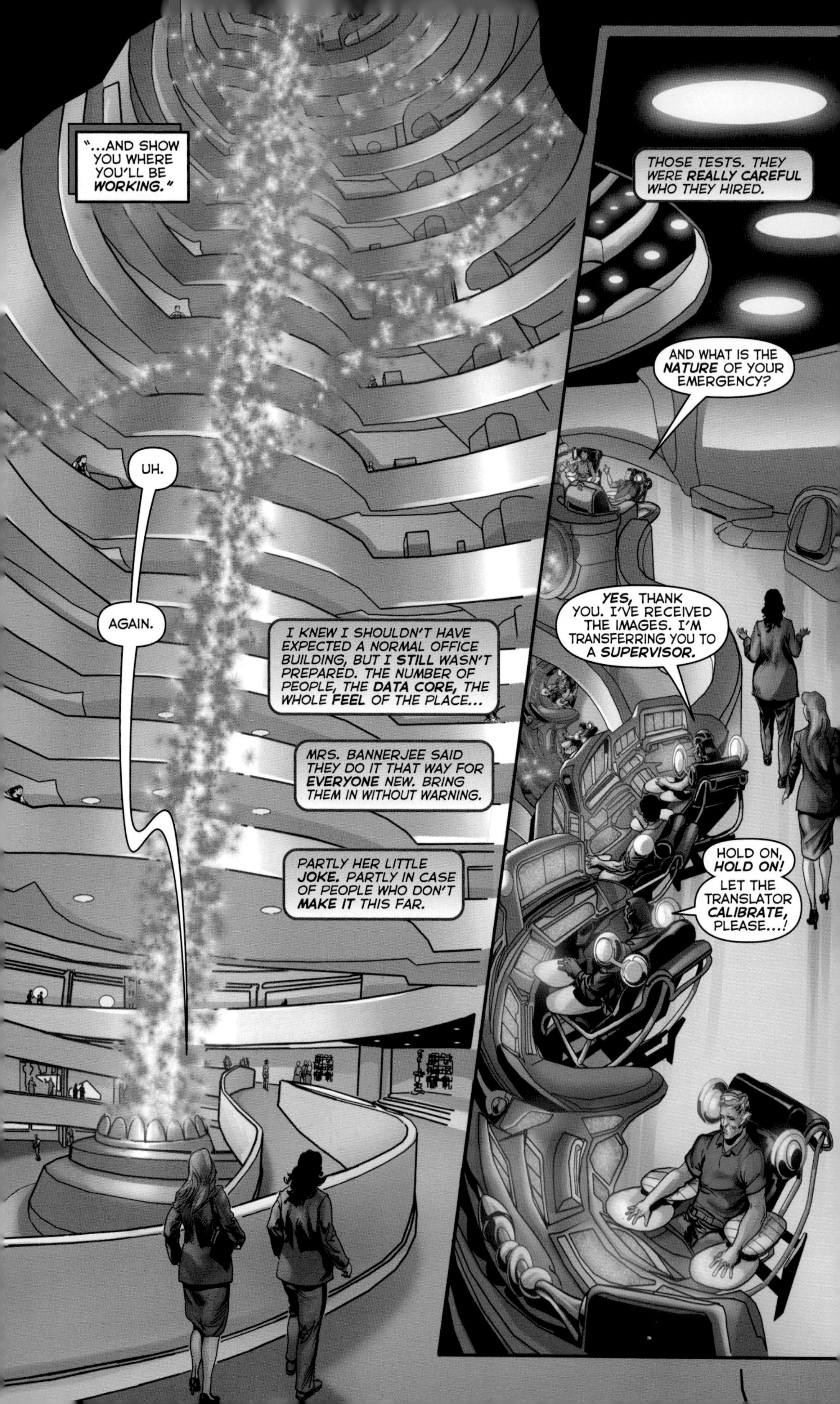
"...AND SHOW YOU WHERE YOU'LL BE **WORKING.**"
UH.
AGAIN.
I KNEW I SHOULDN'T HAVE EXPECTED A NORMAL OFFICE BUILDING, BUT I **STILL** WASN'T PREPARED. THE NUMBER OF PEOPLE, THE **DATA CORE,** THE WHOLE **FEEL** OF THE PLACE...
MRS. BANNERJEE SAID THEY DO IT THAT WAY FOR **EVERYONE** NEW. BRING THEM IN WITHOUT WARNING.
PARTLY HER LITTLE **JOKE.** PARTLY IN CASE OF PEOPLE WHO DON'T **MAKE IT** THIS FAR.
THOSE TESTS. THEY WERE **REALLY CAREFUL** WHO THEY HIRED.
AND WHAT IS THE **NATURE** OF YOUR EMERGENCY?
YES, THANK YOU. I'VE RECEIVED THE IMAGES. I'M TRANSFERRING YOU TO A **SUPERVISOR.**
HOLD ON, **HOLD ON!** LET THE TRANSLATOR **CALIBRATE,** PLEASE...!

AND THIS'LL BE YOUR **STATION.**

THE CHAIR SHOULD AUTOMATICALLY **ADJUST** TO YOUR WEIGHT AND POSTURE. LET ME KNOW IF IT **DOESN'T** -- YOU'LL BE IN IT A LOT, AND WE WANT YOU COMFORTABLE.

AND YOU'LL BE SPENDING A LOT OF TIME WITH YOUR **CO-WORKERS,** AS WELL...

AH, NEW **FISH.** I'M **JEREMY BAINES.**

MICHIKO OHARA.

HEY. **TONI UMTATA.**

NICE -- NICE TO MEET YOU ALL. I'M **MARELLA COWPER.**

YOU'RE **ALL RIGHT?** READY TO GO?

I... **THINK** SO.

GOOD. BECAUSE YOU ALREADY HAVE YOUR **FIRST** CALL.

OH!

CODE AMBER
Location : Austin, TX
Local time: 09:43
Call Init: 09:44

YOU'RE **CONNECTED.** AND WHAT IS THE **NATURE** OF YOUR **EMERGENCY?**

I REALLY, REALLY DIDN'T WANT TO MESS UP. NOT JUST BECAUSE IT WAS A NEW JOB...

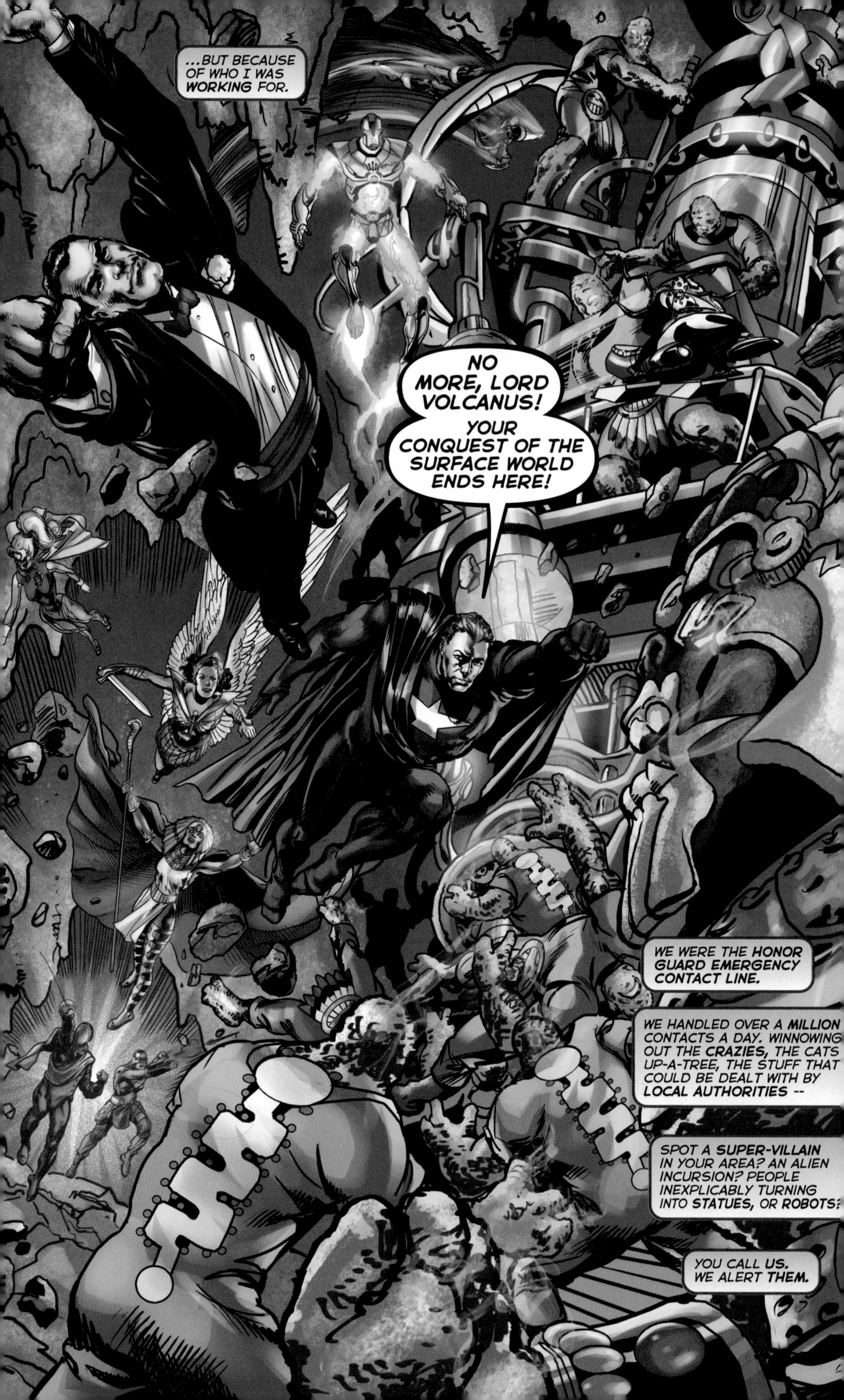
...BUT BECAUSE OF WHO I WAS WORKING FOR.
NO MORE, LORD VOLCANUS! YOUR CONQUEST OF THE SURFACE WORLD ENDS HERE!
WE WERE THE HONOR GUARD EMERGENCY CONTACT LINE.
WE HANDLED OVER A MILLION CONTACTS A DAY. WINNOWING OUT THE CRAZIES, THE CATS UP-A-TREE, THE STUFF THAT COULD BE DEALT WITH BY LOCAL AUTHORITIES --
SPOT A SUPER-VILLAIN IN YOUR AREA? AN ALIEN INCURSION? PEOPLE INEXPLICABLY TURNING INTO STATUES, OR ROBOTS?
YOU CALL US. WE ALERT THEM.

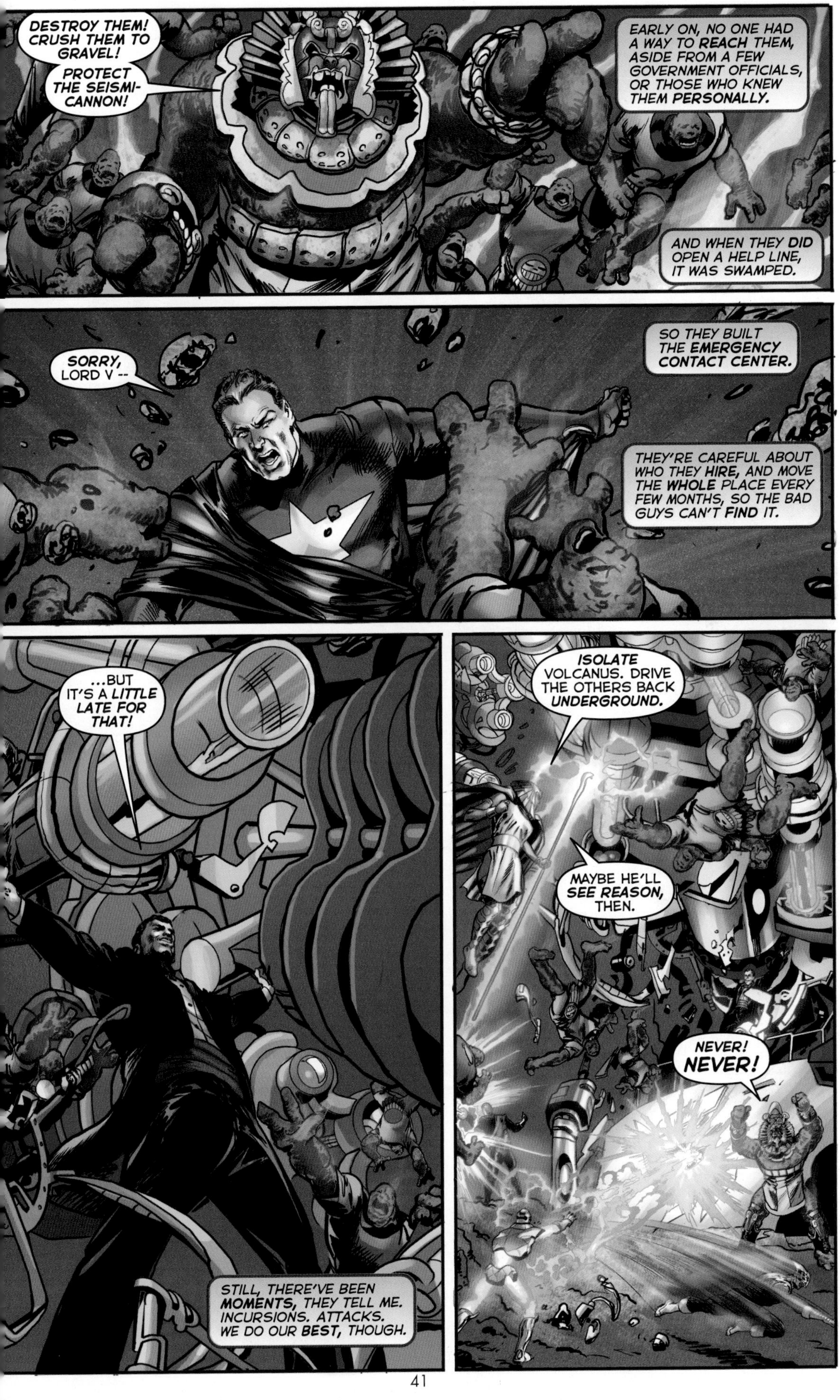
DESTROY THEM! CRUSH THEM TO GRAVEL!
PROTECT THE SEISMI-CANNON!
EARLY ON, NO ONE HAD A WAY TO REACH THEM, ASIDE FROM A FEW GOVERNMENT OFFICIALS, OR THOSE WHO KNEW THEM PERSONALLY.
AND WHEN THEY DID OPEN A HELP LINE, IT WAS SWAMPED.
SORRY, LORD V --
SO THEY BUILT THE EMERGENCY CONTACT CENTER.
THEY'RE CAREFUL ABOUT WHO THEY HIRE, AND MOVE THE WHOLE PLACE EVERY FEW MONTHS, SO THE BAD GUYS CAN'T FIND IT.
...BUT IT'S A LITTLE LATE FOR THAT!
STILL, THERE'VE BEEN MOMENTS, THEY TELL ME. INCURSIONS. ATTACKS. WE DO OUR BEST, THOUGH.
ISOLATE VOLCANUS. DRIVE THE OTHERS BACK UNDERGROUND.
MAYBE HE'LL SEE REASON, THEN.
NEVER! NEVER!

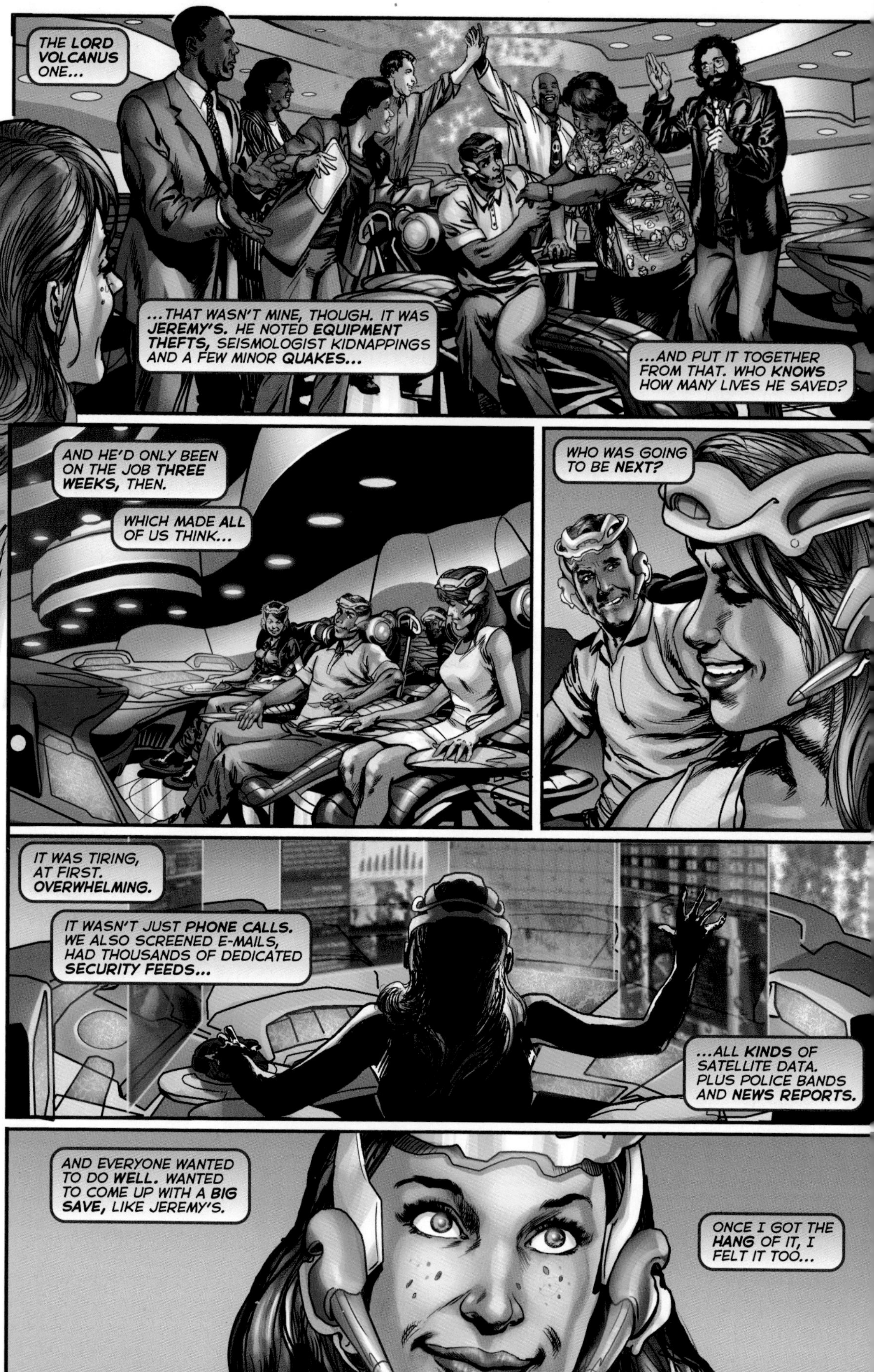
THE LORD VOLCANUS ONE...
...THAT WASN'T MINE, THOUGH. IT WAS JEREMY'S. HE NOTED EQUIPMENT THEFTS, SEISMOLOGIST KIDNAPPINGS AND A FEW MINOR QUAKES...
...AND PUT IT TOGETHER FROM THAT. WHO KNOWS HOW MANY LIVES HE SAVED?
AND HE'D ONLY BEEN ON THE JOB THREE WEEKS, THEN.
WHICH MADE ALL OF US THINK...
WHO WAS GOING TO BE NEXT?
IT WAS TIRING, AT FIRST. OVERWHELMING.
IT WASN'T JUST PHONE CALLS. WE ALSO SCREENED E-MAILS, HAD THOUSANDS OF DEDICATED SECURITY FEEDS...
...ALL KINDS OF SATELLITE DATA. PLUS POLICE BANDS AND NEWS REPORTS.
AND EVERYONE WANTED TO DO WELL. WANTED TO COME UP WITH A BIG SAVE, LIKE JEREMY'S.
ONCE I GOT THE HANG OF IT, I FELT IT TOO...

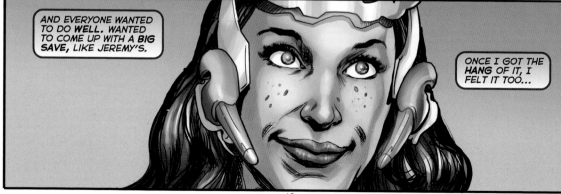

SO. YOU DON'T TALK ABOUT THE NEW *JOB* MUCH.

SELLING NEWSPAPER SUBSCRIPTIONS REALLY *THAT* BAD? LOTTA YELLING AND *HANG-UPS?*

JESS!

IT'S *OKAY,* MOM.

IT'S NOT THAT KIND OF *CALL CENTER,* JESSIE. IT'S LIKE -- AN *INFORMATION LINE,* REALLY. PEOPLE CALL IN, WITH PROBLEMS --

WE WEREN'T SUPPOSED TO TELL PEOPLE MUCH ABOUT THE JOB. NOT EVEN OUR *FAMILIES,* EARLY ON.

WE DIDN'T HAVE TO *LIE,* NOT IF WE DIDN'T WANT TO. WE WERE JUST...ENCOURAGED TO KEEP IT *VAGUE.*

-- WE *HELP* 'EM IF WE CAN, TRANSFER 'EM TO SOMEONE ELSE IF WE *CAN'T.* PLUS A LOT OF *DATA GATHERING,* AND LIKE THAT.

THERE'D BEEN AN ATTACK, ONCE, WHEN *PYRAMID* FIGURED OUT WHERE THE CENTER WAS. AND OPERATORS -- PEOPLE LIKE ME -- *DIED.*

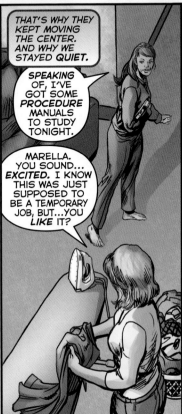

THAT'S WHY THEY KEPT MOVING THE CENTER. AND WHY WE STAYED *QUIET.*

SPEAKING OF, I'VE GOT SOME *PROCEDURE* MANUALS TO STUDY TONIGHT.

MARELLA. YOU SOUND... *EXCITED.* I KNOW THIS WAS JUST SUPPOSED TO BE A TEMPORARY JOB, BUT...YOU *LIKE* IT?

WE *HELP* PEOPLE. THE ORGANIZATION...THEY *CARE,* AND WHAT I DO MATTERS. I REALLY WANT TO BE *GOOD* AT IT, I DON'T WANT TO *MESS UP.*

BUT *YEAH,* MOM... I LIKE IT.

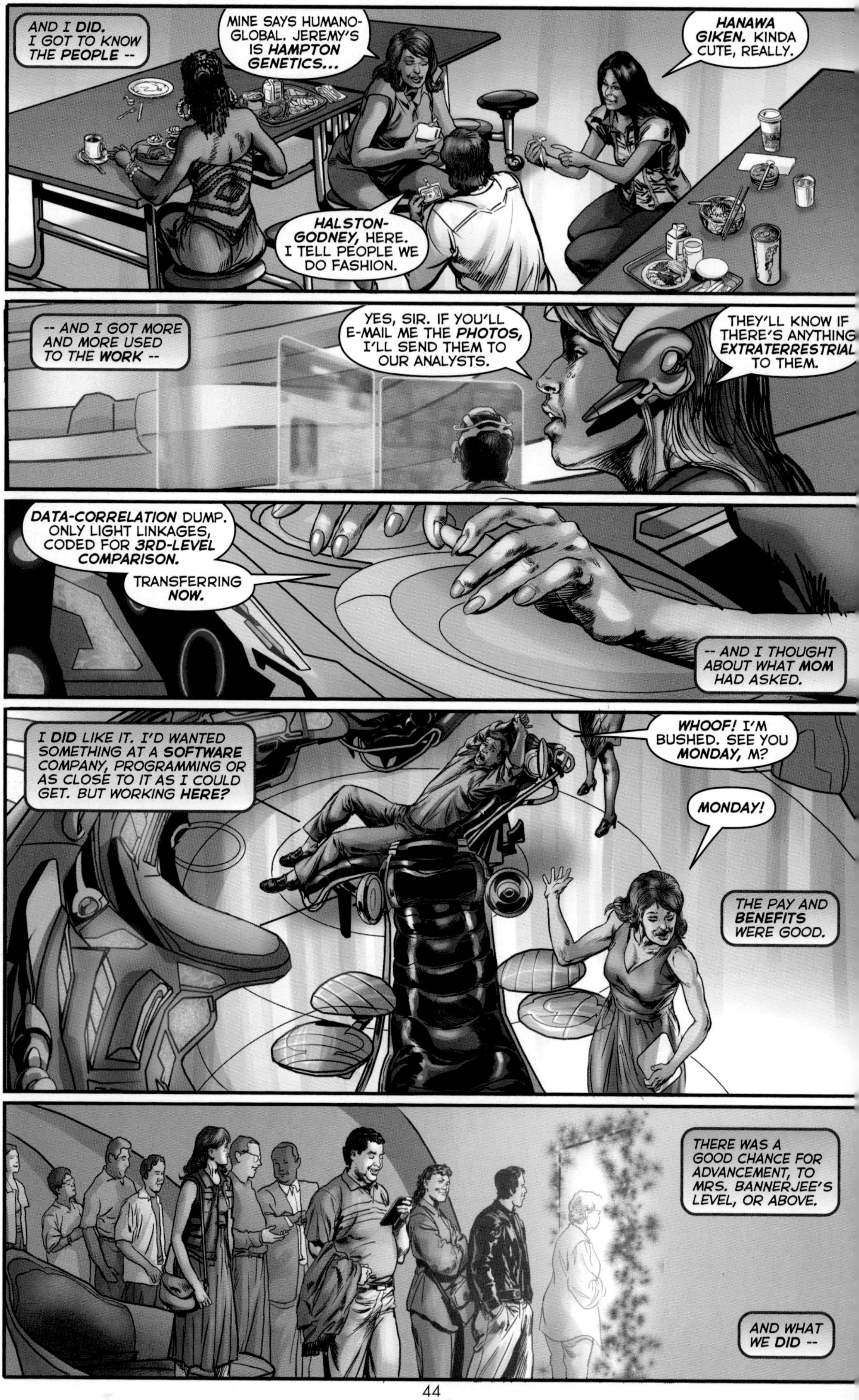
AND I DID. I GOT TO KNOW THE PEOPLE --
MINE SAYS HUMANO-GLOBAL. JEREMY'S IS HAMPTON GENETICS...
HANAWA GIKEN. KINDA CUTE, REALLY.
HALSTON-GODNEY, HERE. I TELL PEOPLE WE DO FASHION.
-- AND I GOT MORE AND MORE USED TO THE WORK --
YES, SIR. IF YOU'LL E-MAIL ME THE PHOTOS, I'LL SEND THEM TO OUR ANALYSTS.
THEY'LL KNOW IF THERE'S ANYTHING EXTRATERRESTRIAL TO THEM.
DATA-CORRELATION DUMP. ONLY LIGHT LINKAGES, CODED FOR 3RD-LEVEL COMPARISON.
TRANSFERRING NOW.
-- AND I THOUGHT ABOUT WHAT MOM HAD ASKED.
I DID LIKE IT. I'D WANTED SOMETHING AT A SOFTWARE COMPANY, PROGRAMMING OR AS CLOSE TO IT AS I COULD GET. BUT WORKING HERE?
WHOOF! I'M BUSHED. SEE YOU MONDAY, M?
MONDAY!
THE PAY AND BENEFITS WERE GOOD.
THERE WAS A GOOD CHANCE FOR ADVANCEMENT, TO MRS. BANNERJEE'S LEVEL, OR ABOVE.
AND WHAT WE DID --

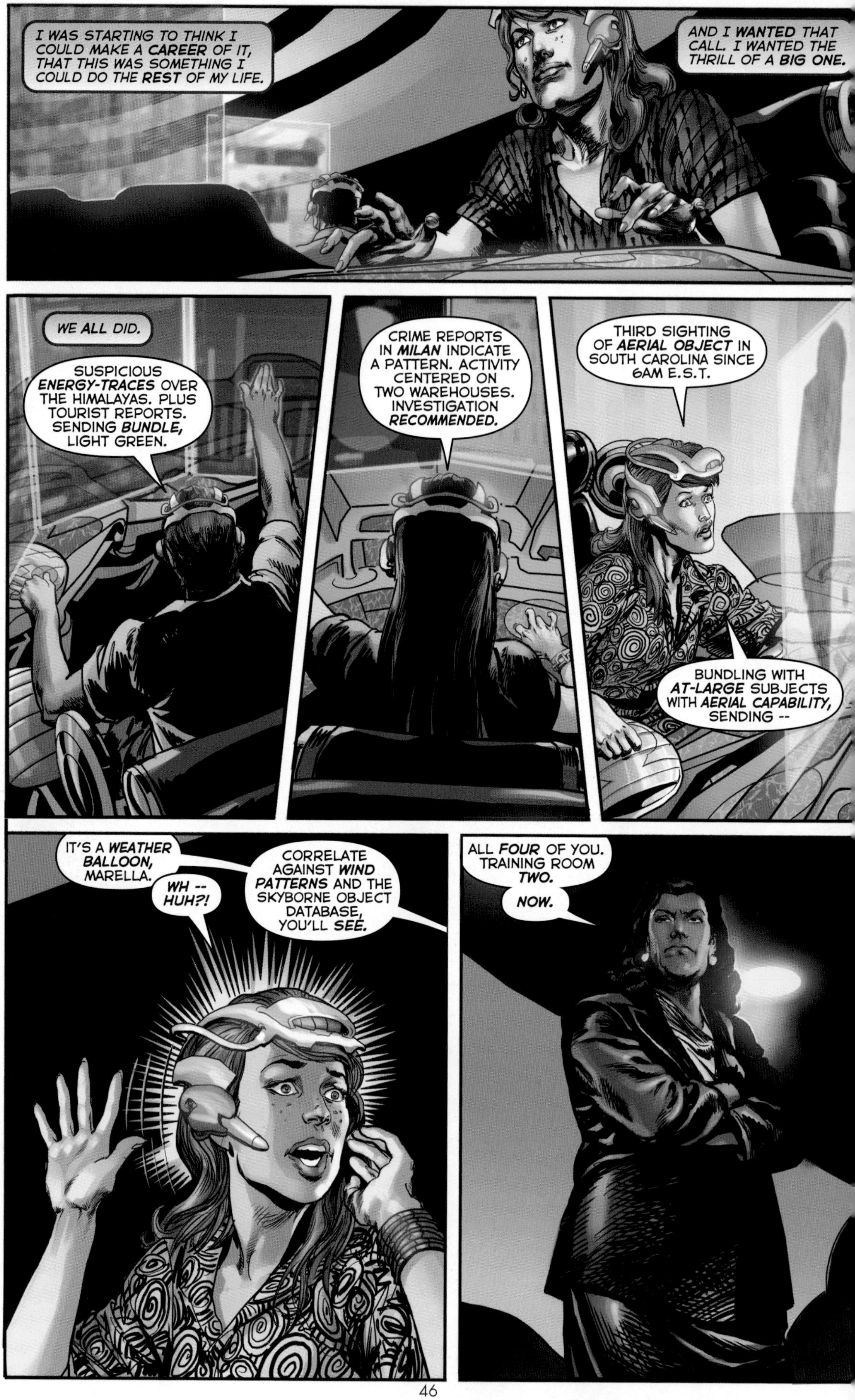

I WAS STARTING TO THINK I COULD MAKE A CAREER OF IT, THAT THIS WAS SOMETHING I COULD DO THE REST OF MY LIFE.
AND I WANTED THAT CALL. I WANTED THE THRILL OF A BIG ONE.
WE ALL DID.
SUSPICIOUS ENERGY-TRACES OVER THE HIMALAYAS. PLUS TOURIST REPORTS. SENDING BUNDLE, LIGHT GREEN.
CRIME REPORTS IN MILAN INDICATE A PATTERN. ACTIVITY CENTERED ON TWO WAREHOUSES. INVESTIGATION RECOMMENDED.
THIRD SIGHTING OF AERIAL OBJECT IN SOUTH CAROLINA SINCE 6AM E.S.T.
BUNDLING WITH AT-LARGE SUBJECTS WITH AERIAL CAPABILITY, SENDING --
IT'S A WEATHER BALLOON, MARELLA.
WH -- HUH?!
CORRELATE AGAINST WIND PATTERNS AND THE SKYBORNE OBJECT DATABASE, YOU'LL SEE.
ALL FOUR OF YOU. TRAINING ROOM TWO.
NOW.

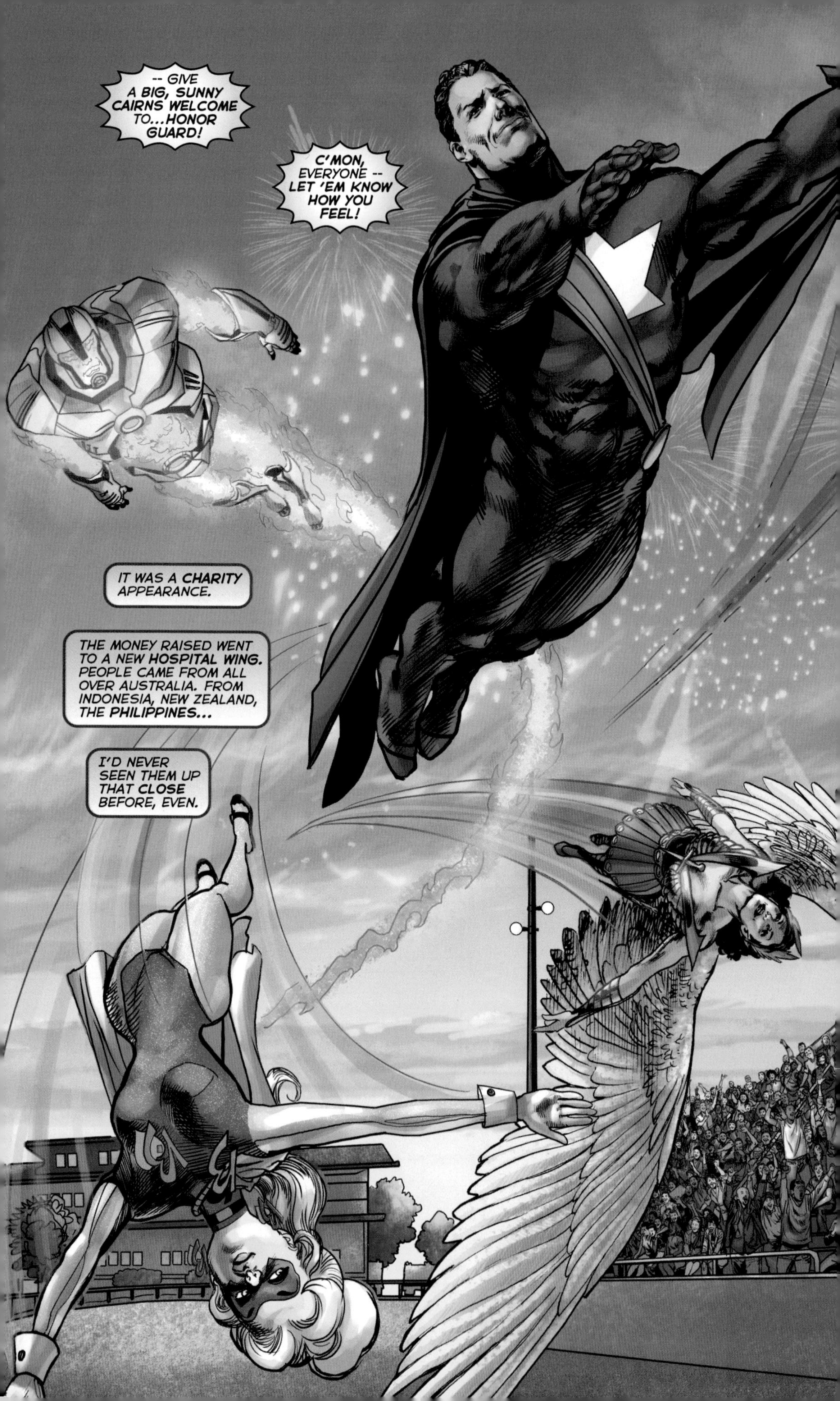

-- GIVE A BIG, SUNNY CAIRNS WELCOME TO...HONOR GUARD!
C'MON, EVERYONE -- LET 'EM KNOW HOW YOU FEEL!
IT WAS A CHARITY APPEARANCE.
THE MONEY RAISED WENT TO A NEW HOSPITAL WING. PEOPLE CAME FROM ALL OVER AUSTRALIA. FROM INDONESIA, NEW ZEALAND, THE PHILIPPINES...
I'D NEVER SEEN THEM UP THAT CLOSE BEFORE, EVEN.

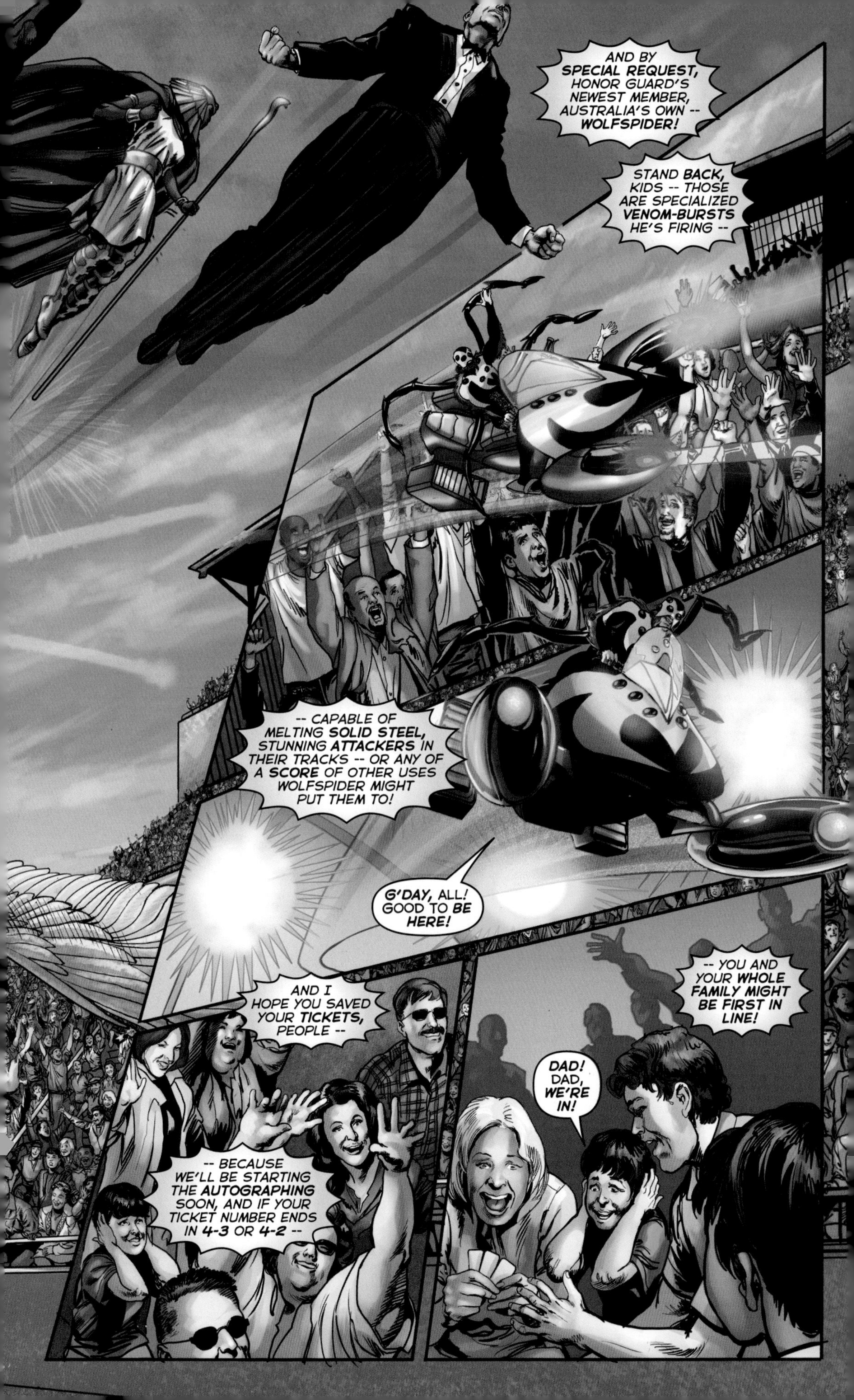
AND BY SPECIAL REQUEST, HONOR GUARD'S NEWEST MEMBER, AUSTRALIA'S OWN -- WOLFSPIDER!
STAND BACK, KIDS -- THOSE ARE SPECIALIZED VENOM-BURSTS HE'S FIRING --
-- CAPABLE OF MELTING SOLID STEEL, STUNNING ATTACKERS IN THEIR TRACKS -- OR ANY OF A SCORE OF OTHER USES WOLFSPIDER MIGHT PUT THEM TO!
G'DAY, ALL! GOOD TO BE HERE!
AND I HOPE YOU SAVED YOUR TICKETS, PEOPLE --
-- BECAUSE WE'LL BE STARTING THE AUTOGRAPHING SOON, AND IF YOUR TICKET NUMBER ENDS IN 4-3 OR 4-2 --
-- YOU AND YOUR WHOLE FAMILY MIGHT BE FIRST IN LINE!
DAD! DAD, WE'RE IN!

MAYBE IT WASN'T SAVING THE *WORLD*, OR STOPPING A SUPERPOWERED INTERNATIONAL *CRIME RING* --

BUT IT'S NOT *BAD*, IS IT?

NOT BAD AT *ALL*.

YOU'RE THE TEAM FROM THE *SUPPORT CENTER*, AREN'T YOU?

CLAUDIA *BANNERJEE'S* PEOPLE?

UH!

AH!

NICE JOB TODAY. EVERYTHING WENT VERY *SMOOTHLY*. I'M TOLD YOU'RE SOME OF OUR MOST *PROMISING* NEW STAFFERS.

UM -- THANKS -- BUT WE'RE NOT EXACTLY *PERFECT* OR ANYTHING --

NONE OF US ARE PERFECT. JUST DO YOUR BEST. THAT'S ALL WE CAN *ASK*.

AND SAY HI TO *MRS. B* FOR ME, HM?

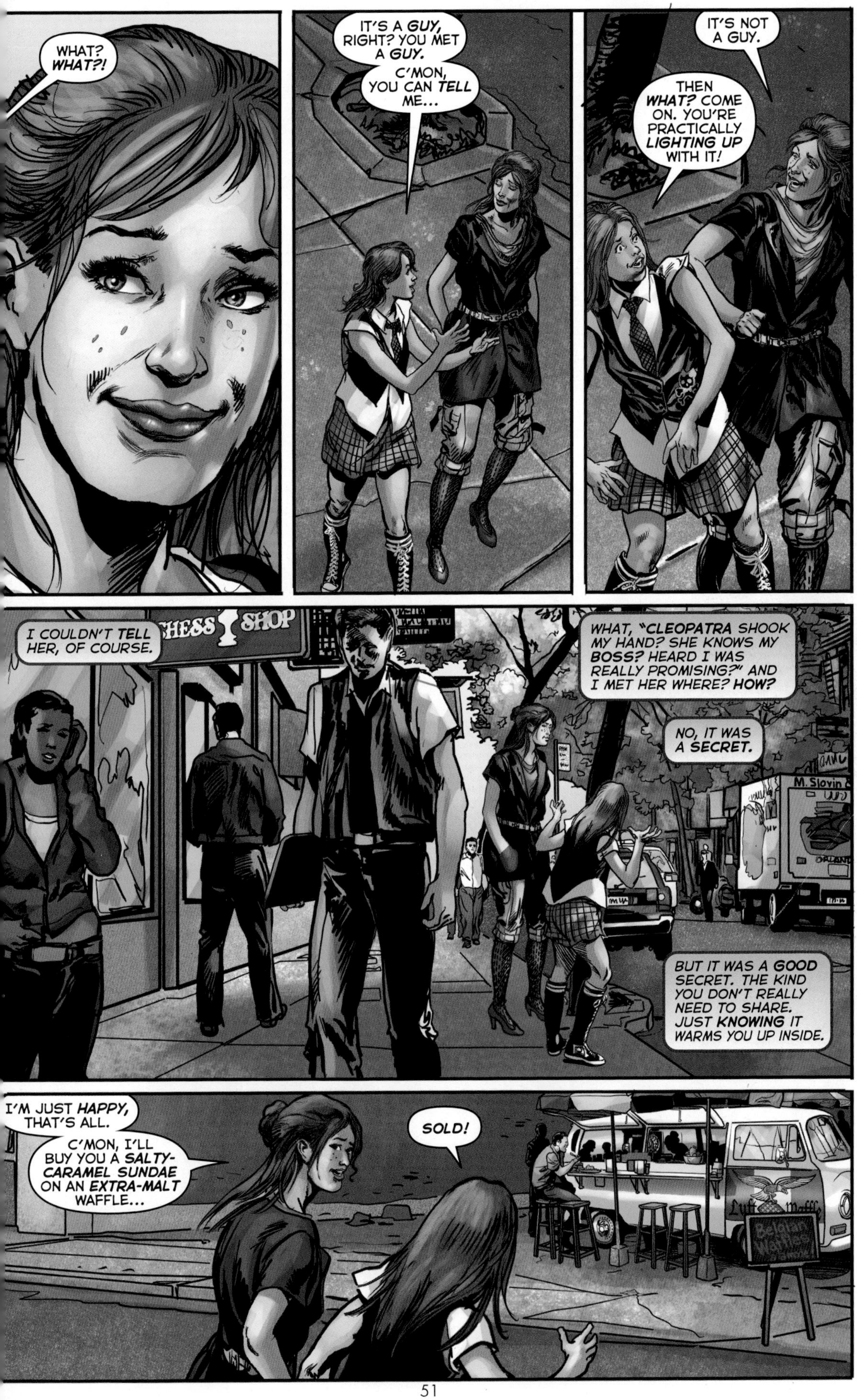
WHAT? WHAT?!
IT'S A GUY, RIGHT? YOU MET A GUY.
C'MON, YOU CAN TELL ME...
IT'S NOT A GUY.
THEN WHAT? COME ON. YOU'RE PRACTICALLY LIGHTING UP WITH IT!
CHESS SHOP
I COULDN'T TELL HER, OF COURSE.
WHAT, "CLEOPATRA SHOOK MY HAND? SHE KNOWS MY BOSS? HEARD I WAS REALLY PROMISING?" AND I MET HER WHERE? HOW?
NO, IT WAS A SECRET.
M. Slovin
BUT IT WAS A GOOD SECRET. THE KIND YOU DON'T REALLY NEED TO SHARE. JUST KNOWING IT WARMS YOU UP INSIDE.
I'M JUST HAPPY, THAT'S ALL.
C'MON, I'LL BUY YOU A SALTY-CARAMEL SUNDAE ON AN EXTRA-MALT WAFFLE...
SOLD!

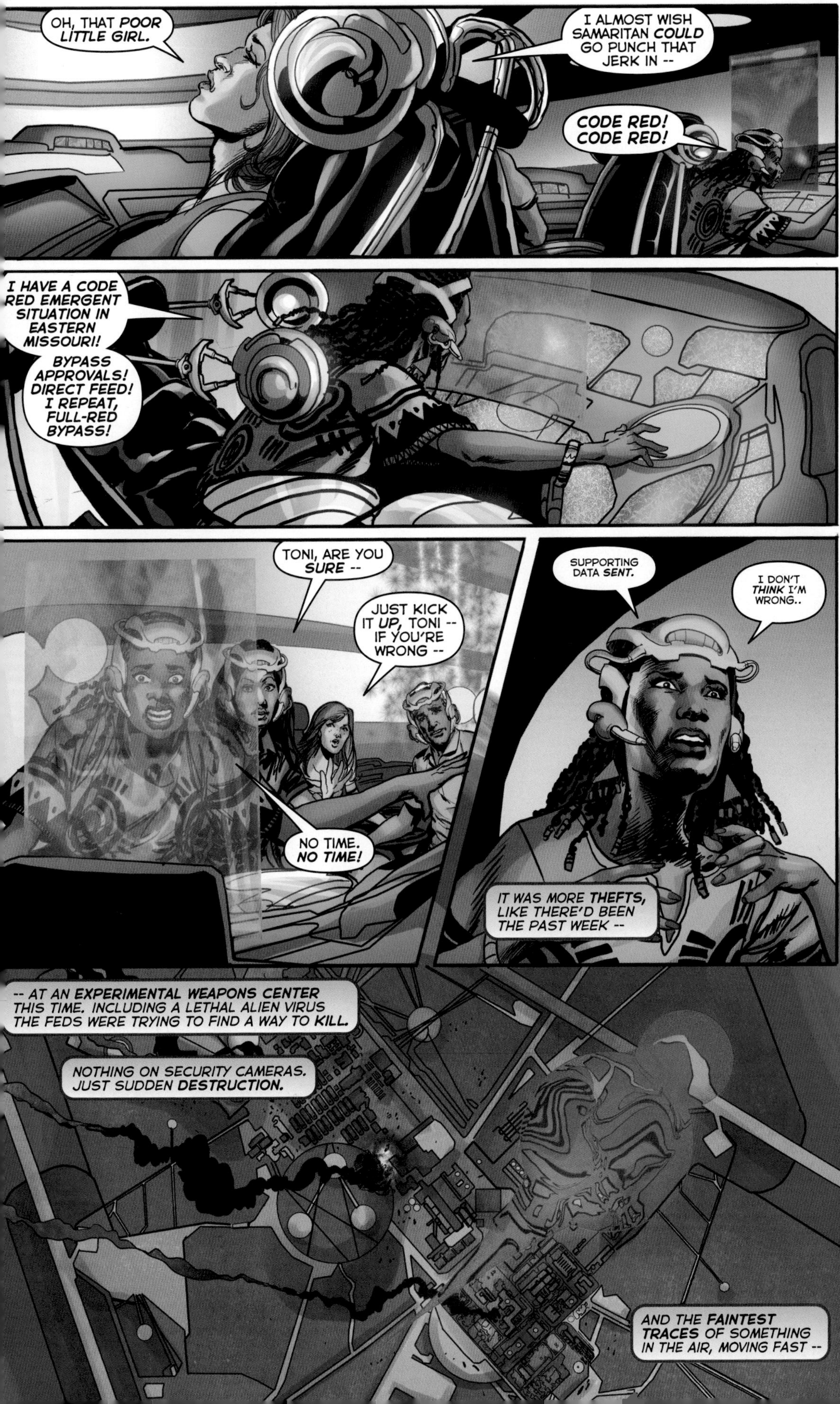
OH, THAT POOR LITTLE GIRL.
I ALMOST WISH SAMARITAN COULD GO PUNCH THAT JERK IN --
CODE RED! CODE RED!
I HAVE A CODE RED EMERGENT SITUATION IN EASTERN MISSOURI!
BYPASS APPROVALS! DIRECT FEED! I REPEAT, FULL-RED BYPASS!
TONI, ARE YOU SURE --
JUST KICK IT UP, TONI -- IF YOU'RE WRONG --
NO TIME. NO TIME!
SUPPORTING DATA SENT.
I DON'T THINK I'M WRONG..
IT WAS MORE THEFTS, LIKE THERE'D BEEN THE PAST WEEK --
-- AT AN EXPERIMENTAL WEAPONS CENTER THIS TIME. INCLUDING A LETHAL ALIEN VIRUS THE FEDS WERE TRYING TO FIND A WAY TO KILL.
NOTHING ON SECURITY CAMERAS. JUST SUDDEN DESTRUCTION.
AND THE FAINTEST TRACES OF SOMETHING IN THE AIR, MOVING FAST --

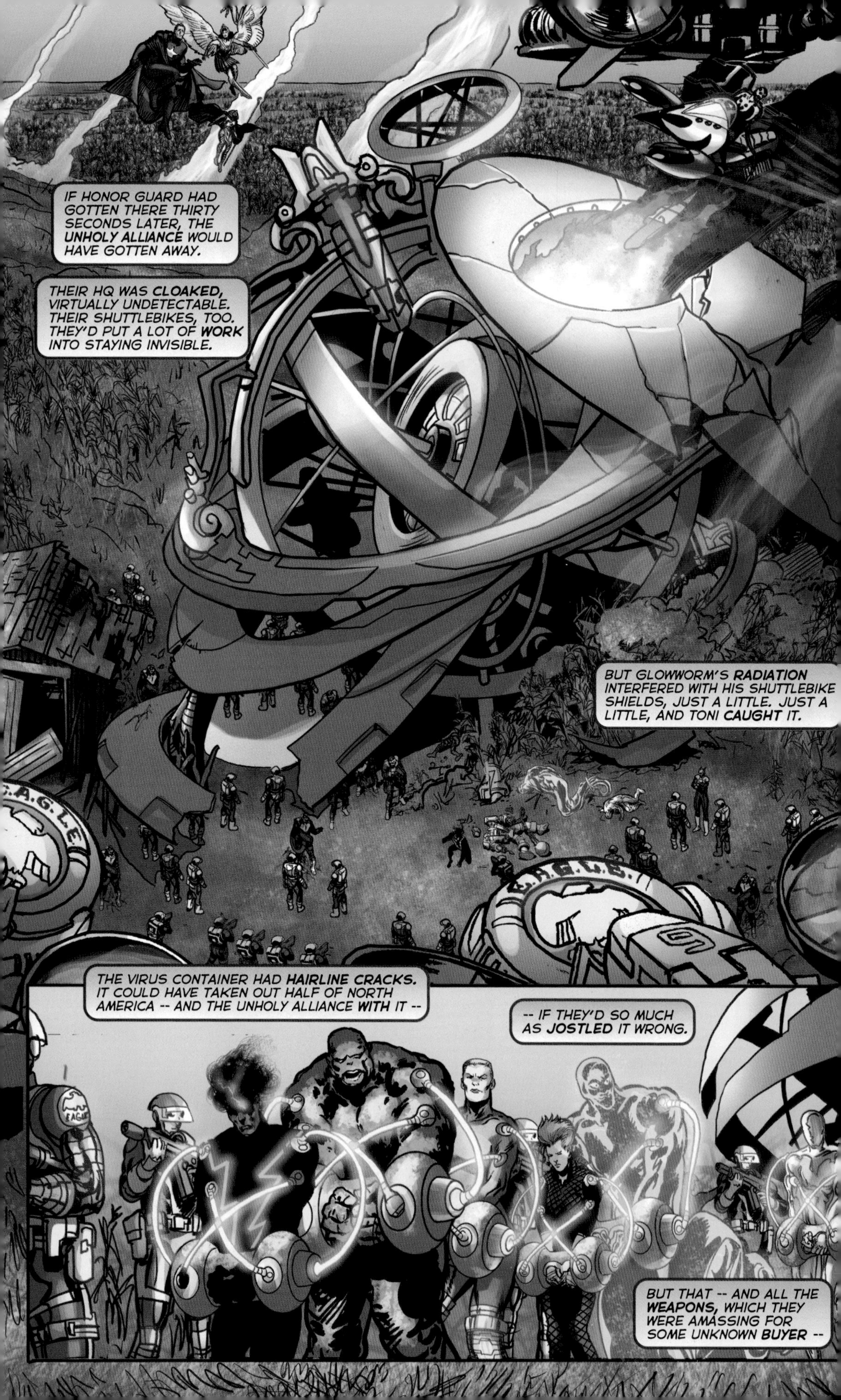
IF HONOR GUARD HAD GOTTEN THERE THIRTY SECONDS LATER, THE UNHOLY ALLIANCE WOULD HAVE GOTTEN AWAY.
THEIR HQ WAS CLOAKED, VIRTUALLY UNDETECTABLE. THEIR SHUTTLEBIKES, TOO. THEY'D PUT A LOT OF WORK INTO STAYING INVISIBLE.
BUT GLOWWORM'S RADIATION INTERFERED WITH HIS SHUTTLEBIKE SHIELDS, JUST A LITTLE. JUST A LITTLE, AND TONI CAUGHT IT.
E.A.G.L.E.
E.A.G.L.E.
THE VIRUS CONTAINER HAD HAIRLINE CRACKS. IT COULD HAVE TAKEN OUT HALF OF NORTH AMERICA -- AND THE UNHOLY ALLIANCE WITH IT --
-- IF THEY'D SO MUCH AS JOSTLED IT WRONG.
EAGLE
BUT THAT -- AND ALL THE WEAPONS, WHICH THEY WERE AMASSING FOR SOME UNKNOWN BUYER --

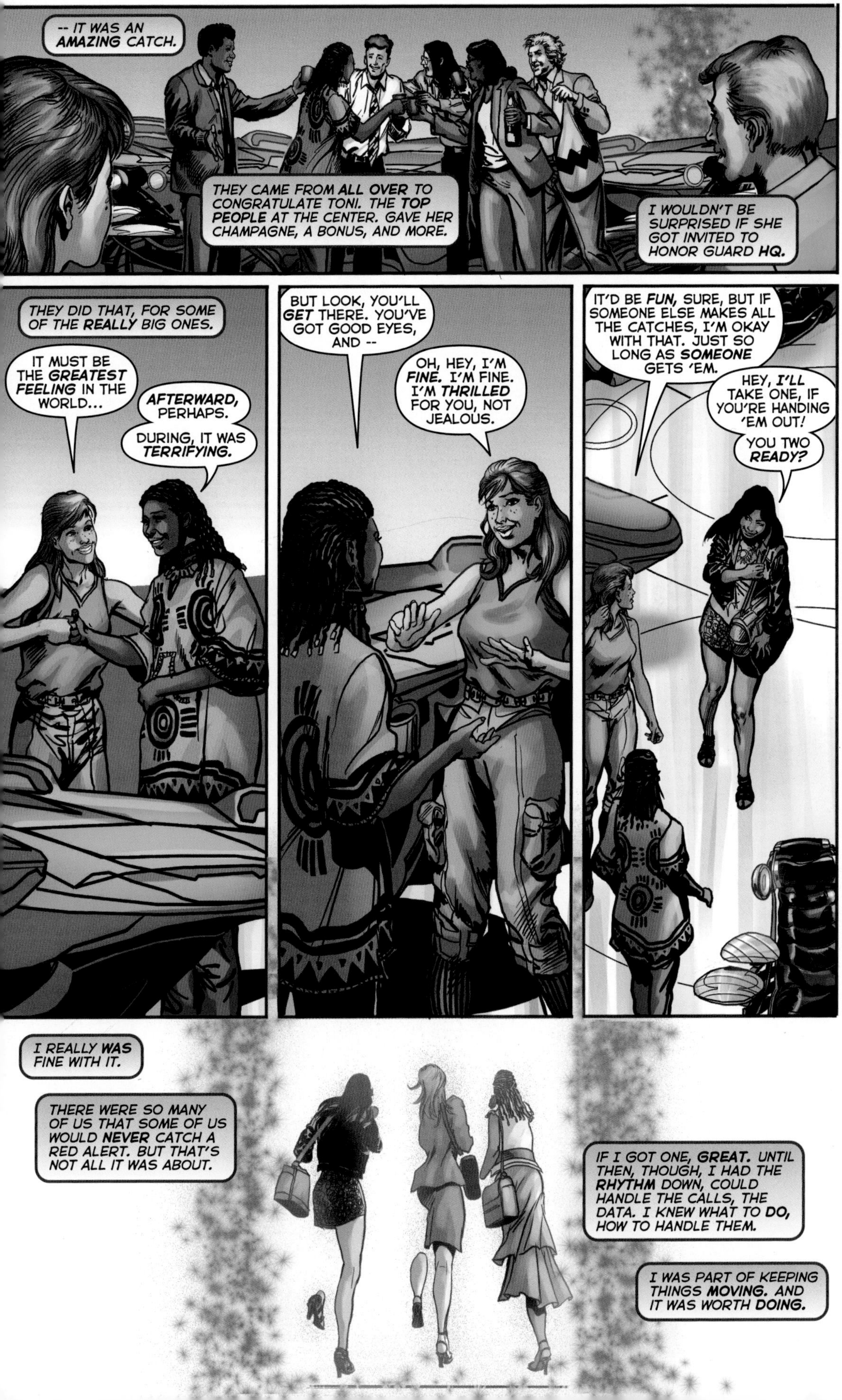
-- IT WAS AN AMAZING CATCH.
THEY CAME FROM ALL OVER TO CONGRATULATE TONI. THE TOP PEOPLE AT THE CENTER. GAVE HER CHAMPAGNE, A BONUS, AND MORE.
I WOULDN'T BE SURPRISED IF SHE GOT INVITED TO HONOR GUARD HQ.
THEY DID THAT, FOR SOME OF THE REALLY BIG ONES.
IT MUST BE THE GREATEST FEELING IN THE WORLD...
AFTERWARD, PERHAPS.
DURING, IT WAS TERRIFYING.
BUT LOOK, YOU'LL GET THERE. YOU'VE GOT GOOD EYES, AND --
OH, HEY, I'M FINE. I'M FINE. I'M THRILLED FOR YOU, NOT JEALOUS.
IT'D BE FUN, SURE, BUT IF SOMEONE ELSE MAKES ALL THE CATCHES, I'M OKAY WITH THAT. JUST SO LONG AS SOMEONE GETS 'EM.
HEY, I'LL TAKE ONE, IF YOU'RE HANDING 'EM OUT!
YOU TWO READY?
I REALLY WAS FINE WITH IT.
THERE WERE SO MANY OF US THAT SOME OF US WOULD NEVER CATCH A RED ALERT. BUT THAT'S NOT ALL IT WAS ABOUT.
IF I GOT ONE, GREAT. UNTIL THEN, THOUGH, I HAD THE RHYTHM DOWN, COULD HANDLE THE CALLS, THE DATA. I KNEW WHAT TO DO, HOW TO HANDLE THEM.
I WAS PART OF KEEPING THINGS MOVING. AND IT WAS WORTH DOING.

AND THERE WERE *OTHER* THINGS ABOUT THE JOB THAT MADE IT FUN, TOO.

I DON'T *BELIEVE* IT. I DON'T BELIEVE WE'RE ACTUALLY *HERE!*

THE LOUVRE FIRST! THE *LOUVRE!*

SURE, WE COULDN'T DO A LOT OF *SHARING* WITH OUR FAMILIES. BUT THE JOB MADE UP FOR IT.

THEY LET US USE THE *TELEPORTERS,* AS LONG AS THERE WASN'T AN EMERGENCY, AND WE SIGNED UP IN *ADVANCE.*

THERE WERE *RULES:* SPEND CASH ONLY, OR USE A COMPANY CARD THEY COULD *DISGUISE.* NO CREDIT CARD ANOMALIES, NO *FOREIGN-TRAVEL* FLAGS.

I GOT TO SEE *ROME, MADRID, LONDON, PARIS...*

I DON'T *BELIEVE* YOU, MICHIKO.

YOU COULD *OUT-SHOP ALL MY* AUNTS COMBINED. AND THEY'RE *OLYMPIC* CALIBER.

MY *GRANDMA,* TOO...

THEY TOOK SECURITY *SERIOUSLY.* BUT THEY MADE SURE THERE WERE *PERKS.* THEY WANTED US TO BE HAPPY. RELAXED. BUT *FOCUSED.*

REALLY, MICHI? *SWEET!*

SO I'VE BEEN TELLING MY MOTHER ABOUT THESE TWO *FOREIGN-EXCHANGE STUDENTS* FROM THE UNIVERSITY.

IF YOU CAN DROP A FEW REFERENCES TO *PACIFIC RIM ECONOMICS,* YOU COULD COME FOR DINNER.

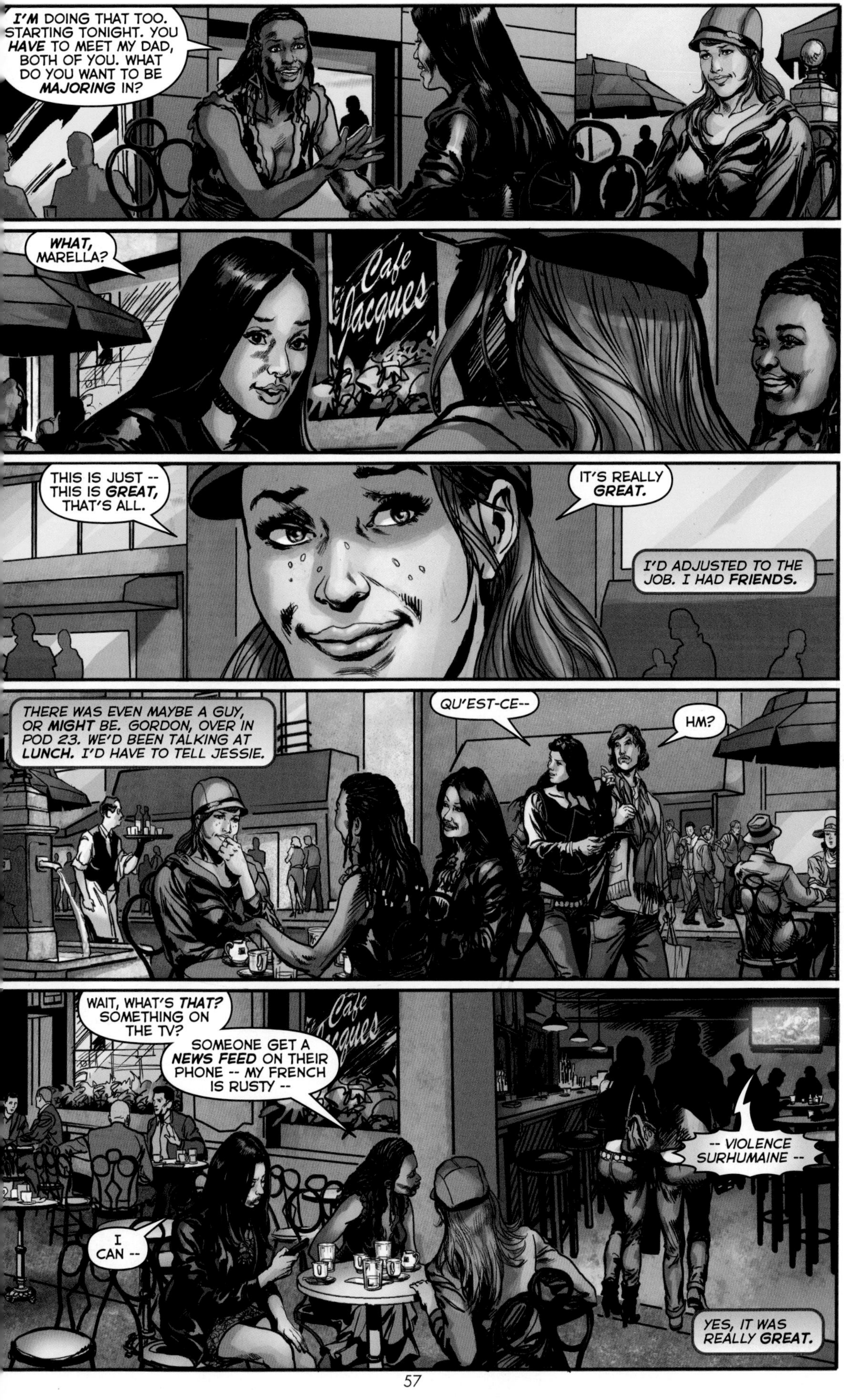
I'M DOING THAT TOO. STARTING TONIGHT. YOU HAVE TO MEET MY DAD, BOTH OF YOU. WHAT DO YOU WANT TO BE MAJORING IN?
WHAT, MARELLA?
Cafe Jacques
THIS IS JUST -- THIS IS GREAT, THAT'S ALL.
IT'S REALLY GREAT.
I'D ADJUSTED TO THE JOB. I HAD FRIENDS.
THERE WAS EVEN MAYBE A GUY, OR MIGHT BE. GORDON, OVER IN POD 23. WE'D BEEN TALKING AT LUNCH. I'D HAVE TO TELL JESSIE.
QU'EST-CE--
HM?
WAIT, WHAT'S THAT? SOMETHING ON THE TV?
SOMEONE GET A NEWS FEED ON THEIR PHONE -- MY FRENCH IS RUSTY --
-- VIOLENCE SURHUMAINE --
I CAN --
YES, IT WAS REALLY GREAT.

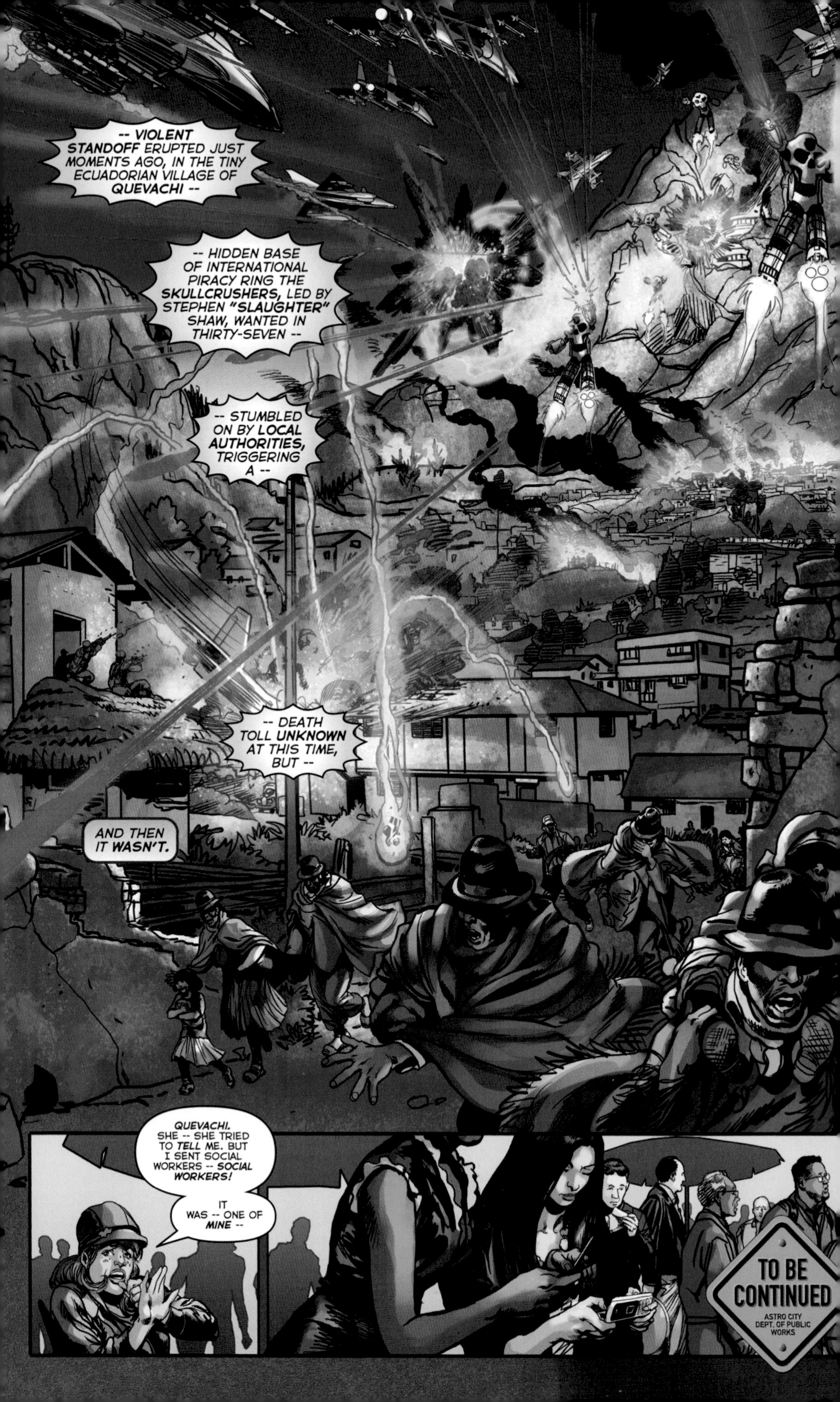

-- VIOLENT STANDOFF ERUPTED JUST MOMENTS AGO, IN THE TINY ECUADORIAN VILLAGE OF QUEVACHI --
-- HIDDEN BASE OF INTERNATIONAL PIRACY RING THE SKULLCRUSHERS, LED BY STEPHEN "SLAUGHTER" SHAW, WANTED IN THIRTY-SEVEN --
-- STUMBLED ON BY LOCAL AUTHORITIES, TRIGGERING A --
-- DEATH TOLL UNKNOWN AT THIS TIME, BUT --
AND THEN IT WASN'T.
QUEVACHI. SHE -- SHE TRIED TO TELL ME. BUT I SENT SOCIAL WORKERS -- SOCIAL WORKERS!
IT WAS -- ONE OF MINE --
TO BE CONTINUED
ASTRO CITY DEPT. OF PUBLIC WORKS

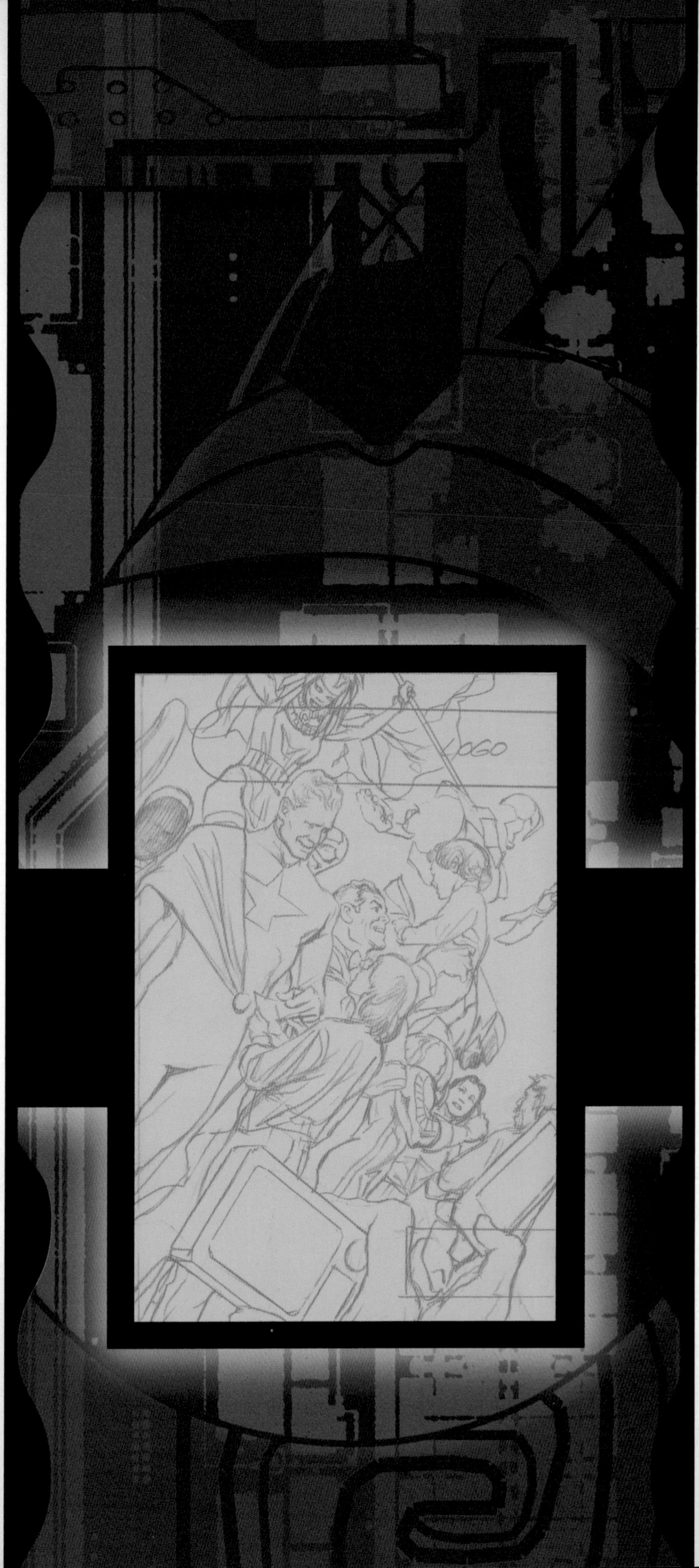
LOGO

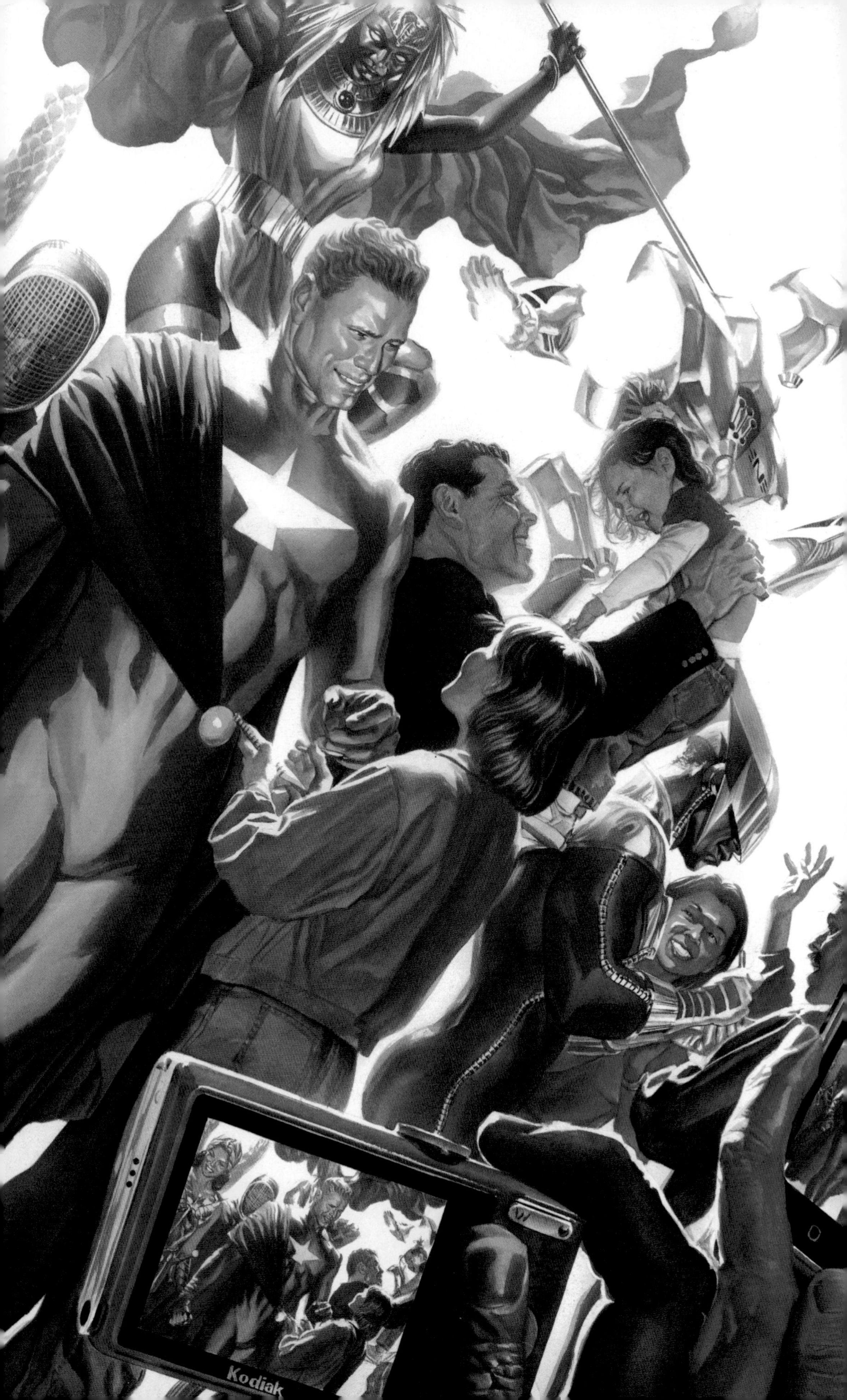
Kodiak

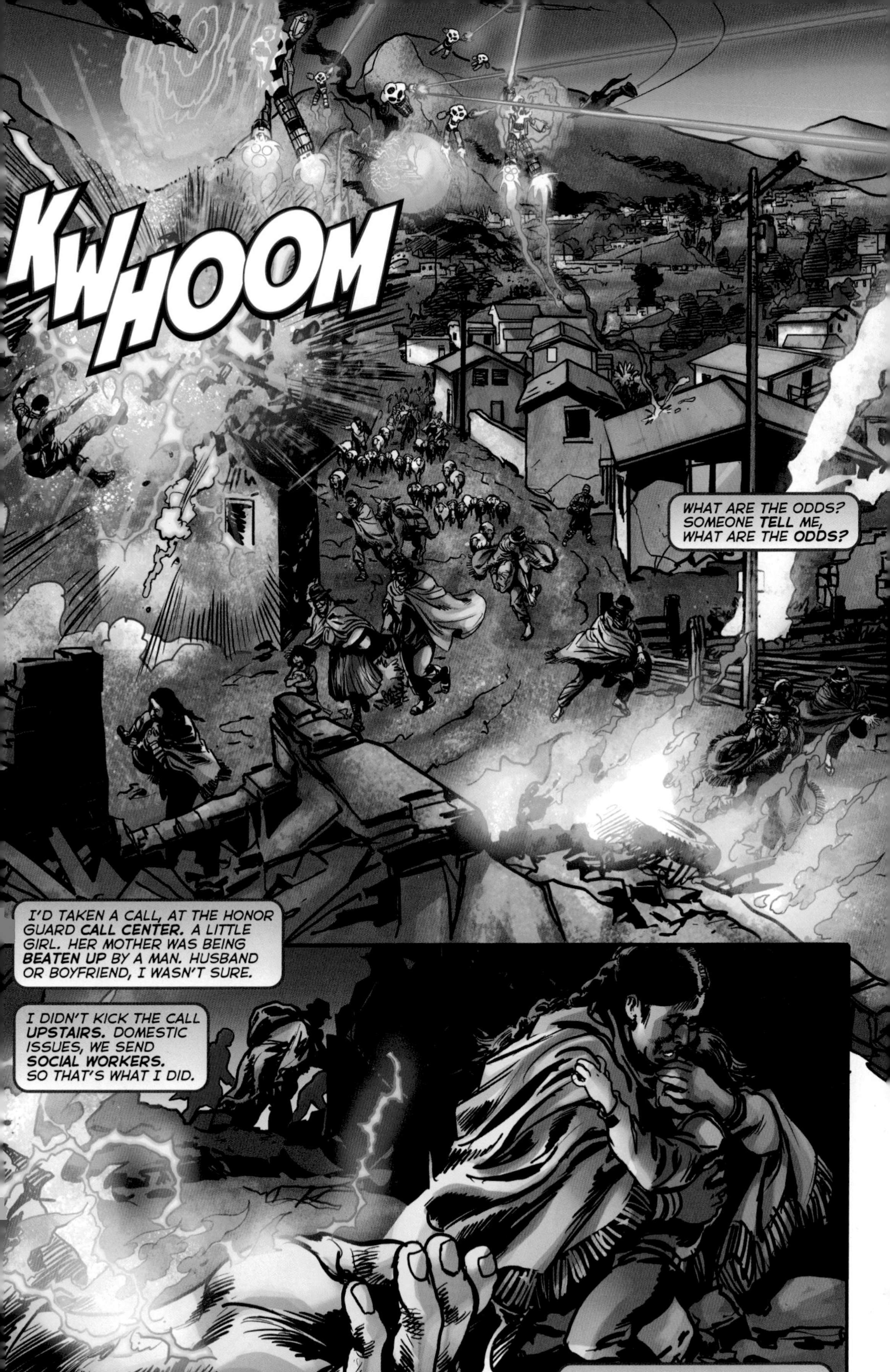
KWHOOM
WHAT ARE THE ODDS? SOMEONE TELL ME, WHAT ARE THE ODDS?
I'D TAKEN A CALL, AT THE HONOR GUARD CALL CENTER. A LITTLE GIRL. HER MOTHER WAS BEING BEATEN UP BY A MAN. HUSBAND OR BOYFRIEND, I WASN'T SURE.
I DIDN'T KICK THE CALL UPSTAIRS. DOMESTIC ISSUES, WE SEND SOCIAL WORKERS. SO THAT'S WHAT I DID.
SOCIAL WORKERS. TO A LITTLE MOUNTAIN VILLAGE IN ECUADOR. AND LESS THAN TWO DAYS LATER...

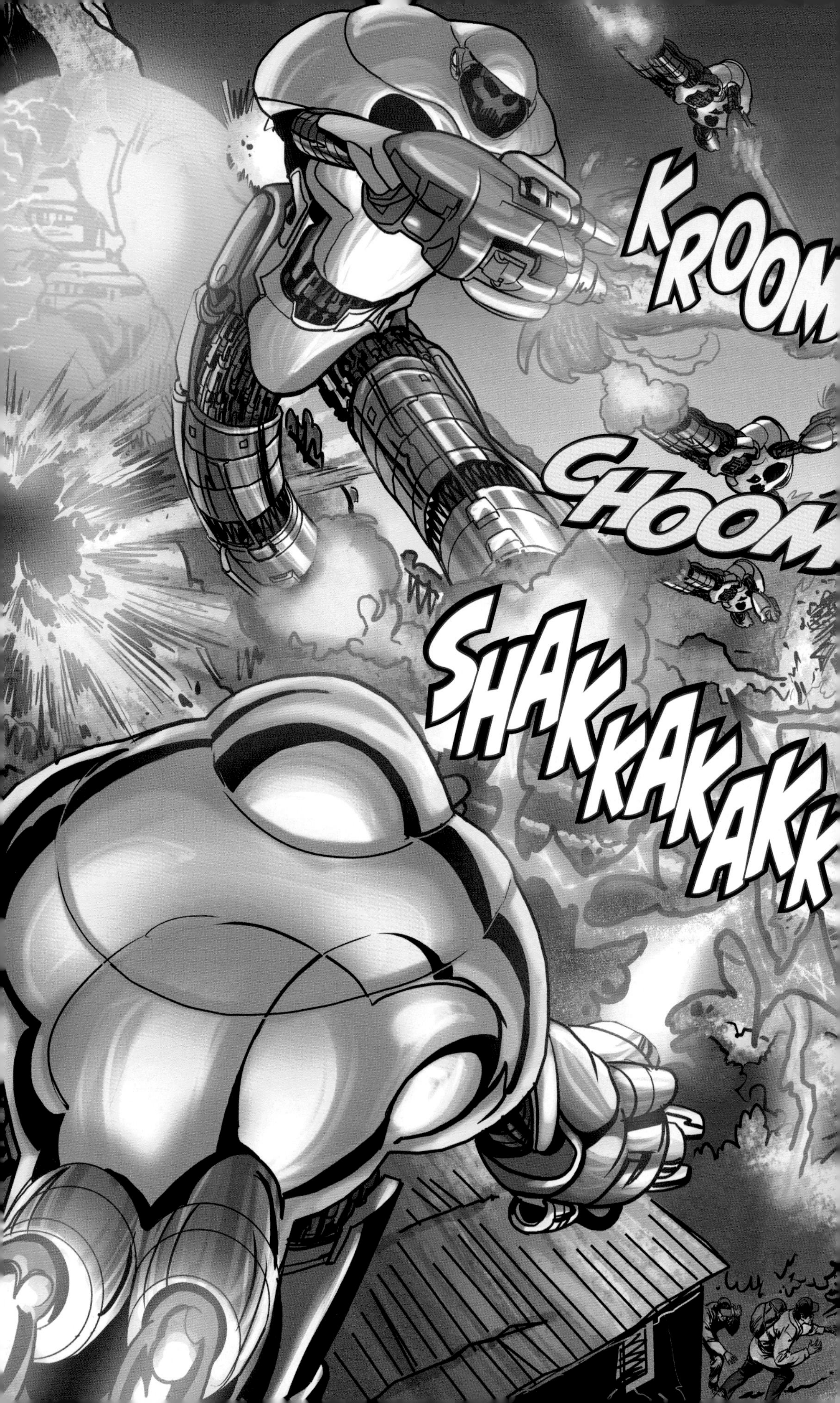
KROOM
CHOOM
SHAKKAKAKK

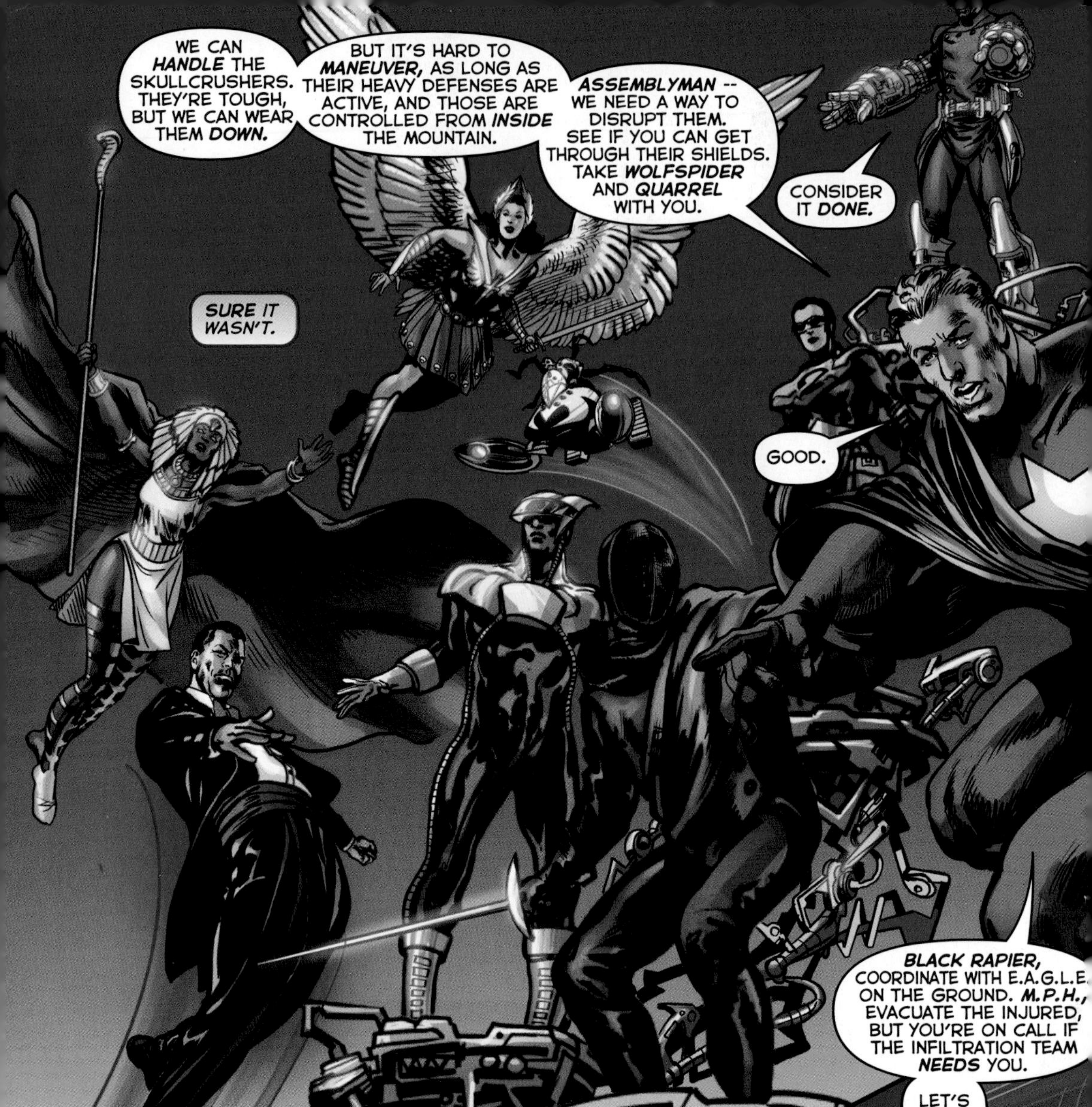
WE CAN HANDLE THE SKULLCRUSHERS. THEY'RE TOUGH, BUT WE CAN WEAR THEM DOWN.
BUT IT'S HARD TO MANEUVER, AS LONG AS THEIR HEAVY DEFENSES ARE ACTIVE, AND THOSE ARE CONTROLLED FROM INSIDE THE MOUNTAIN.
ASSEMBLYMAN -- WE NEED A WAY TO DISRUPT THEM. SEE IF YOU CAN GET THROUGH THEIR SHIELDS. TAKE WOLFSPIDER AND QUARREL WITH YOU.
CONSIDER IT DONE.
SURE IT WASN'T.
GOOD.
BLACK RAPIER, COORDINATE WITH E.A.G.L.E. ON THE GROUND. M.P.H., EVACUATE THE INJURED, BUT YOU'RE ON CALL IF THE INFILTRATION TEAM NEEDS YOU.
LET'S GO.

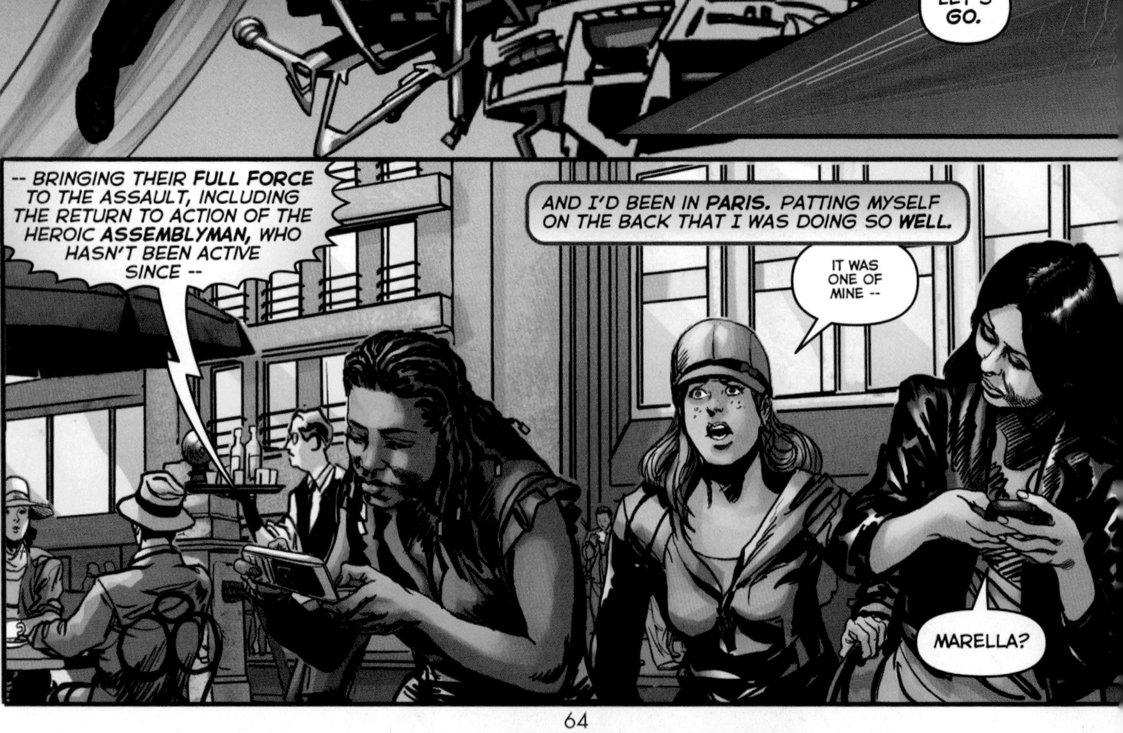
-- BRINGING THEIR FULL FORCE TO THE ASSAULT, INCLUDING THE RETURN TO ACTION OF THE HEROIC ASSEMBLYMAN, WHO HASN'T BEEN ACTIVE SINCE --
AND I'D BEEN IN PARIS. PATTING MYSELF ON THE BACK THAT I WAS DOING SO WELL.
IT WAS ONE OF MINE --
MARELLA?

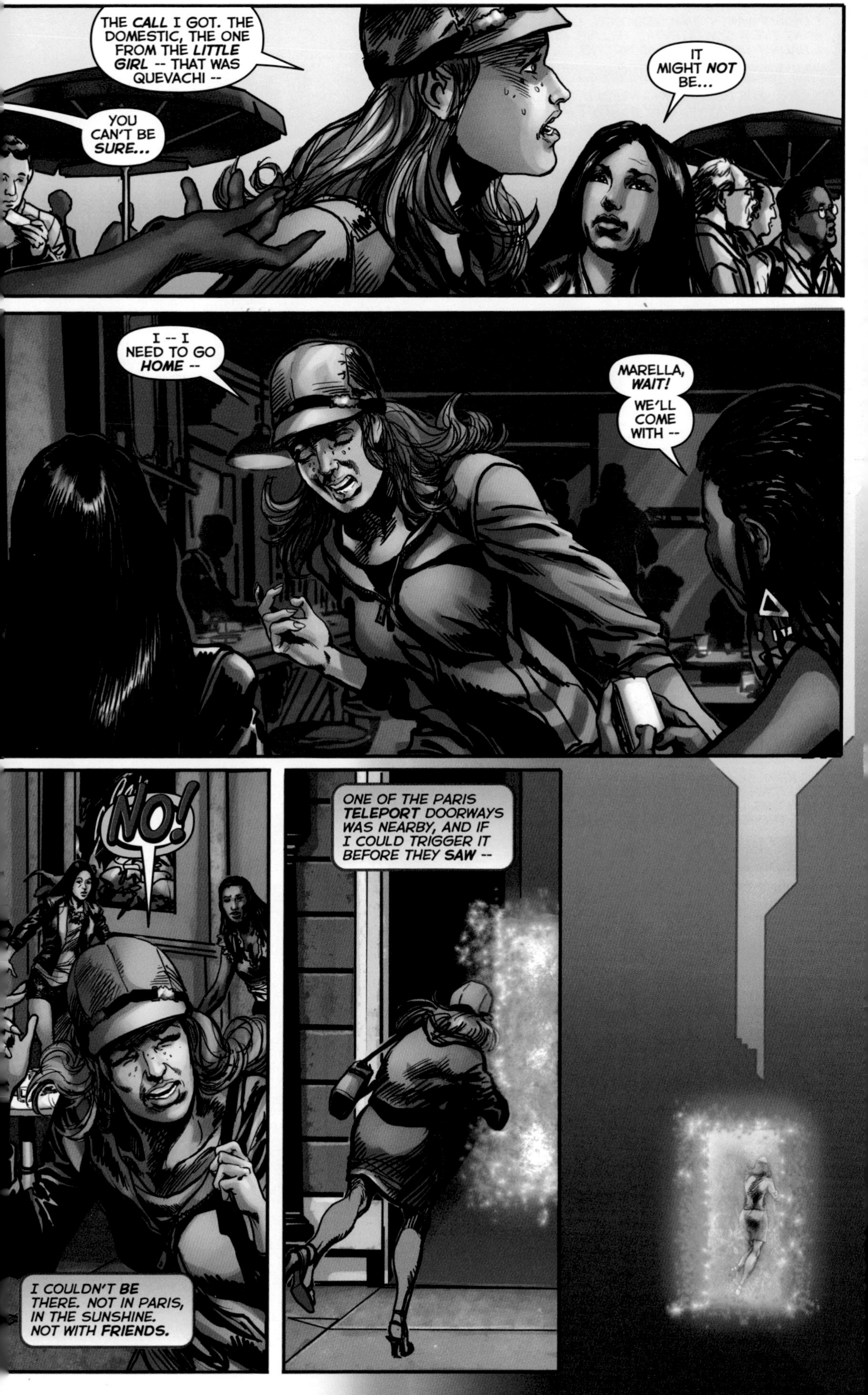
THE CALL I GOT. THE DOMESTIC, THE ONE FROM THE LITTLE GIRL -- THAT WAS QUEVACHI --
YOU CAN'T BE SURE...
IT MIGHT NOT BE...
I -- I NEED TO GO HOME --
MARELLA, WAIT!
WE'LL COME WITH --
NO!
I COULDN'T BE THERE. NOT IN PARIS, IN THE SUNSHINE. NOT WITH FRIENDS.
ONE OF THE PARIS TELEPORT DOORWAYS WAS NEARBY, AND IF I COULD TRIGGER IT BEFORE THEY SAW --

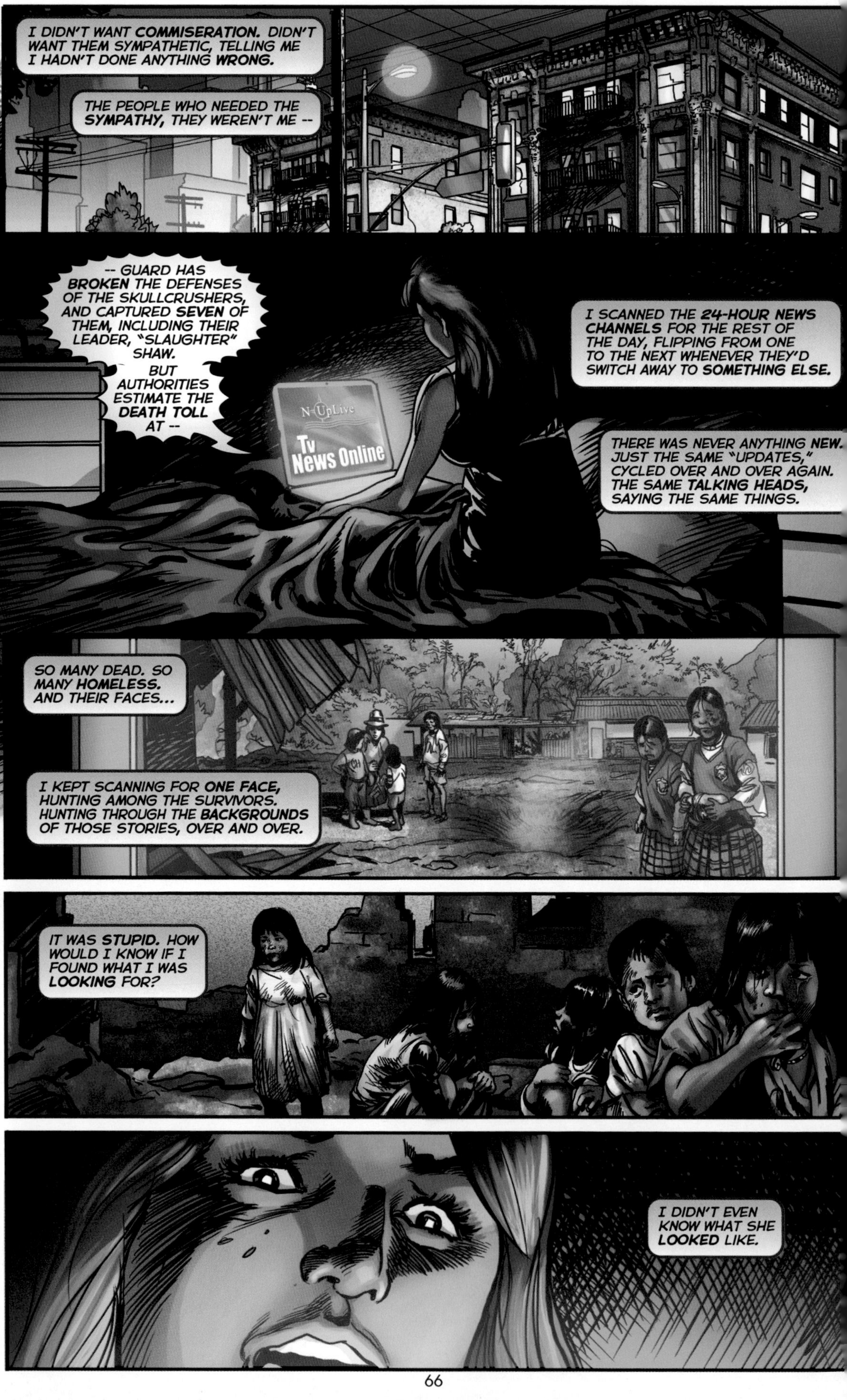

I DIDN'T WANT COMMISERATION. DIDN'T WANT THEM SYMPATHETIC, TELLING ME I HADN'T DONE ANYTHING WRONG.
THE PEOPLE WHO NEEDED THE SYMPATHY, THEY WEREN'T ME --
-- GUARD HAS BROKEN THE DEFENSES OF THE SKULLCRUSHERS, AND CAPTURED SEVEN OF THEM, INCLUDING THEIR LEADER, "SLAUGHTER" SHAW.
BUT AUTHORITIES ESTIMATE THE DEATH TOLL AT --
N UpLive
Tv News Online
I SCANNED THE 24-HOUR NEWS CHANNELS FOR THE REST OF THE DAY, FLIPPING FROM ONE TO THE NEXT WHENEVER THEY'D SWITCH AWAY TO SOMETHING ELSE.
THERE WAS NEVER ANYTHING NEW. JUST THE SAME "UPDATES," CYCLED OVER AND OVER AGAIN. THE SAME TALKING HEADS, SAYING THE SAME THINGS.
SO MANY DEAD. SO MANY HOMELESS. AND THEIR FACES...
I KEPT SCANNING FOR ONE FACE, HUNTING AMONG THE SURVIVORS. HUNTING THROUGH THE BACKGROUNDS OF THOSE STORIES, OVER AND OVER.
IT WAS STUPID. HOW WOULD I KNOW IF I FOUND WHAT I WAS LOOKING FOR?
I DIDN'T EVEN KNOW WHAT SHE LOOKED LIKE.

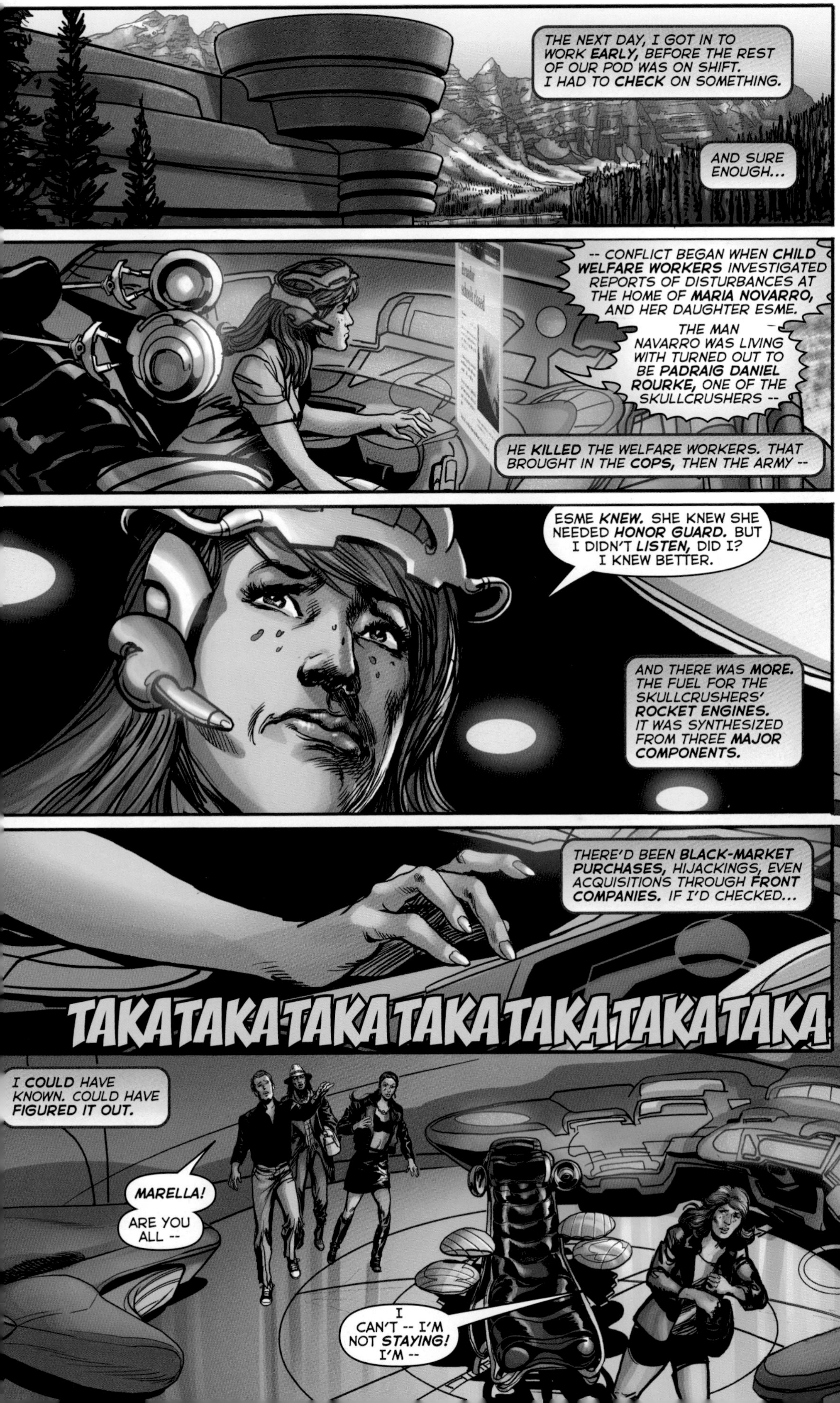
THE NEXT DAY, I GOT IN TO WORK EARLY, BEFORE THE REST OF OUR POD WAS ON SHIFT. I HAD TO CHECK ON SOMETHING.
AND SURE ENOUGH...
-- CONFLICT BEGAN WHEN CHILD WELFARE WORKERS INVESTIGATED REPORTS OF DISTURBANCES AT THE HOME OF MARIA NOVARRO, AND HER DAUGHTER ESME.
THE MAN NAVARRO WAS LIVING WITH TURNED OUT TO BE PADRAIG DANIEL ROURKE, ONE OF THE SKULLCRUSHERS --
HE KILLED THE WELFARE WORKERS. THAT BROUGHT IN THE COPS, THEN THE ARMY --
ESME KNEW. SHE KNEW SHE NEEDED HONOR GUARD. BUT I DIDN'T LISTEN, DID I? I KNEW BETTER.
AND THERE WAS MORE. THE FUEL FOR THE SKULLCRUSHERS' ROCKET ENGINES. IT WAS SYNTHESIZED FROM THREE MAJOR COMPONENTS.
THERE'D BEEN BLACK-MARKET PURCHASES, HIJACKINGS, EVEN ACQUISITIONS THROUGH FRONT COMPANIES. IF I'D CHECKED...
TAKATAKATAKATAKATAKATAKATAKA
I COULD HAVE KNOWN. COULD HAVE FIGURED IT OUT.
MARELLA!
ARE YOU ALL --
I CAN'T -- I'M NOT STAYING! I'M --

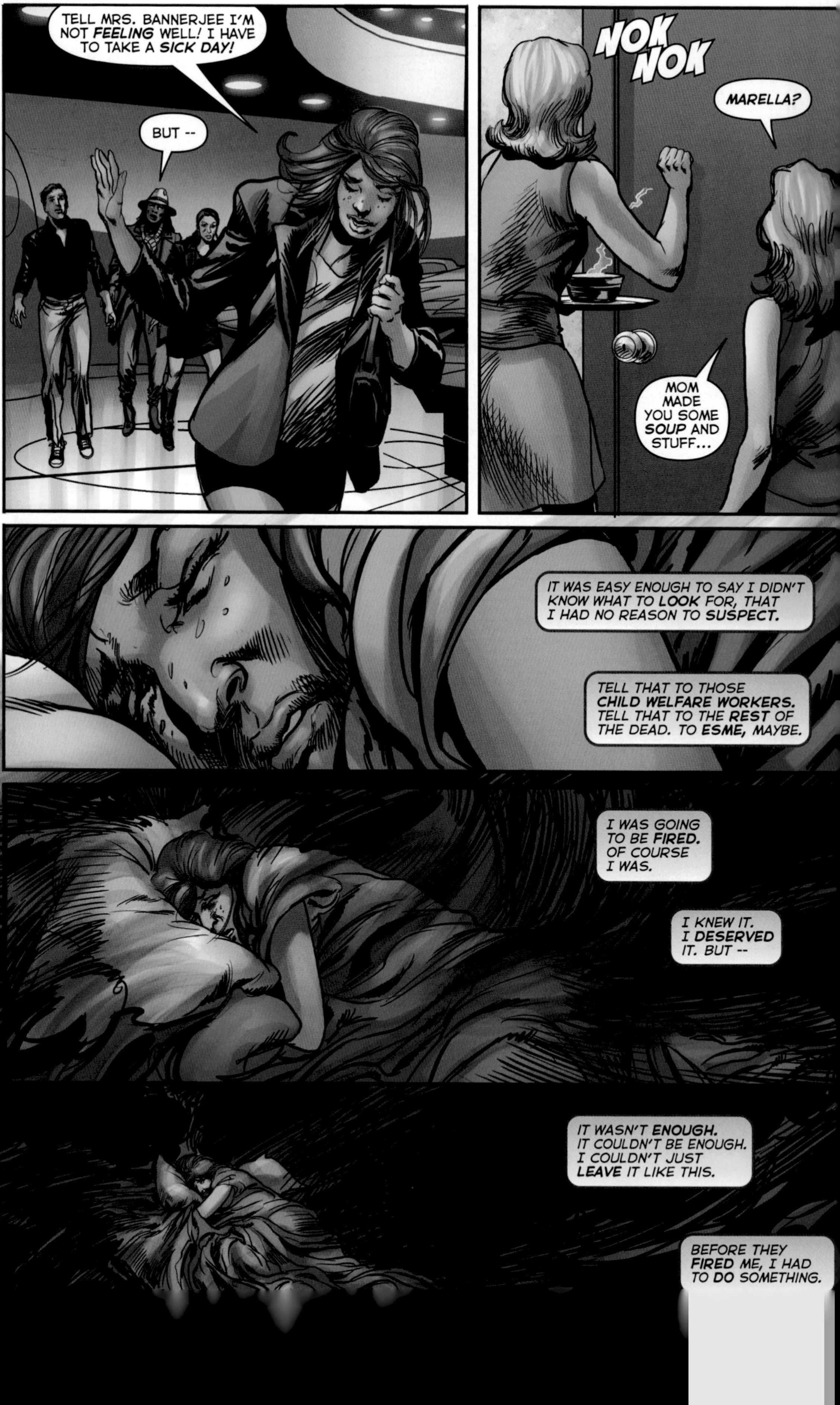
TELL MRS. BANNERJEE I'M NOT FEELING WELL! I HAVE TO TAKE A SICK DAY!
BUT --
NOK NOK
MARELLA?
MOM MADE YOU SOME SOUP AND STUFF...
IT WAS EASY ENOUGH TO SAY I DIDN'T KNOW WHAT TO LOOK FOR, THAT I HAD NO REASON TO SUSPECT.
TELL THAT TO THOSE CHILD WELFARE WORKERS. TELL THAT TO THE REST OF THE DEAD. TO ESME, MAYBE.
I WAS GOING TO BE FIRED. OF COURSE I WAS.
I KNEW IT. I DESERVED IT. BUT --
IT WASN'T ENOUGH. IT COULDN'T BE ENOUGH. I COULDN'T JUST LEAVE IT LIKE THIS.
BEFORE THEY FIRED ME, I HAD TO DO SOMETHING.

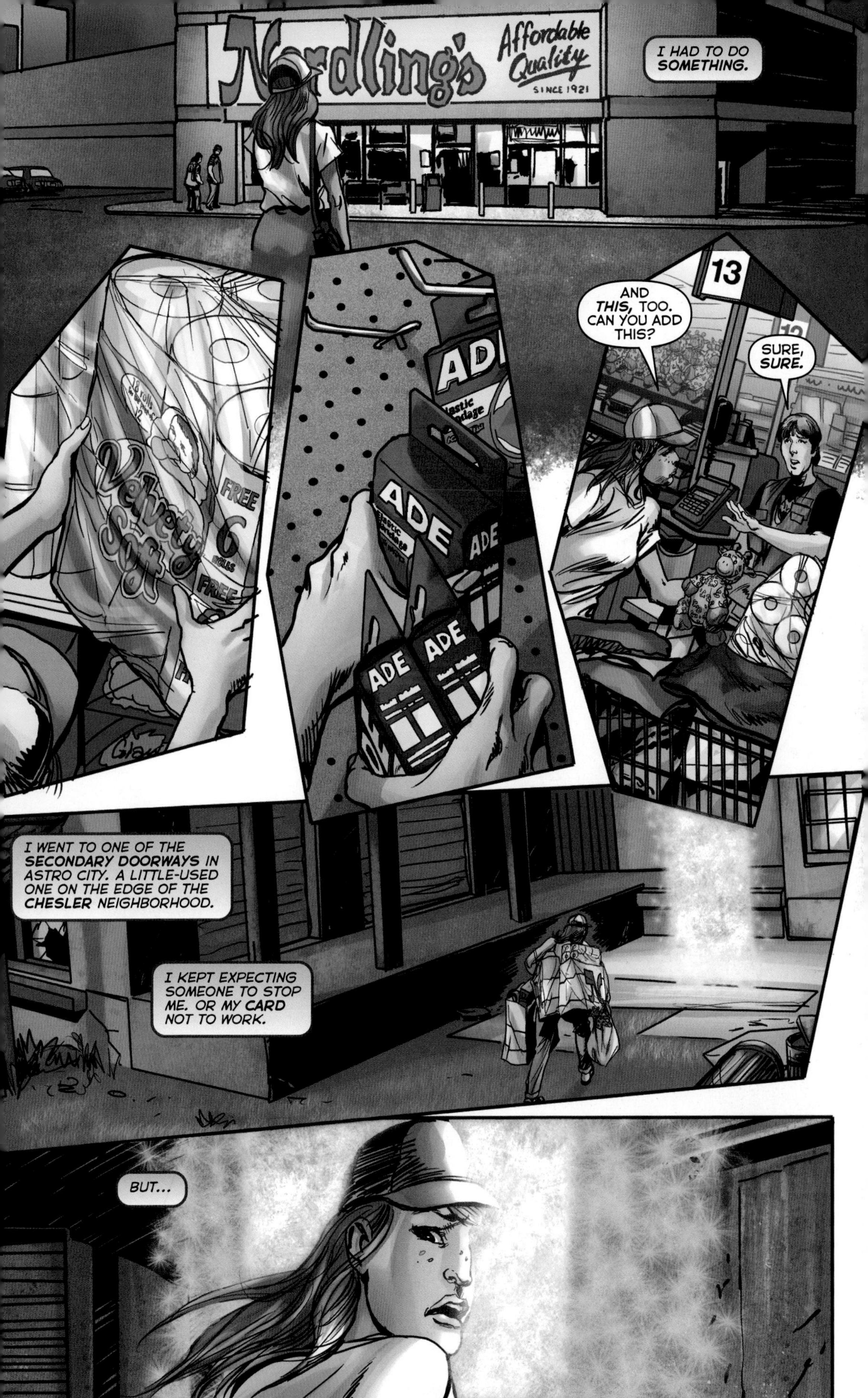

Nordling's
Affordable Quality
SINCE 1921
I HAD TO DO SOMETHING.
Velvety Soft
FREE
6 ROLLS
ADE
Elastic Bandage
13
AND THIS, TOO. CAN YOU ADD THIS?
SURE, SURE.
I WENT TO ONE OF THE SECONDARY DOORWAYS IN ASTRO CITY. A LITTLE-USED ONE ON THE EDGE OF THE CHESLER NEIGHBORHOOD.
I KEPT EXPECTING SOMEONE TO STOP ME. OR MY CARD NOT TO WORK.
BUT...

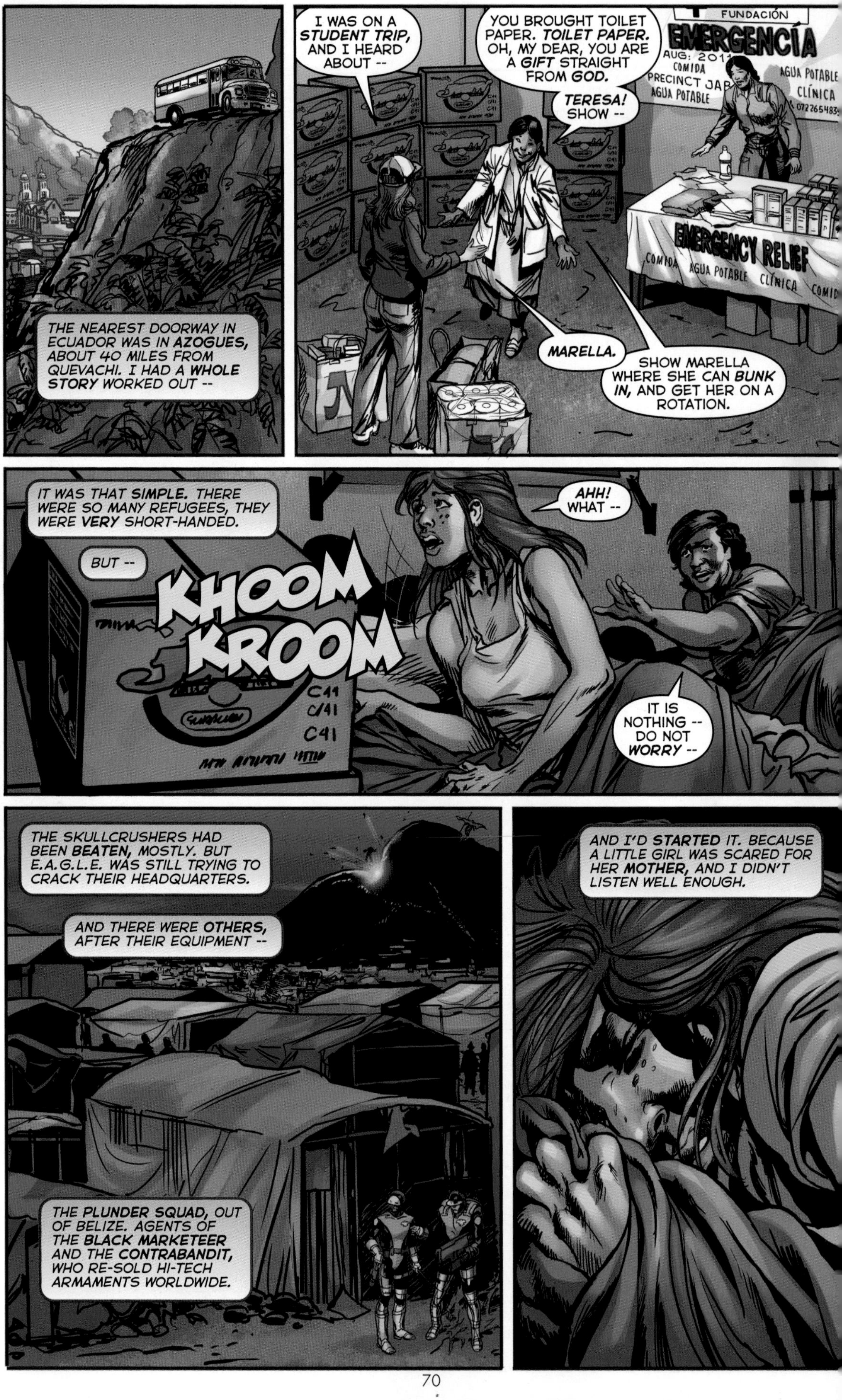
THE NEAREST DOORWAY IN ECUADOR WAS IN AZOGUES, ABOUT 40 MILES FROM QUEVACHI. I HAD A WHOLE STORY WORKED OUT --
I WAS ON A STUDENT TRIP, AND I HEARD ABOUT --
YOU BROUGHT TOILET PAPER. TOILET PAPER. OH, MY DEAR, YOU ARE A GIFT STRAIGHT FROM GOD.
TERESA! SHOW --
MARELLA.
SHOW MARELLA WHERE SHE CAN BUNK IN, AND GET HER ON A ROTATION.
FUNDACIÓN
EMERGENCIA
AUG: 2011
COMIDA
PRECINCT JAB
AGUA POTABLE
AGUA POTABLE
CLÍNICA
EMERGENCY RELIEF
COMIDA AGUA POTABLE CLÍNICA COMIDA
IT WAS THAT SIMPLE. THERE WERE SO MANY REFUGEES, THEY WERE VERY SHORT-HANDED.
BUT --
KHOOM KROOM
AHH! WHAT --
IT IS NOTHING -- DO NOT WORRY --
C41
C41
C41
THE SKULLCRUSHERS HAD BEEN BEATEN, MOSTLY. BUT E.A.G.L.E. WAS STILL TRYING TO CRACK THEIR HEADQUARTERS.
AND THERE WERE OTHERS, AFTER THEIR EQUIPMENT --
THE PLUNDER SQUAD, OUT OF BELIZE. AGENTS OF THE BLACK MARKETEER AND THE CONTRABANDIT, WHO RE-SOLD HI-TECH ARMAMENTS WORLDWIDE.
AND I'D STARTED IT. BECAUSE A LITTLE GIRL WAS SCARED FOR HER MOTHER, AND I DIDN'T LISTEN WELL ENOUGH.

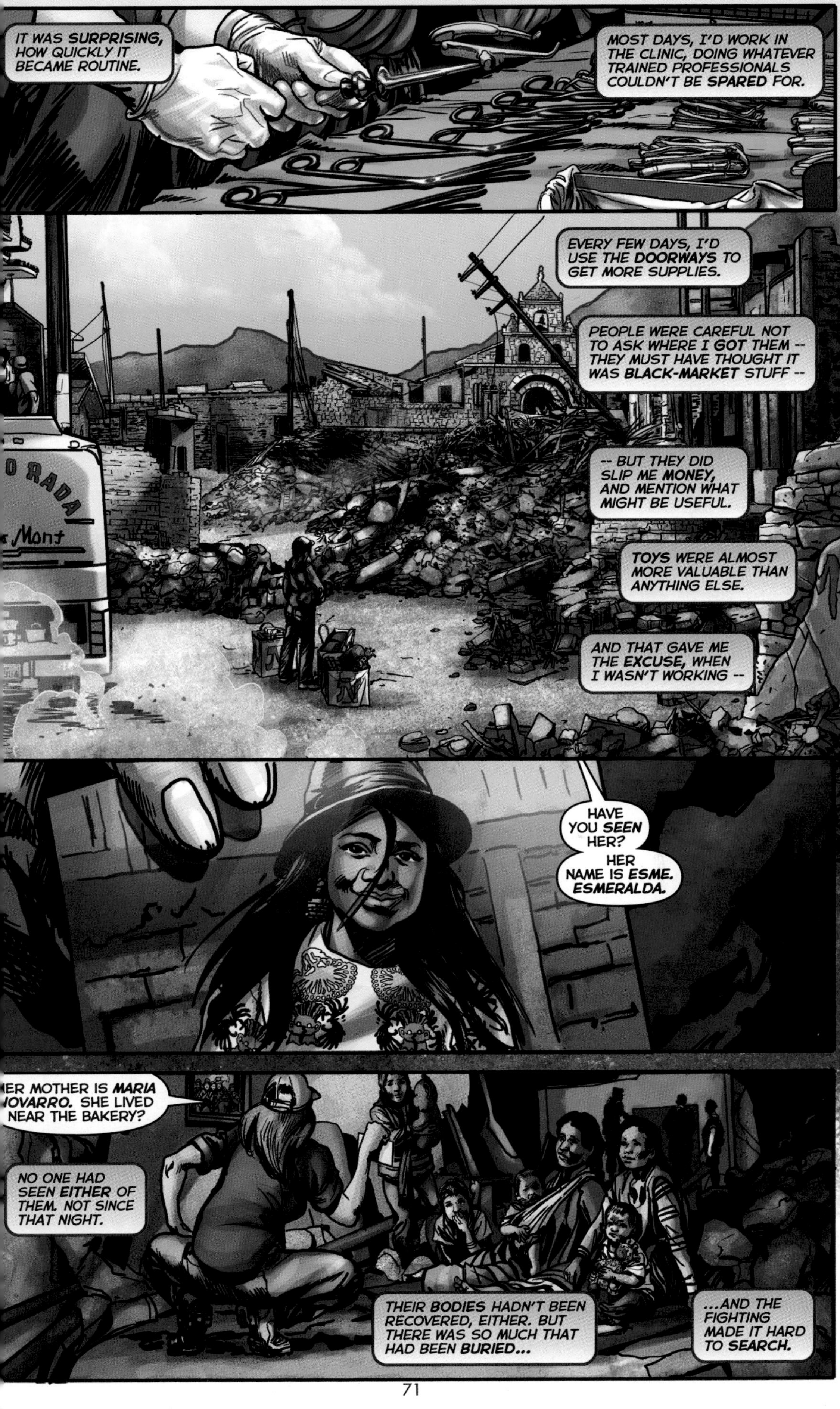

IT WAS SURPRISING, HOW QUICKLY IT BECAME ROUTINE.
MOST DAYS, I'D WORK IN THE CLINIC, DOING WHATEVER TRAINED PROFESSIONALS COULDN'T BE SPARED FOR.
EVERY FEW DAYS, I'D USE THE DOORWAYS TO GET MORE SUPPLIES.
PEOPLE WERE CAREFUL NOT TO ASK WHERE I GOT THEM -- THEY MUST HAVE THOUGHT IT WAS BLACK-MARKET STUFF --
-- BUT THEY DID SLIP ME MONEY, AND MENTION WHAT MIGHT BE USEFUL.
TOYS WERE ALMOST MORE VALUABLE THAN ANYTHING ELSE.
AND THAT GAVE ME THE EXCUSE, WHEN I WASN'T WORKING --
HAVE YOU SEEN HER?
HER NAME IS ESME. ESMERALDA.
ER MOTHER IS MARIA OVARRO. SHE LIVED NEAR THE BAKERY?
NO ONE HAD SEEN EITHER OF THEM. NOT SINCE THAT NIGHT.
THEIR BODIES HADN'T BEEN RECOVERED, EITHER. BUT THERE WAS SO MUCH THAT HAD BEEN BURIED...
...AND THE FIGHTING MADE IT HARD TO SEARCH.

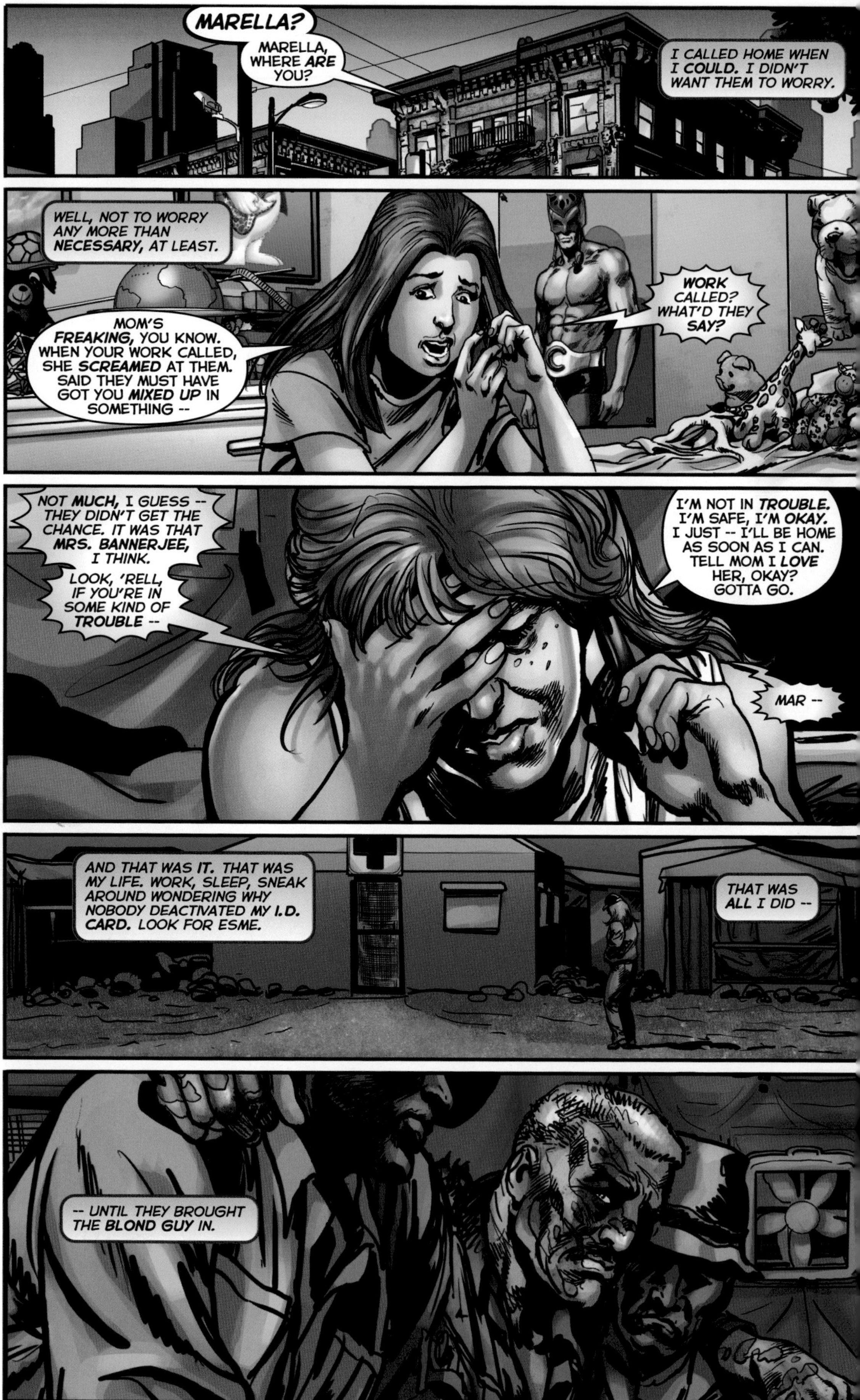
MARELLA?
MARELLA, WHERE ARE YOU?
I CALLED HOME WHEN I COULD. I DIDN'T WANT THEM TO WORRY.
WELL, NOT TO WORRY ANY MORE THAN NECESSARY, AT LEAST.
MOM'S FREAKING, YOU KNOW. WHEN YOUR WORK CALLED, SHE SCREAMED AT THEM. SAID THEY MUST HAVE GOT YOU MIXED UP IN SOMETHING --
WORK CALLED? WHAT'D THEY SAY?
NOT MUCH, I GUESS -- THEY DIDN'T GET THE CHANCE. IT WAS THAT MRS. BANNERJEE, I THINK.
LOOK, 'RELL, IF YOU'RE IN SOME KIND OF TROUBLE --
I'M NOT IN TROUBLE. I'M SAFE, I'M OKAY. I JUST -- I'LL BE HOME AS SOON AS I CAN. TELL MOM I LOVE HER, OKAY? GOTTA GO.
MAR --
AND THAT WAS IT. THAT WAS MY LIFE. WORK, SLEEP, SNEAK AROUND WONDERING WHY NOBODY DEACTIVATED MY I.D. CARD. LOOK FOR ESME.
THAT WAS ALL I DID --
-- UNTIL THEY BROUGHT THE BLOND GUY IN.

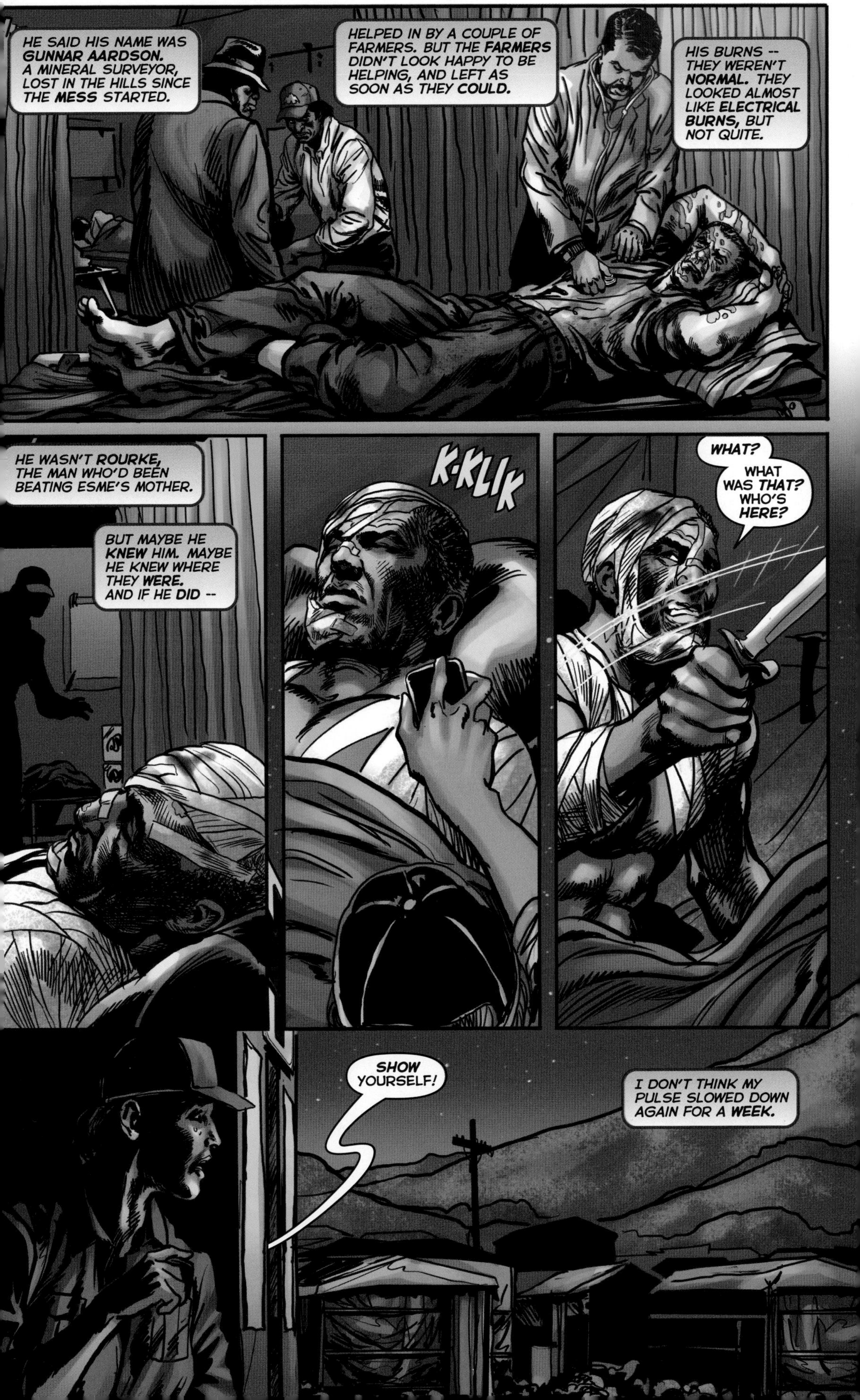

HE SAID HIS NAME WAS GUNNAR AARDSON. A MINERAL SURVEYOR, LOST IN THE HILLS SINCE THE MESS STARTED.
HELPED IN BY A COUPLE OF FARMERS. BUT THE FARMERS DIDN'T LOOK HAPPY TO BE HELPING, AND LEFT AS SOON AS THEY COULD.
HIS BURNS -- THEY WEREN'T NORMAL. THEY LOOKED ALMOST LIKE ELECTRICAL BURNS, BUT NOT QUITE.
HE WASN'T ROURKE, THE MAN WHO'D BEEN BEATING ESME'S MOTHER.
BUT MAYBE HE KNEW HIM. MAYBE HE KNEW WHERE THEY WERE. AND IF HE DID --
K-KLIK
WHAT?
WHAT WAS THAT? WHO'S HERE?
SHOW YOURSELF!
I DON'T THINK MY PULSE SLOWED DOWN AGAIN FOR A WEEK.

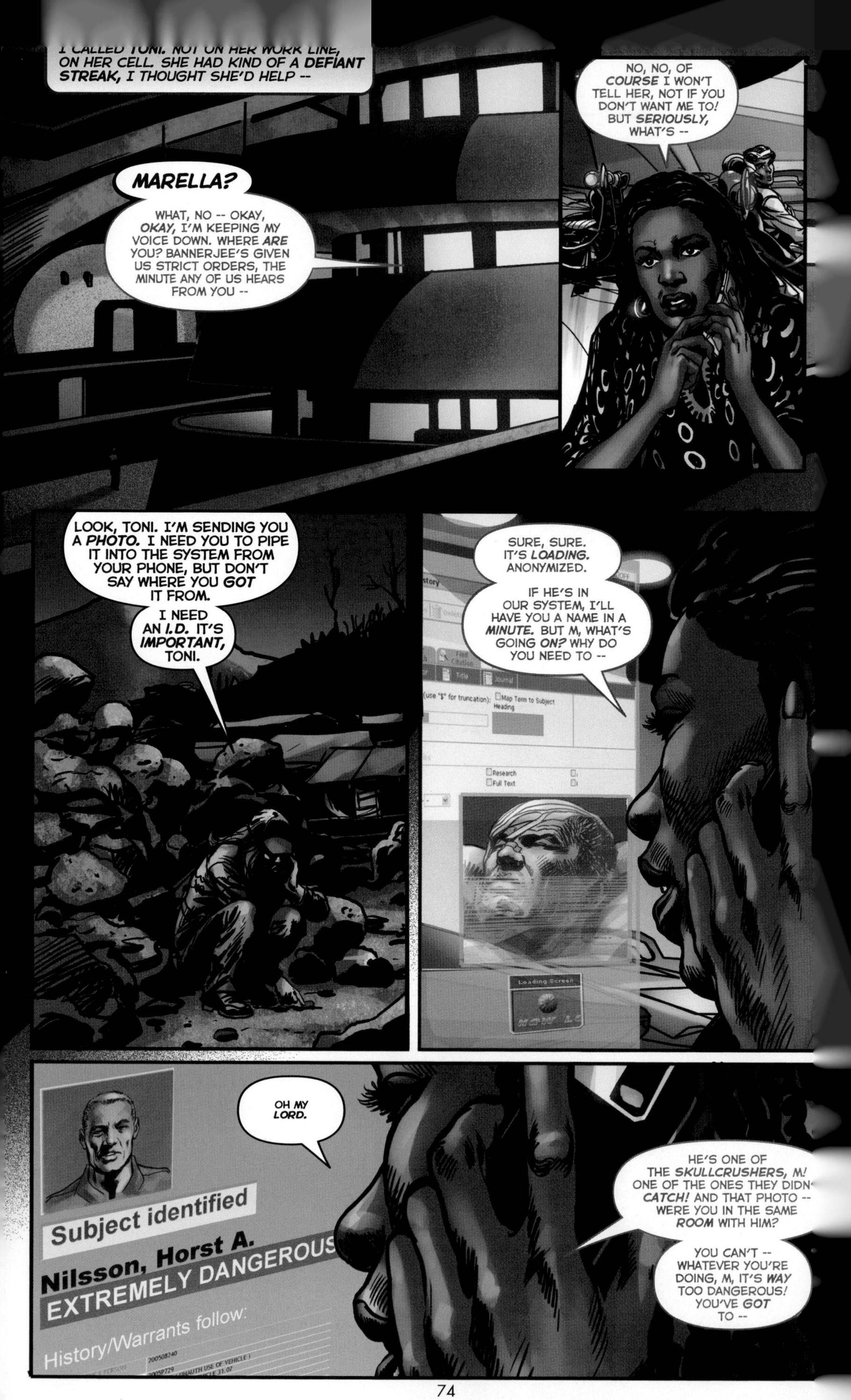

I CALLED TONI. NOT ON HER WORK LINE, ON HER CELL. SHE HAD KIND OF A DEFIANT STREAK, I THOUGHT SHE'D HELP --
MARELLA?
WHAT, NO -- OKAY, OKAY, I'M KEEPING MY VOICE DOWN. WHERE ARE YOU? BANNERJEE'S GIVEN US STRICT ORDERS, THE MINUTE ANY OF US HEARS FROM YOU --
NO, NO, OF COURSE I WON'T TELL HER, NOT IF YOU DON'T WANT ME TO! BUT SERIOUSLY, WHAT'S --
LOOK, TONI. I'M SENDING YOU A PHOTO. I NEED YOU TO PIPE IT INTO THE SYSTEM FROM YOUR PHONE, BUT DON'T SAY WHERE YOU GOT IT FROM.
I NEED AN I.D. IT'S IMPORTANT, TONI.
SURE, SURE. IT'S LOADING. ANONYMIZED.
IF HE'S IN OUR SYSTEM, I'LL HAVE YOU A NAME IN A MINUTE. BUT M, WHAT'S GOING ON? WHY DO YOU NEED TO --
Map Term to Subject Heading
Research
Full Text
Loading Screen
Subject identified
Nilsson, Horst A.
EXTREMELY DANGEROUS
History/Warrants follow:
OH MY LORD.
HE'S ONE OF THE SKULLCRUSHERS, M! ONE OF THE ONES THEY DIDN'T CATCH! AND THAT PHOTO -- WERE YOU IN THE SAME ROOM WITH HIM?
YOU CAN'T -- WHATEVER YOU'RE DOING, M, IT'S WAY TOO DANGEROUS! YOU'VE GOT TO --

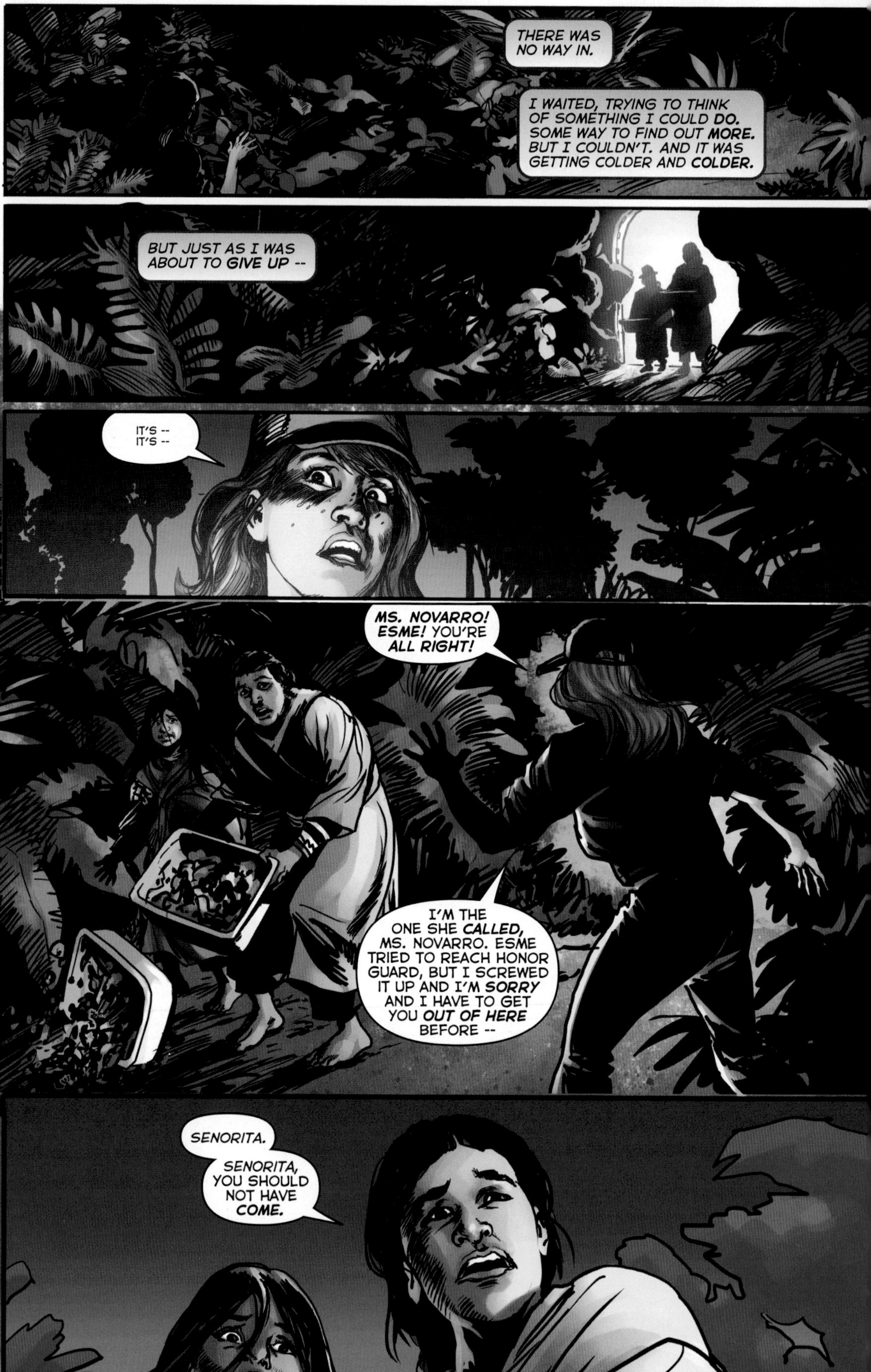
THERE WAS NO WAY IN.
I WAITED, TRYING TO THINK OF SOMETHING I COULD DO. SOME WAY TO FIND OUT MORE. BUT I COULDN'T. AND IT WAS GETTING COLDER AND COLDER.
BUT JUST AS I WAS ABOUT TO GIVE UP --
IT'S -- IT'S --
MS. NOVARRO! ESME! YOU'RE ALL RIGHT!
I'M THE ONE SHE CALLED, MS. NOVARRO. ESME TRIED TO REACH HONOR GUARD, BUT I SCREWED IT UP AND I'M SORRY AND I HAVE TO GET YOU OUT OF HERE BEFORE --
SENORITA.
SENORITA, YOU SHOULD NOT HAVE COME.

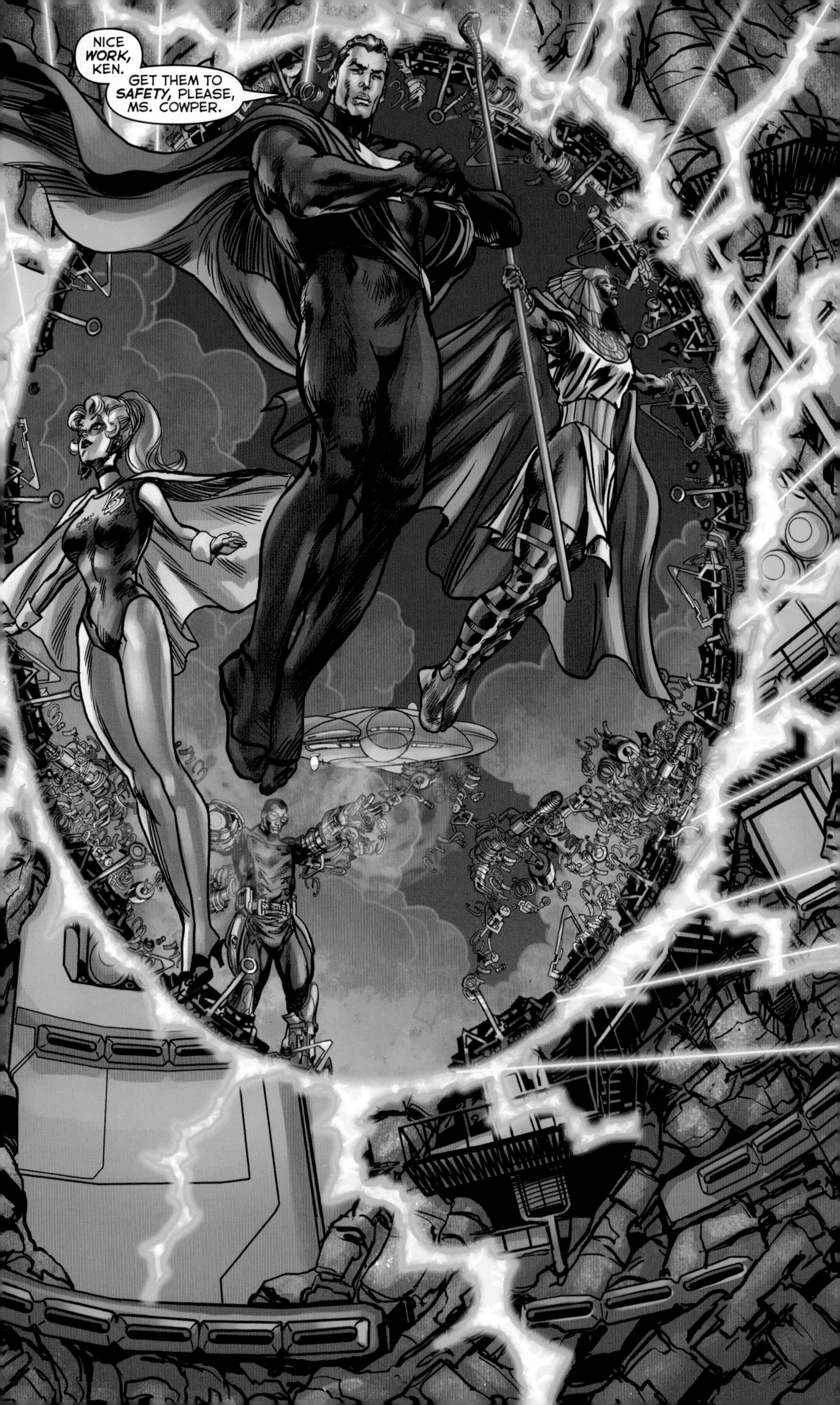

NICE WORK, KEN.
GET THEM TO SAFETY, PLEASE, MS. COWPER.

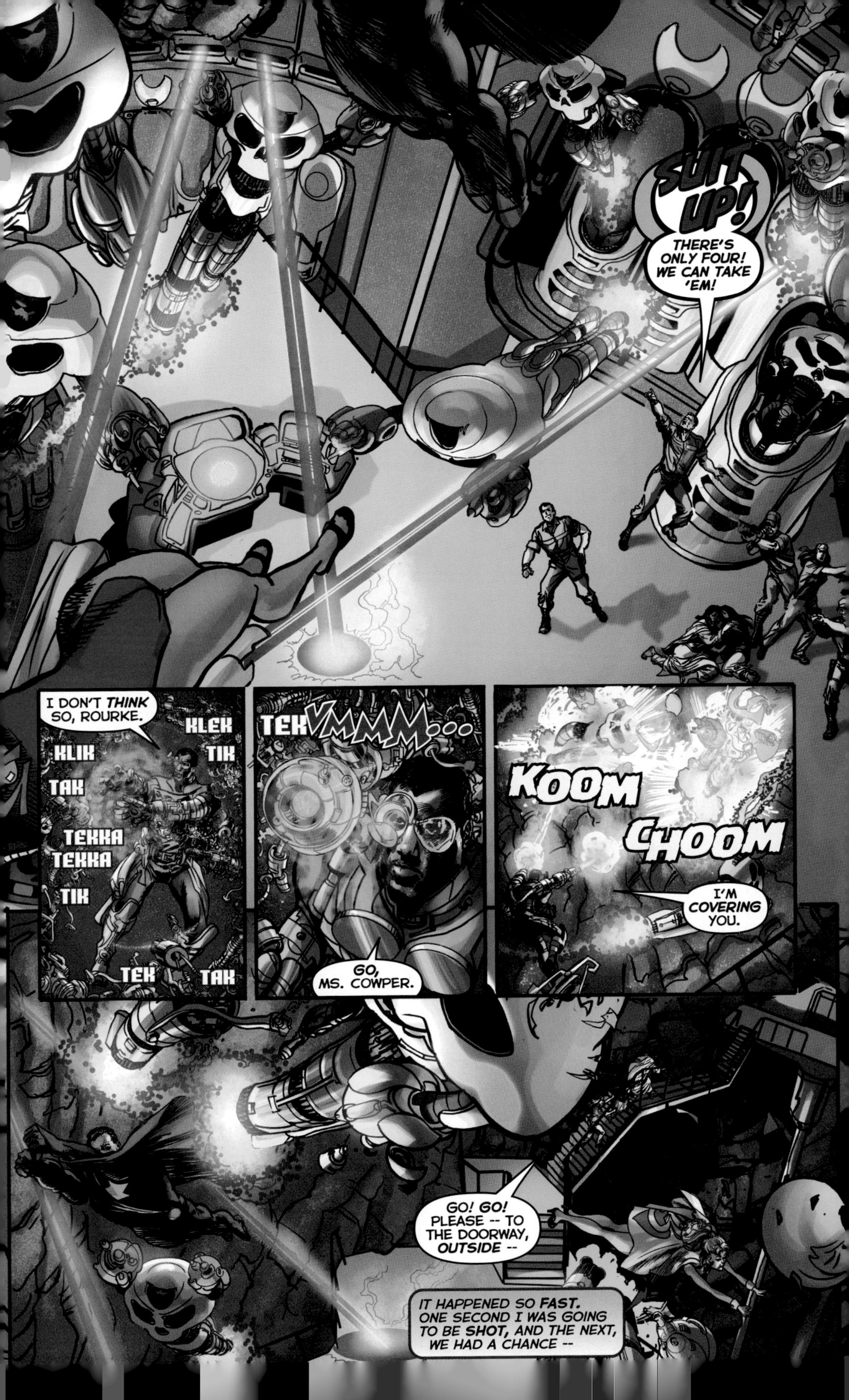
SUIT UP!
THERE'S ONLY FOUR! WE CAN TAKE 'EM!
I DON'T THINK SO, ROURKE.
KLEK
TIK
KLIK
TAK
TEKKA
TEKKA
TIK
TEK
TAK
TEKVMMM...
GO, MS. COWPER.
KOOM
CHOOM
I'M COVERING YOU.
GO! GO! PLEASE -- TO THE DOORWAY, OUTSIDE --
IT HAPPENED SO FAST. ONE SECOND I WAS GOING TO BE SHOT, AND THE NEXT, WE HAD A CHANCE --

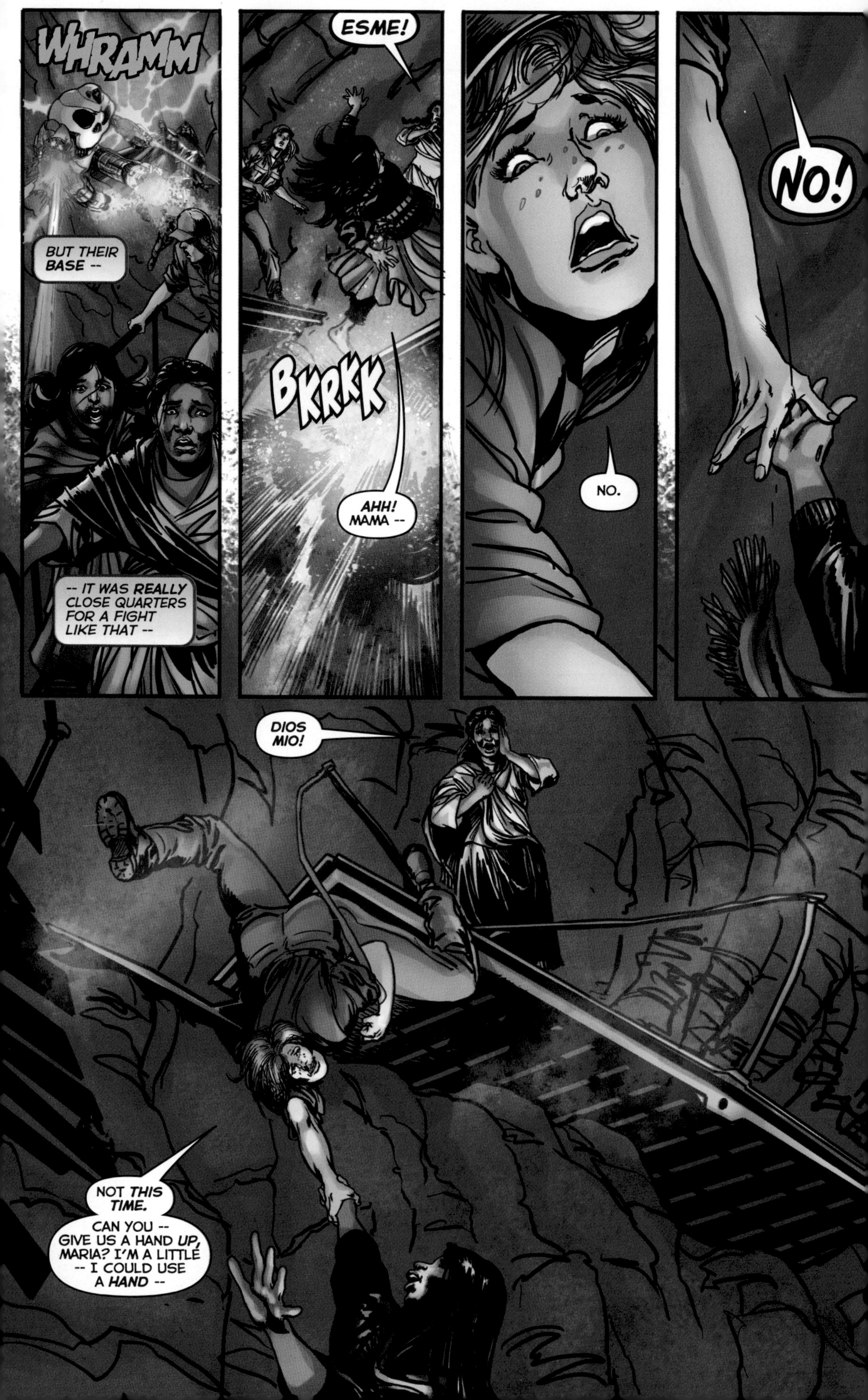
WHRAMM
BUT THEIR BASE --
-- IT WAS REALLY CLOSE QUARTERS FOR A FIGHT LIKE THAT --
ESME!
BKRKK
AHH! MAMA --
NO.
NO!
DIOS MIO!
NOT THIS TIME.
CAN YOU -- GIVE US A HAND UP, MARIA? I'M A LITTLE -- I COULD USE A HAND --

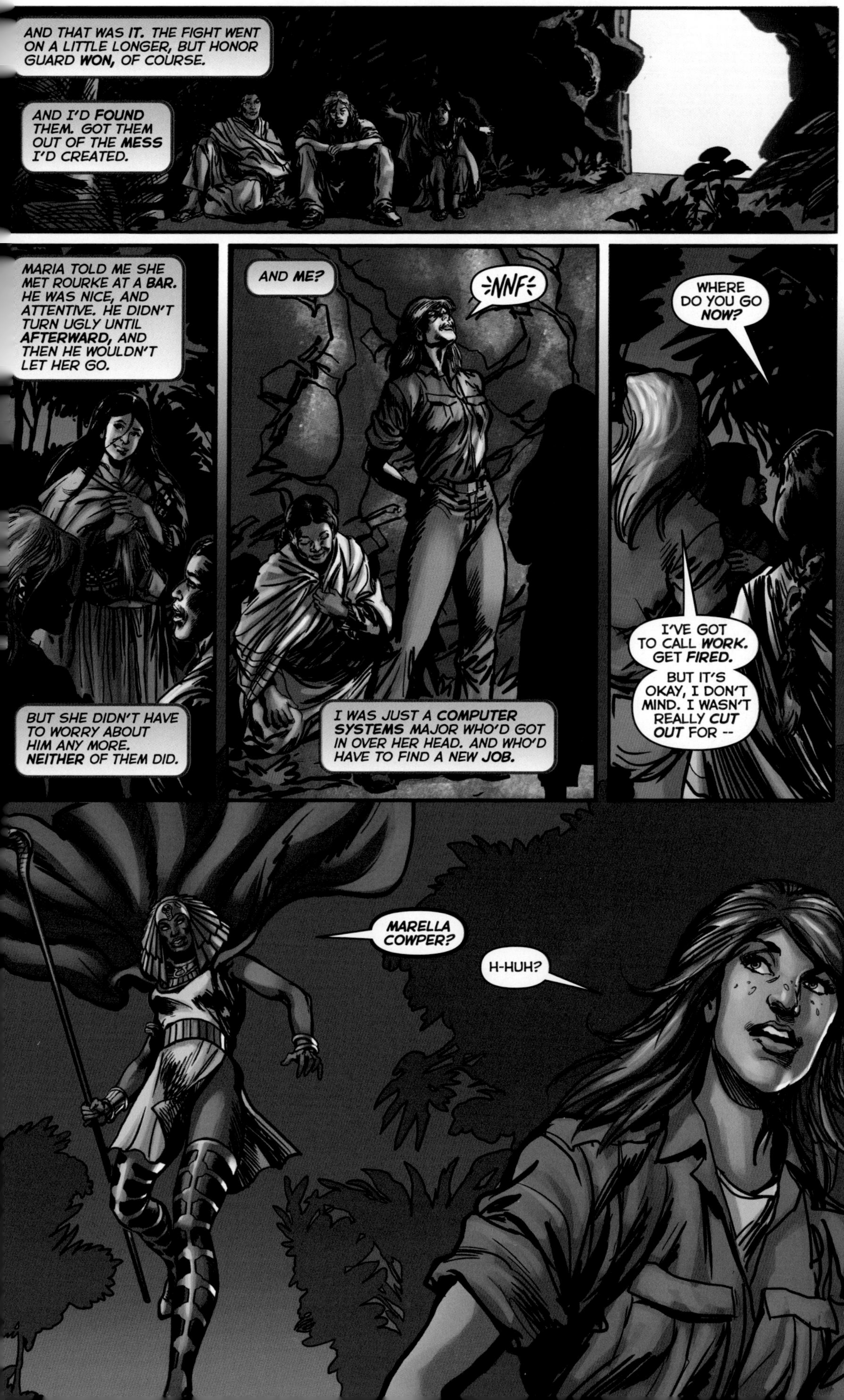
AND THAT WAS IT. THE FIGHT WENT ON A LITTLE LONGER, BUT HONOR GUARD WON, OF COURSE.
AND I'D FOUND THEM. GOT THEM OUT OF THE MESS I'D CREATED.
MARIA TOLD ME SHE MET ROURKE AT A BAR. HE WAS NICE, AND ATTENTIVE. HE DIDN'T TURN UGLY UNTIL AFTERWARD, AND THEN HE WOULDN'T LET HER GO.
BUT SHE DIDN'T HAVE TO WORRY ABOUT HIM ANY MORE. NEITHER OF THEM DID.
AND ME?
NNF
I WAS JUST A COMPUTER SYSTEMS MAJOR WHO'D GOT IN OVER HER HEAD. AND WHO'D HAVE TO FIND A NEW JOB.
WHERE DO YOU GO NOW?
I'VE GOT TO CALL WORK. GET FIRED.
BUT IT'S OKAY, I DON'T MIND. I WASN'T REALLY CUT OUT FOR --
MARELLA COWPER?
H-HUH?

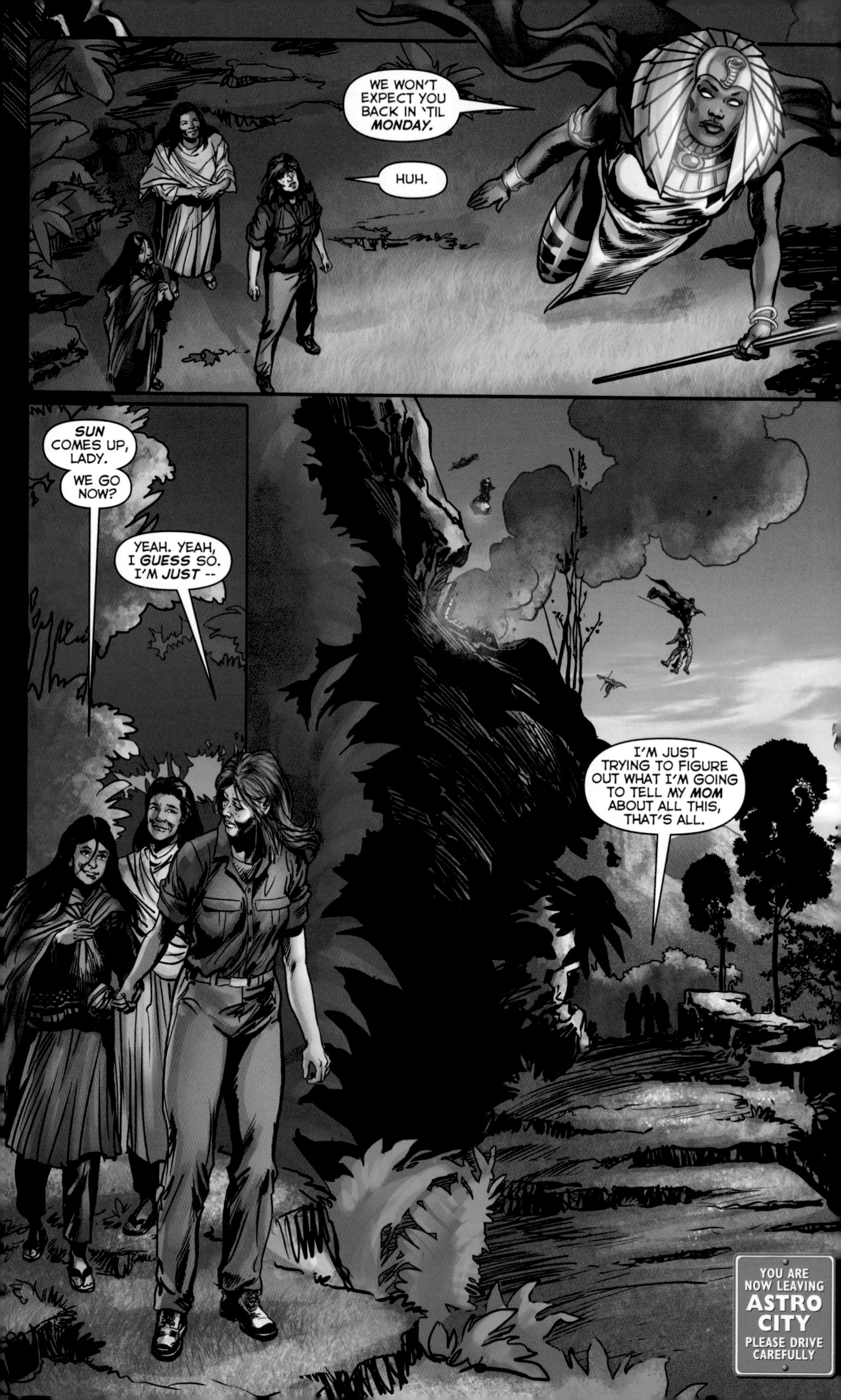
WE WON'T EXPECT YOU BACK IN 'TIL *MONDAY.*
HUH.
SUN COMES UP, LADY.
WE GO NOW?
YEAH. YEAH, I *GUESS* SO. I'M *JUST* --
I'M JUST TRYING TO FIGURE OUT WHAT I'M GOING TO TELL MY *MOM* ABOUT ALL THIS, THAT'S ALL.
YOU ARE NOW LEAVING ASTRO CITY PLEASE DRIVE CAREFULLY

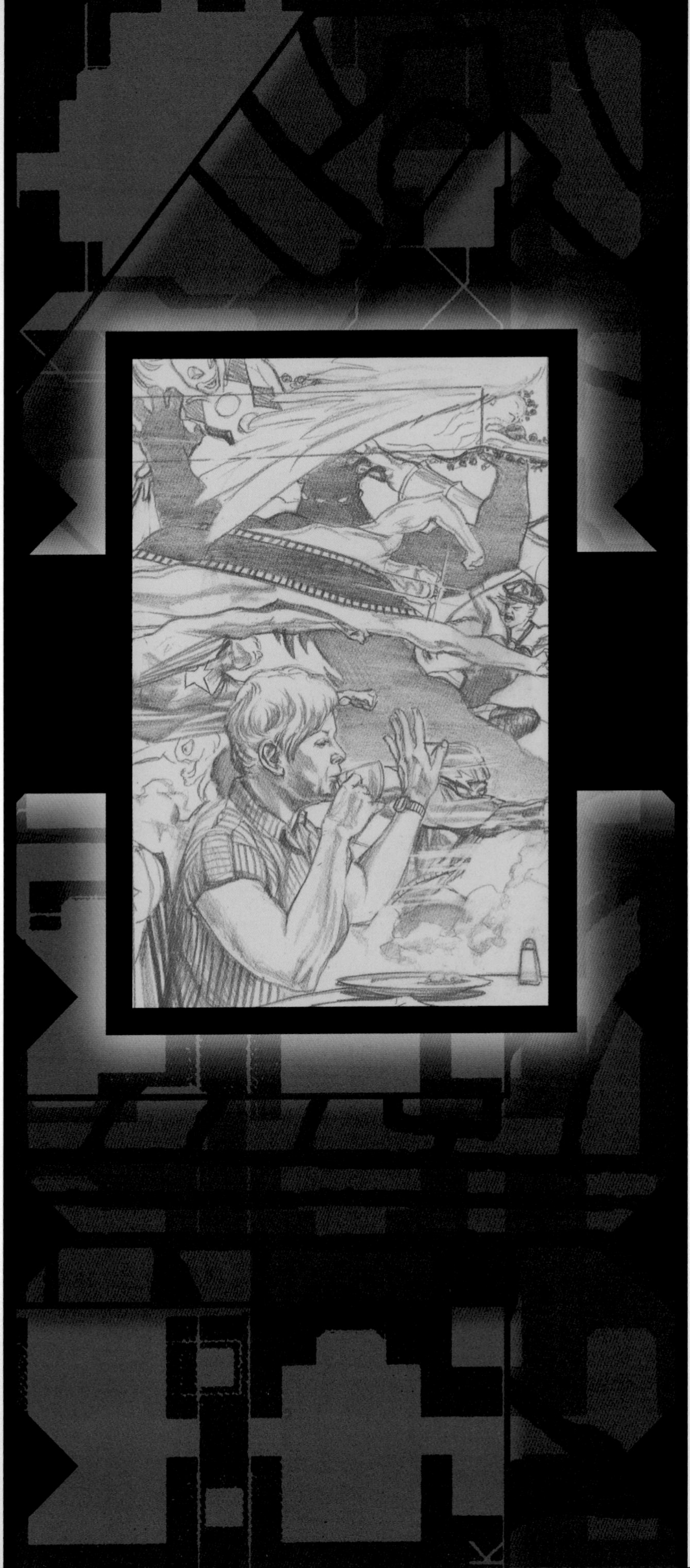

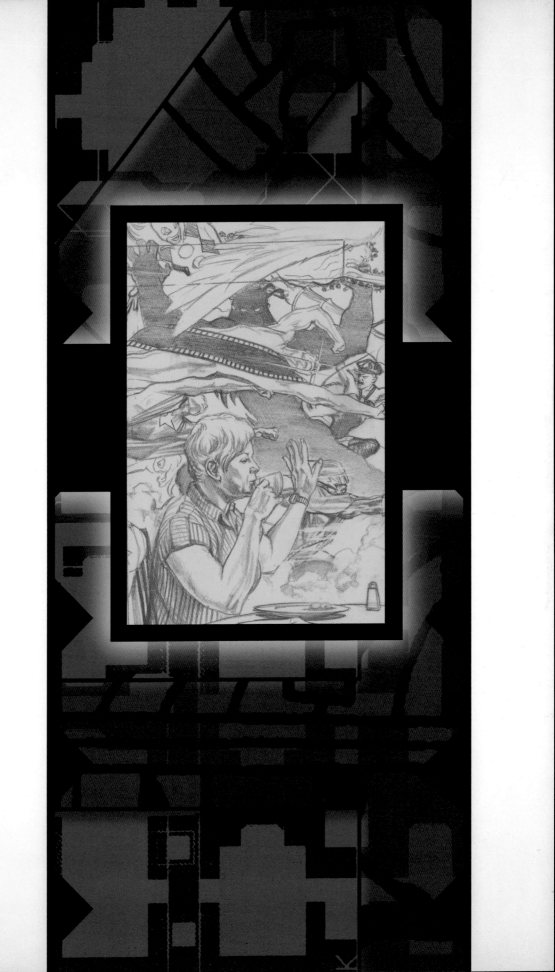

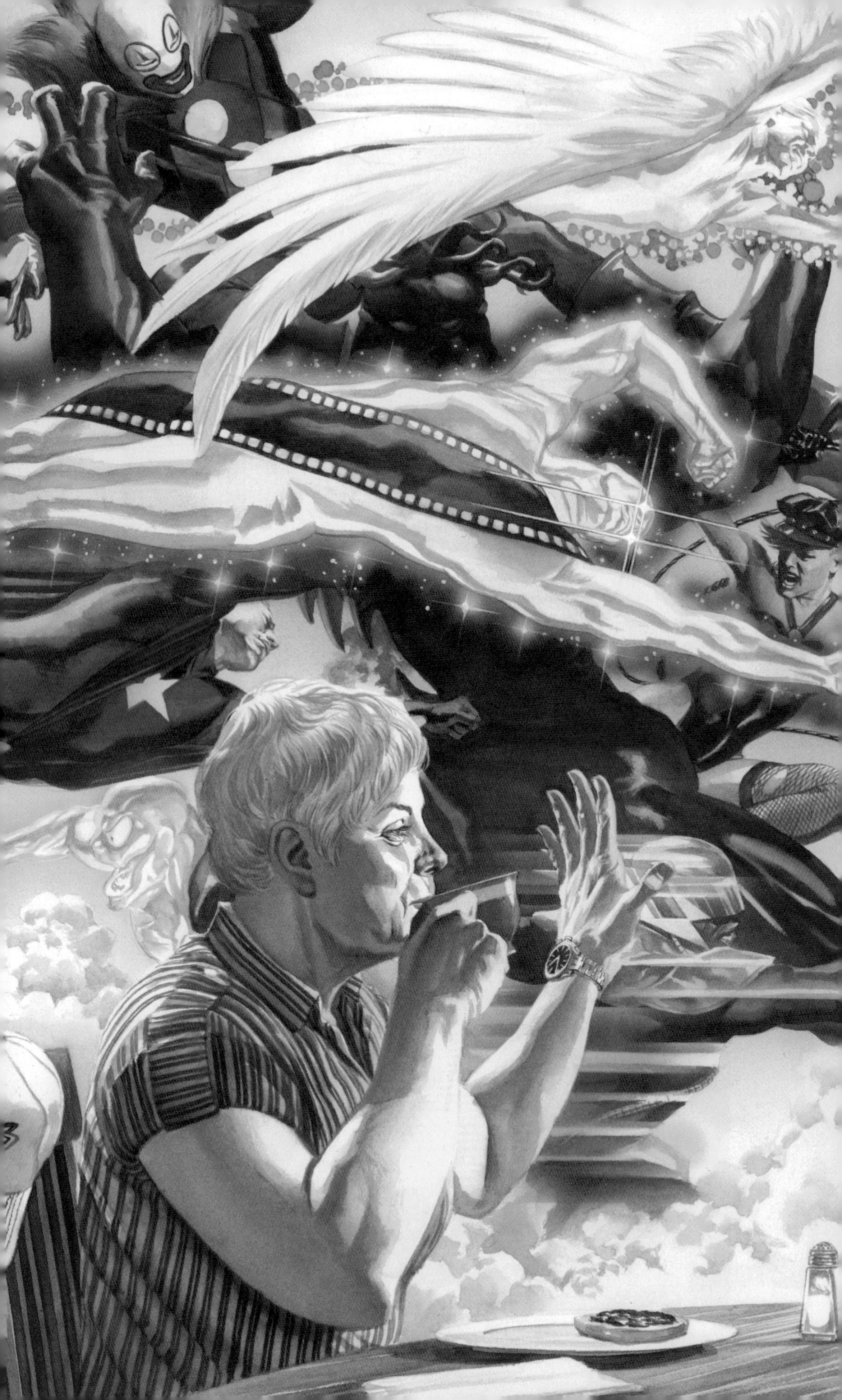

THE MILLRACE IS MY FAVORITE SPOT IN ASTRO CITY. I MAKE IT A POINT TO HAVE BREAKFAST HERE AFTER I FINISH ANY JOB, WHENEVER IT'S POSSIBLE.

I'D JUST FINISHED WORKING ON A MOVIE -- A PIECE OF CRAP ACTION-FEST I WOULDN'T RECOMMEND TO MY WORST ENEMY -- AND MY AGENT WAS SORTING THROUGH THE AVAILABLE GIGS ON OFFER. I MIGHT BE WORKING AGAIN AS SOON AS MONDAY.

BUT IN THE MEANTIME, I HAD A CHANCE TO GET HOME, RELAX, INDULGE.

AT MY AGE, WITH MY JOB, MY LIFE, IT'S THE LITTLE THINGS THAT COUNT MOST.

THE VIEW.

THE BREEZE OFF THE RIVER.

THE SMELL OF GOOD COFFEE AND THE MURMUR OF CONVERSATION, WASHING AROUND ME LIKE THE TWITTERING OF A FLOCK OF BIRDS.

AND THE BEST SCRATCH-MADE ENGLISH MUFFINS IN TOWN, TOPPED WITH --

On the Sidelines

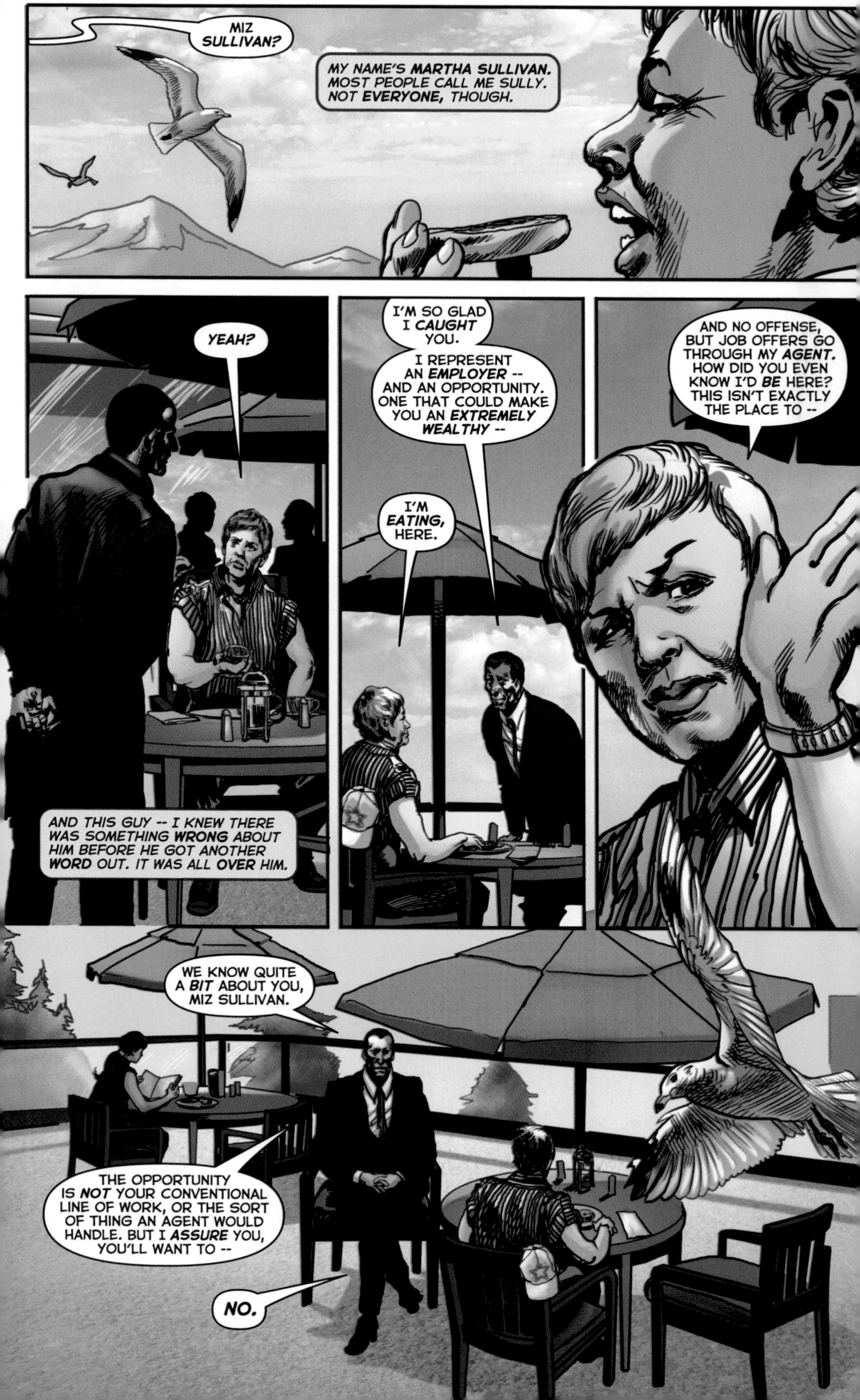
MIZ SULLIVAN?
MY NAME'S MARTHA SULLIVAN. MOST PEOPLE CALL ME SULLY. NOT EVERYONE, THOUGH.
YEAH?
AND THIS GUY -- I KNEW THERE WAS SOMETHING WRONG ABOUT HIM BEFORE HE GOT ANOTHER WORD OUT. IT WAS ALL OVER HIM.
I'M SO GLAD I CAUGHT YOU.
I REPRESENT AN EMPLOYER -- AND AN OPPORTUNITY. ONE THAT COULD MAKE YOU AN EXTREMELY WEALTHY --
I'M EATING, HERE.
AND NO OFFENSE, BUT JOB OFFERS GO THROUGH MY AGENT. HOW DID YOU EVEN KNOW I'D BE HERE? THIS ISN'T EXACTLY THE PLACE TO --
WE KNOW QUITE A BIT ABOUT YOU, MIZ SULLIVAN.
THE OPPORTUNITY IS NOT YOUR CONVENTIONAL LINE OF WORK, OR THE SORT OF THING AN AGENT WOULD HANDLE. BUT I ASSURE YOU, YOU'LL WANT TO --
NO.

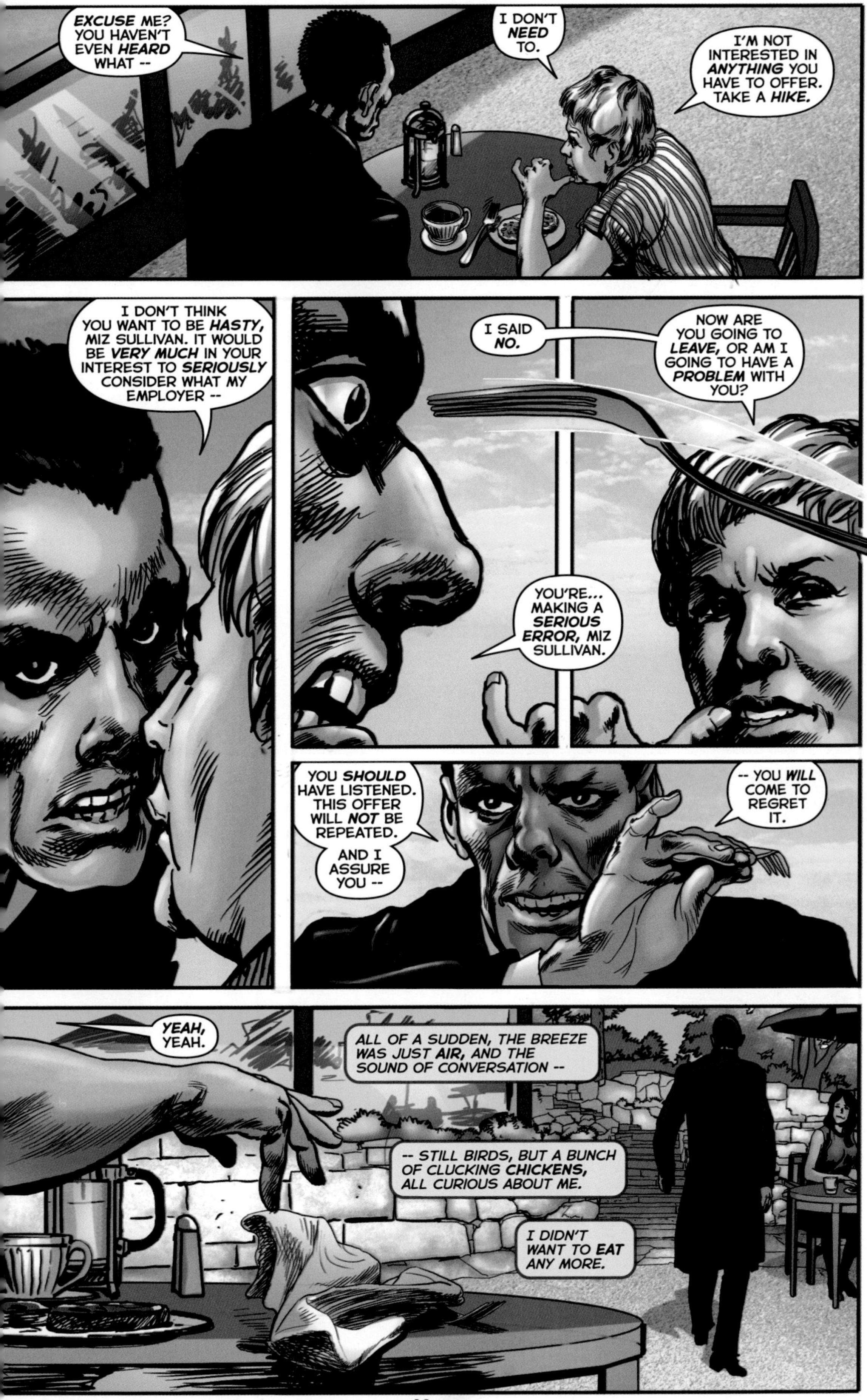
EXCUSE ME? YOU HAVEN'T EVEN HEARD WHAT --
I DON'T NEED TO.
I'M NOT INTERESTED IN ANYTHING YOU HAVE TO OFFER. TAKE A HIKE.
I DON'T THINK YOU WANT TO BE HASTY, MIZ SULLIVAN. IT WOULD BE VERY MUCH IN YOUR INTEREST TO SERIOUSLY CONSIDER WHAT MY EMPLOYER --
I SAID NO.
NOW ARE YOU GOING TO LEAVE, OR AM I GOING TO HAVE A PROBLEM WITH YOU?
YOU'RE... MAKING A SERIOUS ERROR, MIZ SULLIVAN.
YOU SHOULD HAVE LISTENED. THIS OFFER WILL NOT BE REPEATED.
AND I ASSURE YOU --
-- YOU WILL COME TO REGRET IT.
YEAH, YEAH.
ALL OF A SUDDEN, THE BREEZE WAS JUST AIR, AND THE SOUND OF CONVERSATION --
-- STILL BIRDS, BUT A BUNCH OF CLUCKING CHICKENS, ALL CURIOUS ABOUT ME.
I DIDN'T WANT TO EAT ANY MORE.

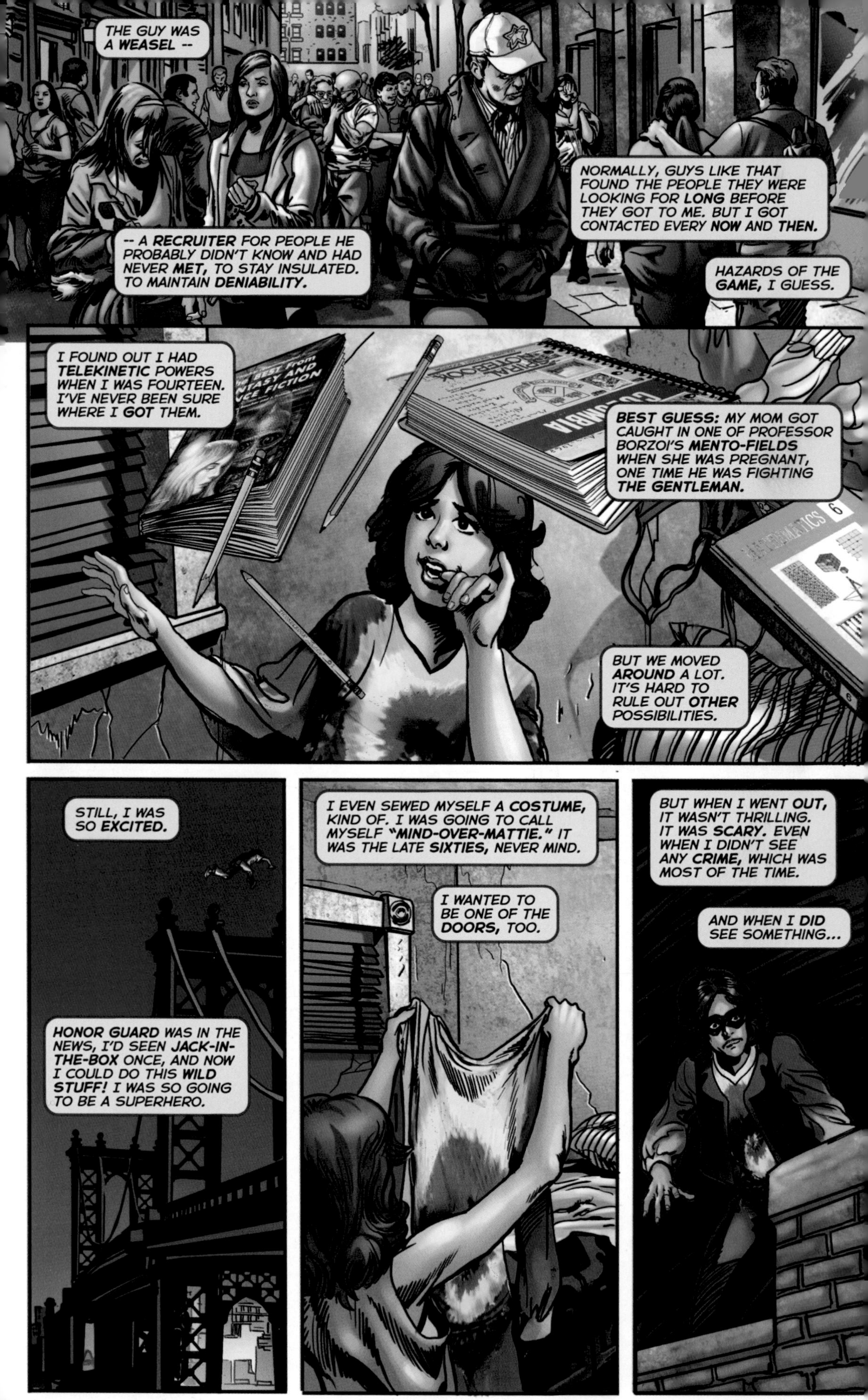
THE GUY WAS A WEASEL --
-- A RECRUITER FOR PEOPLE HE PROBABLY DIDN'T KNOW AND HAD NEVER MET, TO STAY INSULATED. TO MAINTAIN DENIABILITY.
NORMALLY, GUYS LIKE THAT FOUND THE PEOPLE THEY WERE LOOKING FOR LONG BEFORE THEY GOT TO ME. BUT I GOT CONTACTED EVERY NOW AND THEN.
HAZARDS OF THE GAME, I GUESS.
I FOUND OUT I HAD TELEKINETIC POWERS WHEN I WAS FOURTEEN. I'VE NEVER BEEN SURE WHERE I GOT THEM.
BEST GUESS: MY MOM GOT CAUGHT IN ONE OF PROFESSOR BORZOI'S MENTO-FIELDS WHEN SHE WAS PREGNANT, ONE TIME HE WAS FIGHTING THE GENTLEMAN.
BUT WE MOVED AROUND A LOT. IT'S HARD TO RULE OUT OTHER POSSIBILITIES.
STILL, I WAS SO EXCITED.
HONOR GUARD WAS IN THE NEWS, I'D SEEN JACK-IN-THE-BOX ONCE, AND NOW I COULD DO THIS WILD STUFF! I WAS SO GOING TO BE A SUPERHERO.
I EVEN SEWED MYSELF A COSTUME, KIND OF. I WAS GOING TO CALL MYSELF "MIND-OVER-MATTIE." IT WAS THE LATE SIXTIES, NEVER MIND.
I WANTED TO BE ONE OF THE DOORS, TOO.
BUT WHEN I WENT OUT, IT WASN'T THRILLING. IT WAS SCARY. EVEN WHEN I DIDN'T SEE ANY CRIME, WHICH WAS MOST OF THE TIME.
AND WHEN I DID SEE SOMETHING...

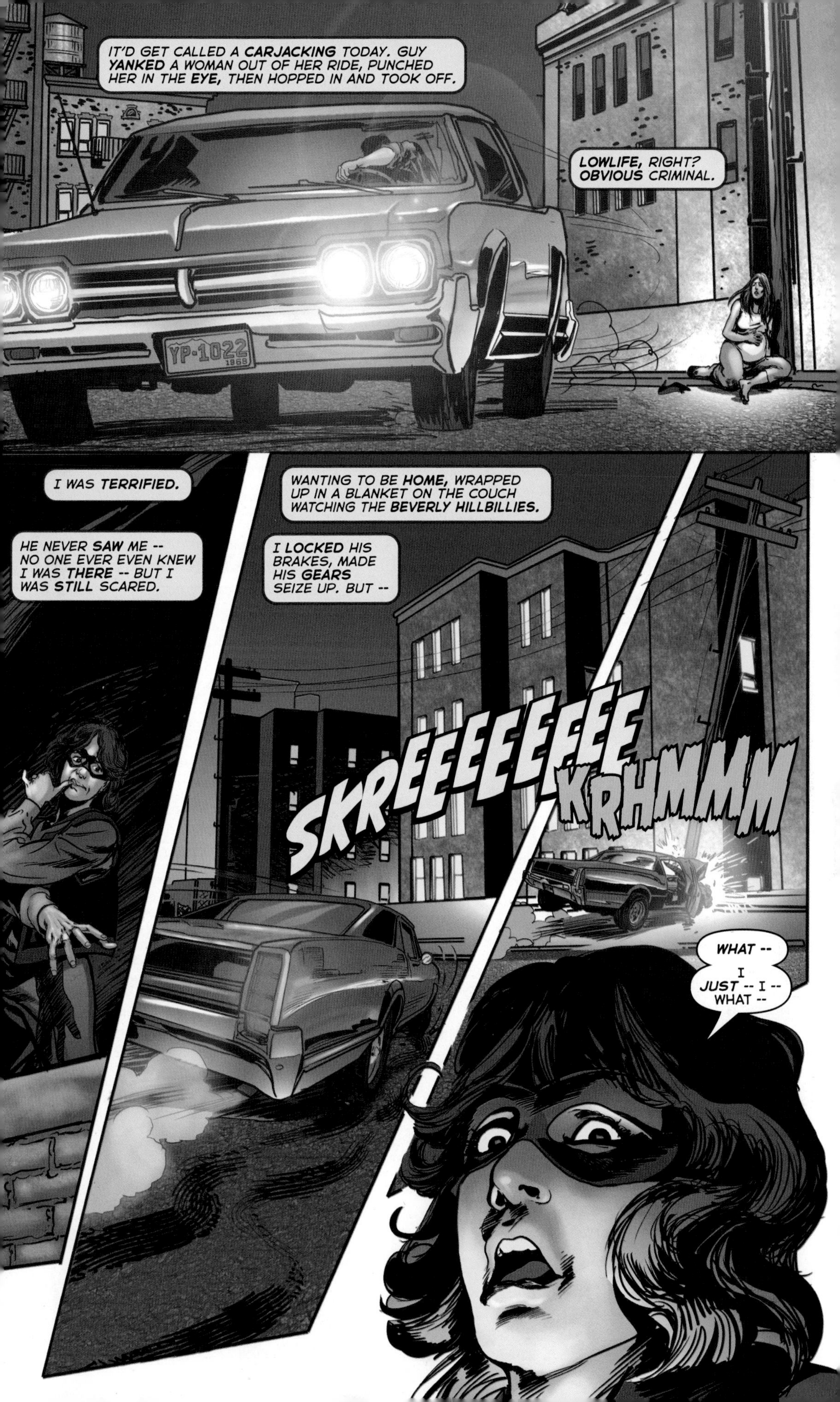

IT'D GET CALLED A CARJACKING TODAY. GUY YANKED A WOMAN OUT OF HER RIDE, PUNCHED HER IN THE EYE, THEN HOPPED IN AND TOOK OFF.
LOWLIFE, RIGHT? OBVIOUS CRIMINAL.
YP-1022
1969
I WAS TERRIFIED.
HE NEVER SAW ME -- NO ONE EVER EVEN KNEW I WAS THERE -- BUT I WAS STILL SCARED.
WANTING TO BE HOME, WRAPPED UP IN A BLANKET ON THE COUCH WATCHING THE BEVERLY HILLBILLIES.
I LOCKED HIS BRAKES, MADE HIS GEARS SEIZE UP. BUT --
SKREEEEEEEEE
KRHMMM
WHAT --
I JUST -- I -- WHAT --

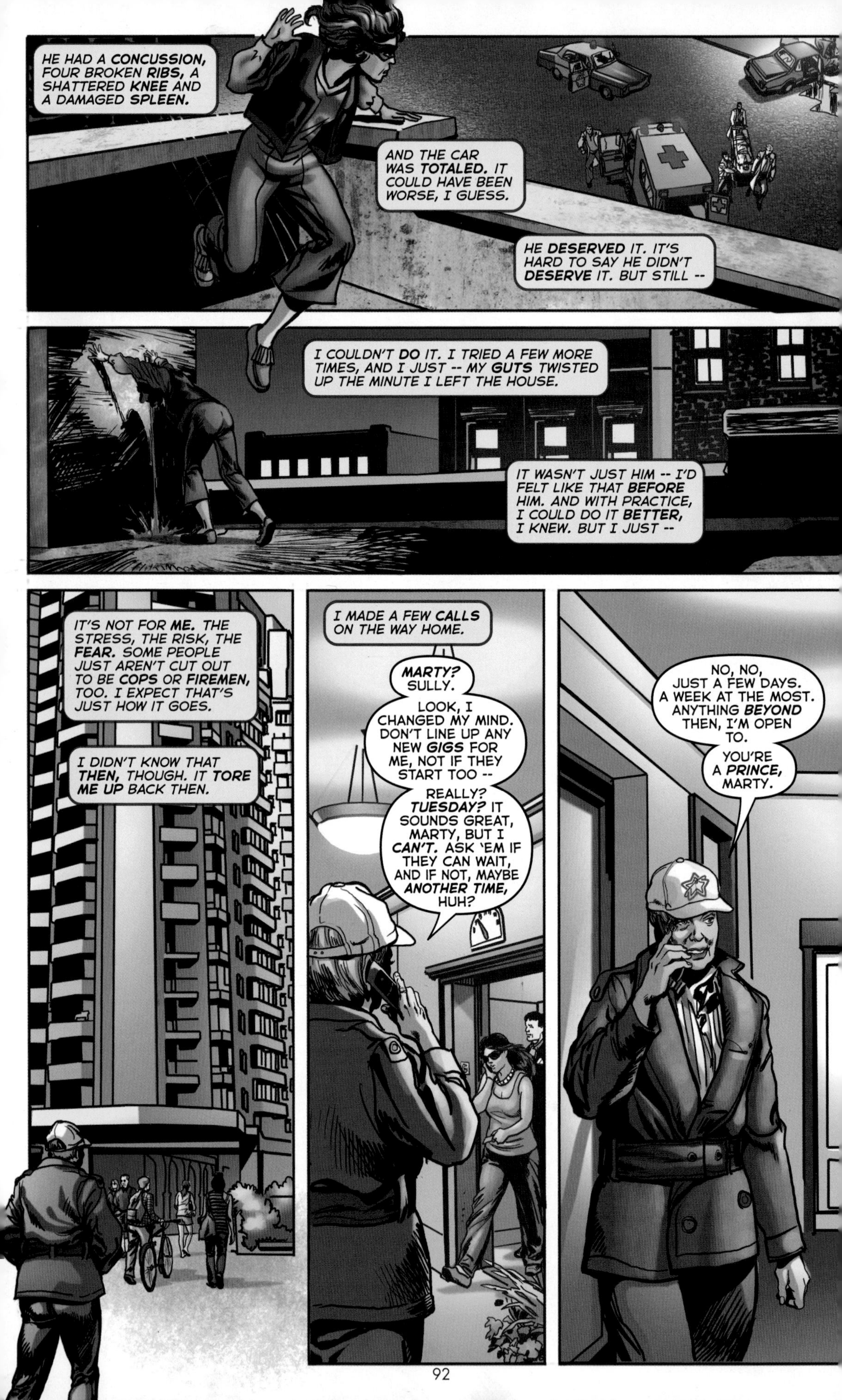
HE HAD A CONCUSSION, FOUR BROKEN RIBS, A SHATTERED KNEE AND A DAMAGED SPLEEN.
AND THE CAR WAS TOTALED. IT COULD HAVE BEEN WORSE, I GUESS.
HE DESERVED IT. IT'S HARD TO SAY HE DIDN'T DESERVE IT. BUT STILL --
I COULDN'T DO IT. I TRIED A FEW MORE TIMES, AND I JUST -- MY GUTS TWISTED UP THE MINUTE I LEFT THE HOUSE.
IT WASN'T JUST HIM -- I'D FELT LIKE THAT BEFORE HIM. AND WITH PRACTICE, I COULD DO IT BETTER, I KNEW. BUT I JUST --
IT'S NOT FOR ME. THE STRESS, THE RISK, THE FEAR. SOME PEOPLE JUST AREN'T CUT OUT TO BE COPS OR FIREMEN, TOO. I EXPECT THAT'S JUST HOW IT GOES.
I DIDN'T KNOW THAT THEN, THOUGH. IT TORE ME UP BACK THEN.
I MADE A FEW CALLS ON THE WAY HOME.
MARTY? SULLY.
LOOK, I CHANGED MY MIND. DON'T LINE UP ANY NEW GIGS FOR ME, NOT IF THEY START TOO --
REALLY? TUESDAY? IT SOUNDS GREAT, MARTY, BUT I CAN'T. ASK 'EM IF THEY CAN WAIT, AND IF NOT, MAYBE ANOTHER TIME, HUH?
NO, NO, JUST A FEW DAYS. A WEEK AT THE MOST. ANYTHING BEYOND THEN, I'M OPEN TO.
YOU'RE A PRINCE, MARTY.

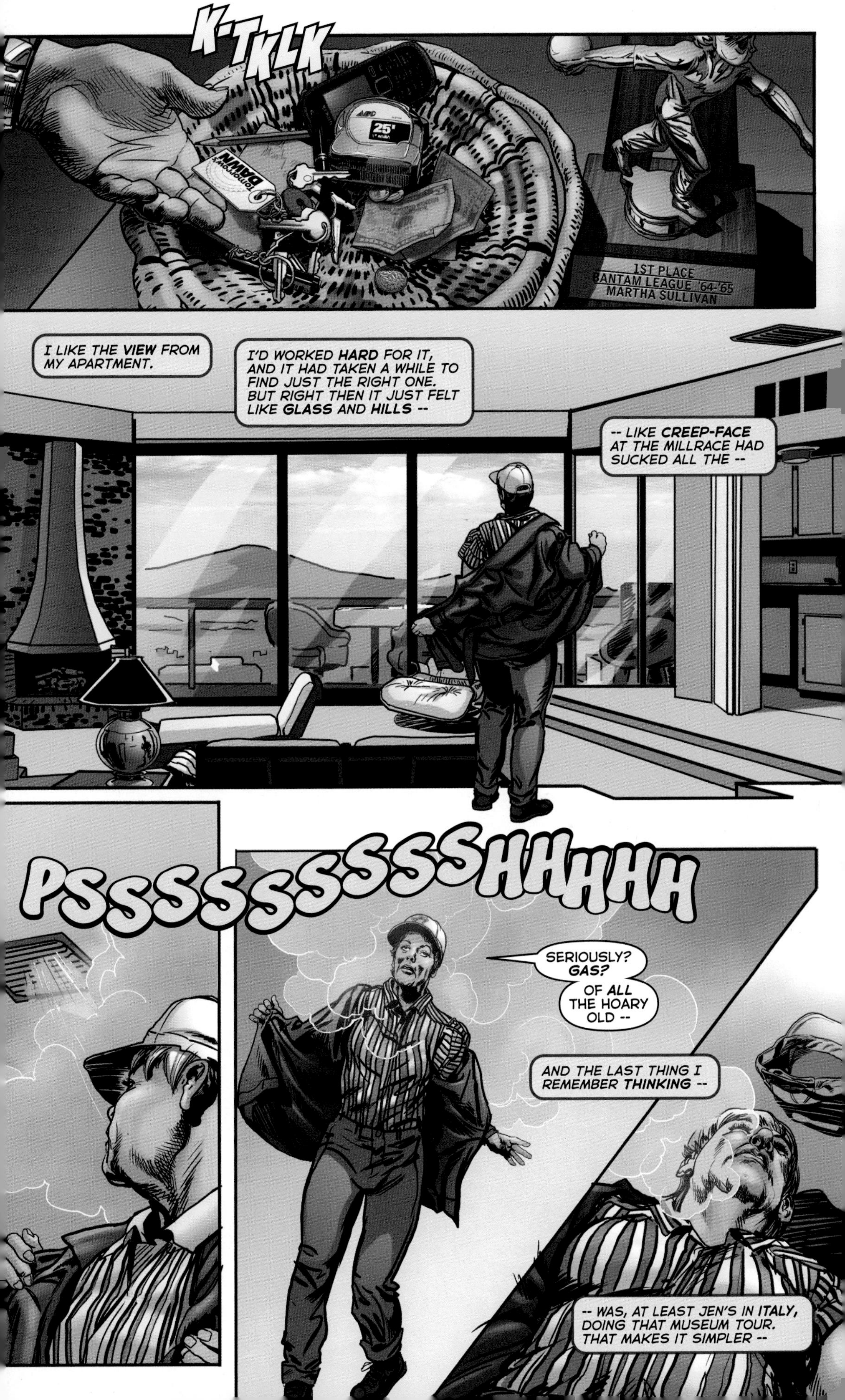
K-TKLK
1ST PLACE
BANTAM LEAGUE '64-'65
MARTHA SULLIVAN
I LIKE THE VIEW FROM MY APARTMENT.
I'D WORKED HARD FOR IT, AND IT HAD TAKEN A WHILE TO FIND JUST THE RIGHT ONE. BUT RIGHT THEN IT JUST FELT LIKE GLASS AND HILLS --
-- LIKE CREEP-FACE AT THE MILLRACE HAD SUCKED ALL THE --
PSSSSSSSSSHHHHH
SERIOUSLY? GAS?
OF ALL THE HOARY OLD --
AND THE LAST THING I REMEMBER THINKING --
-- WAS, AT LEAST JEN'S IN ITALY, DOING THAT MUSEUM TOUR. THAT MAKES IT SIMPLER --

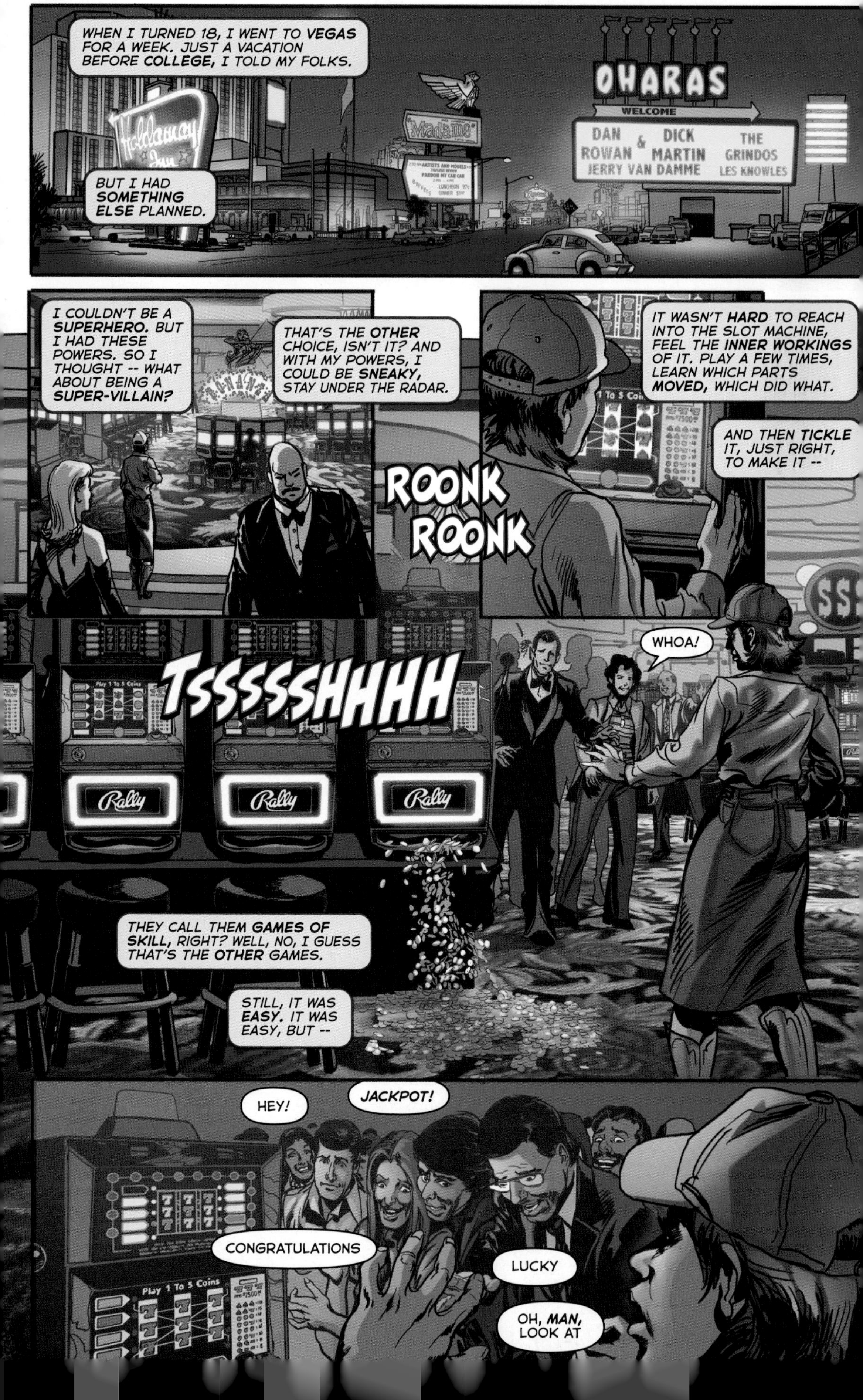

WHEN I TURNED 18, I WENT TO VEGAS FOR A WEEK. JUST A VACATION BEFORE COLLEGE, I TOLD MY FOLKS.
BUT I HAD SOMETHING ELSE PLANNED.
OHARAS
WELCOME
DAN ROWAN & DICK MARTIN
THE GRINDOS
JERRY VAN DAMME
LES KNOWLES
Madame
PARDON MY CAN CAN
I COULDN'T BE A SUPERHERO. BUT I HAD THESE POWERS. SO I THOUGHT -- WHAT ABOUT BEING A SUPER-VILLAIN?
THAT'S THE OTHER CHOICE, ISN'T IT? AND WITH MY POWERS, I COULD BE SNEAKY, STAY UNDER THE RADAR.
IT WASN'T HARD TO REACH INTO THE SLOT MACHINE, FEEL THE INNER WORKINGS OF IT. PLAY A FEW TIMES, LEARN WHICH PARTS MOVED, WHICH DID WHAT.
AND THEN TICKLE IT, JUST RIGHT, TO MAKE IT --
ROONK ROONK
TSSSSSHHHH
Rally
Rally
Rally
WHOA!
THEY CALL THEM GAMES OF SKILL, RIGHT? WELL, NO, I GUESS THAT'S THE OTHER GAMES.
STILL, IT WAS EASY. IT WAS EASY, BUT --
HEY!
JACKPOT!
CONGRATULATIONS
LUCKY
OH, MAN, LOOK AT
Play 1 To 5 Coins

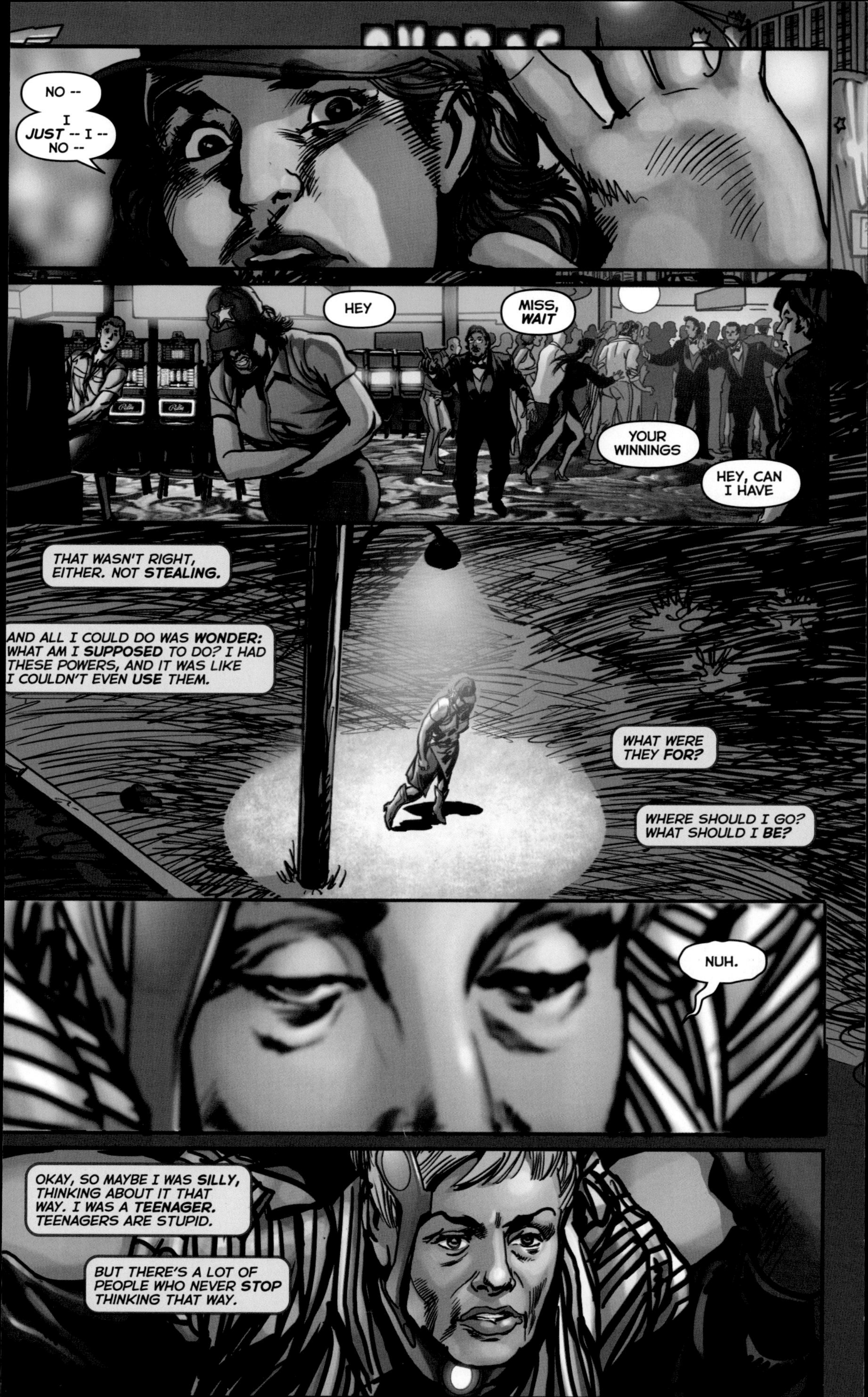
NO --
I JUST -- I -- NO --
HEY
MISS, WAIT
YOUR WINNINGS
HEY, CAN I HAVE
THAT WASN'T RIGHT, EITHER. NOT STEALING.
AND ALL I COULD DO WAS WONDER: WHAT AM I SUPPOSED TO DO? I HAD THESE POWERS, AND IT WAS LIKE I COULDN'T EVEN USE THEM.
WHAT WERE THEY FOR?
WHERE SHOULD I GO? WHAT SHOULD I BE?
NUH.
OKAY, SO MAYBE I WAS SILLY, THINKING ABOUT IT THAT WAY. I WAS A TEENAGER. TEENAGERS ARE STUPID.
BUT THERE'S A LOT OF PEOPLE WHO NEVER STOP THINKING THAT WAY.

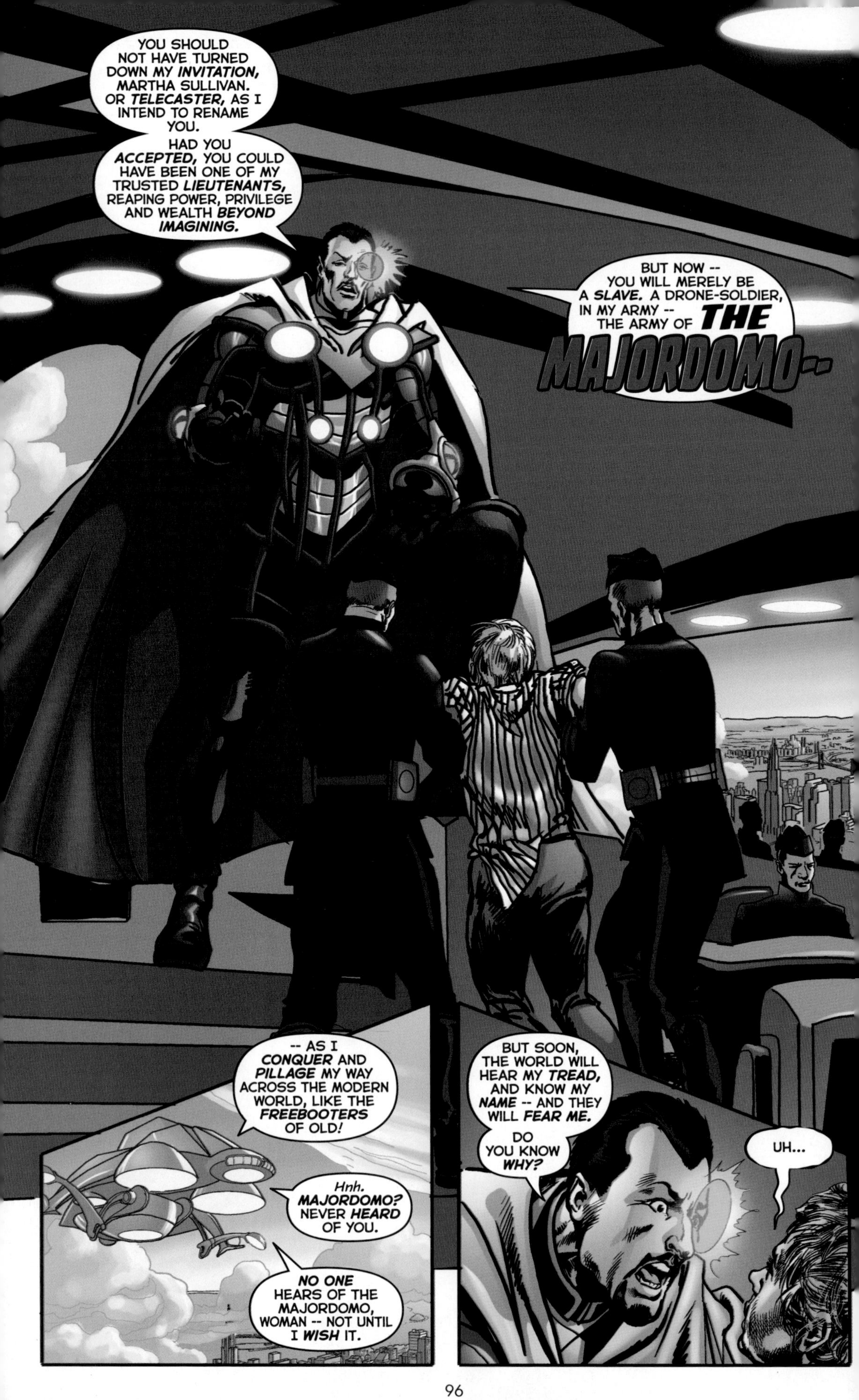

YOU SHOULD NOT HAVE TURNED DOWN MY INVITATION, MARTHA SULLIVAN. OR TELECASTER, AS I INTEND TO RENAME YOU.
HAD YOU ACCEPTED, YOU COULD HAVE BEEN ONE OF MY TRUSTED LIEUTENANTS, REAPING POWER, PRIVILEGE AND WEALTH BEYOND IMAGINING.
BUT NOW -- YOU WILL MERELY BE A SLAVE. A DRONE-SOLDIER, IN MY ARMY -- THE ARMY OF THE MAJORDOMO--
-- AS I CONQUER AND PILLAGE MY WAY ACROSS THE MODERN WORLD, LIKE THE FREEBOOTERS OF OLD!
Hnh. MAJORDOMO? NEVER HEARD OF YOU.
NO ONE HEARS OF THE MAJORDOMO, WOMAN -- NOT UNTIL I WISH IT.
BUT SOON, THE WORLD WILL HEAR MY TREAD, AND KNOW MY NAME -- AND THEY WILL FEAR ME.
DO YOU KNOW WHY?
UH...

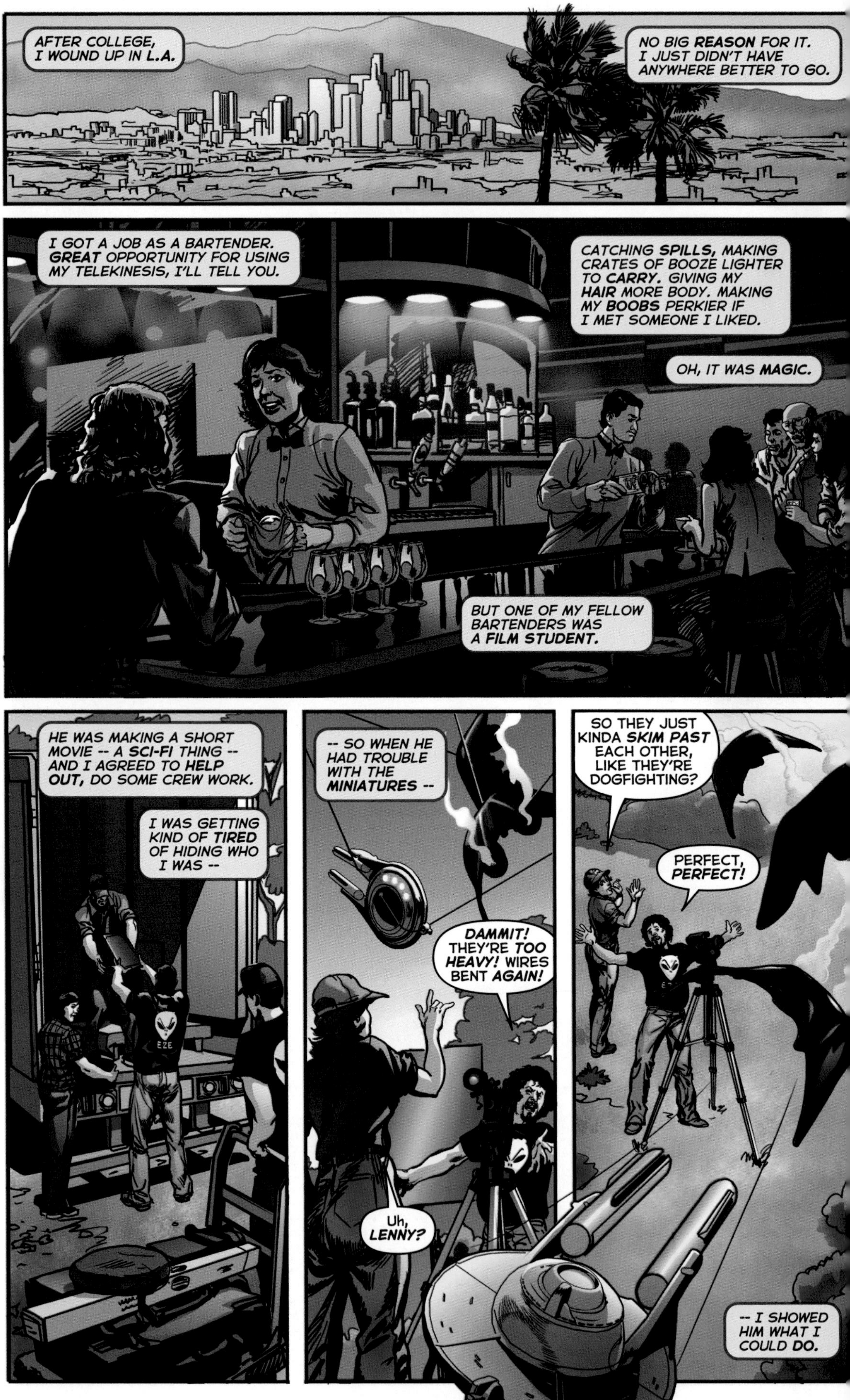
AFTER COLLEGE, I WOUND UP IN L.A.
NO BIG REASON FOR IT. I JUST DIDN'T HAVE ANYWHERE BETTER TO GO.
I GOT A JOB AS A BARTENDER. GREAT OPPORTUNITY FOR USING MY TELEKINESIS, I'LL TELL YOU.
CATCHING SPILLS, MAKING CRATES OF BOOZE LIGHTER TO CARRY. GIVING MY HAIR MORE BODY. MAKING MY BOOBS PERKIER IF I MET SOMEONE I LIKED.
OH, IT WAS MAGIC.
BUT ONE OF MY FELLOW BARTENDERS WAS A FILM STUDENT.
HE WAS MAKING A SHORT MOVIE -- A SCI-FI THING -- AND I AGREED TO HELP OUT, DO SOME CREW WORK.
I WAS GETTING KIND OF TIRED OF HIDING WHO I WAS --
-- SO WHEN HE HAD TROUBLE WITH THE MINIATURES --
DAMMIT! THEY'RE TOO HEAVY! WIRES BENT AGAIN!
Uh, LENNY?
SO THEY JUST KINDA SKIM PAST EACH OTHER, LIKE THEY'RE DOGFIGHTING?
PERFECT, PERFECT!
-- I SHOWED HIM WHAT I COULD DO.

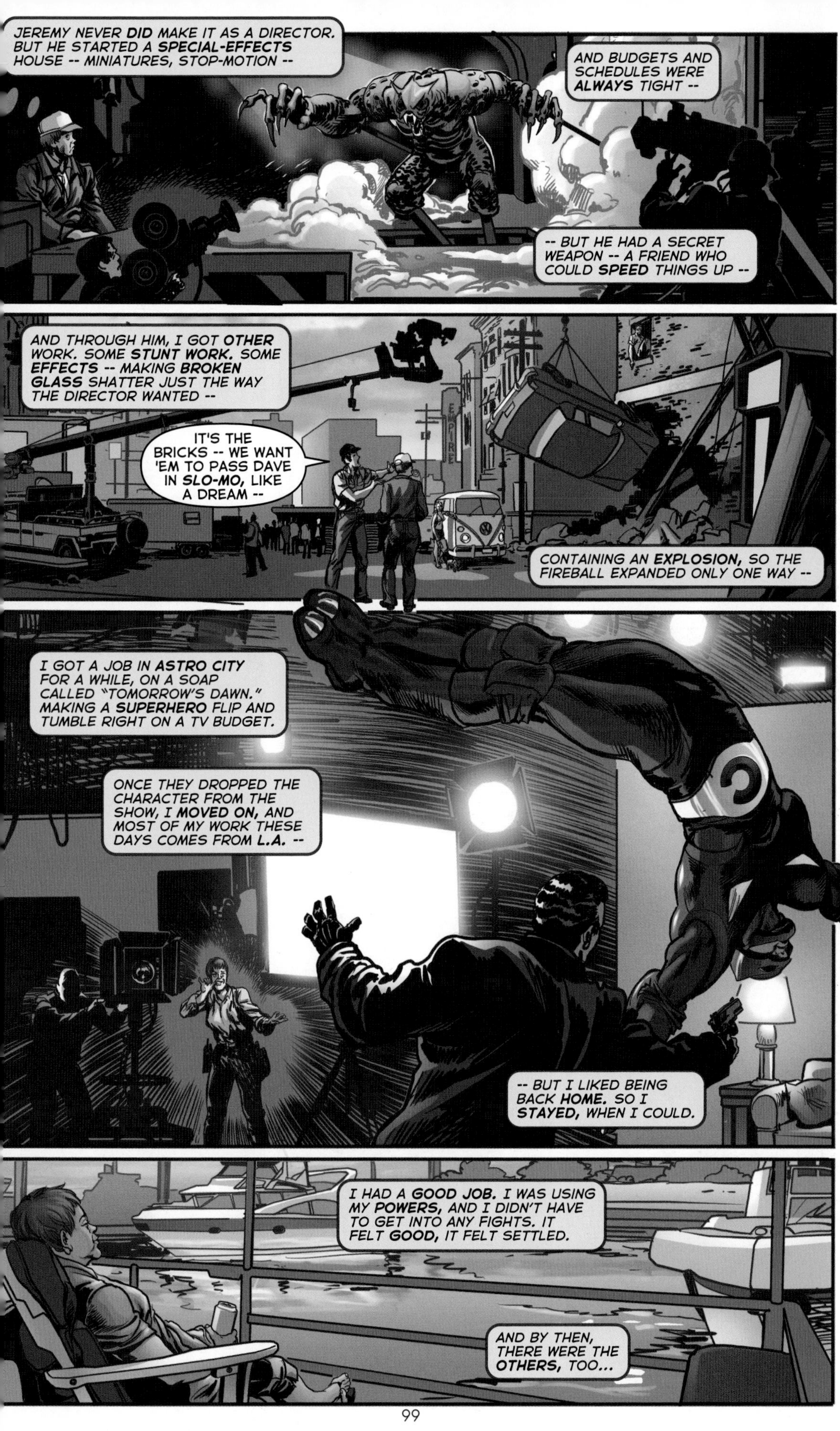
JEREMY NEVER DID MAKE IT AS A DIRECTOR. BUT HE STARTED A SPECIAL-EFFECTS HOUSE -- MINIATURES, STOP-MOTION --
AND BUDGETS AND SCHEDULES WERE ALWAYS TIGHT --
-- BUT HE HAD A SECRET WEAPON -- A FRIEND WHO COULD SPEED THINGS UP --
AND THROUGH HIM, I GOT OTHER WORK. SOME STUNT WORK. SOME EFFECTS -- MAKING BROKEN GLASS SHATTER JUST THE WAY THE DIRECTOR WANTED --
IT'S THE BRICKS -- WE WANT 'EM TO PASS DAVE IN SLO-MO, LIKE A DREAM --
EMPIRE
CONTAINING AN EXPLOSION, SO THE FIREBALL EXPANDED ONLY ONE WAY --
I GOT A JOB IN ASTRO CITY FOR A WHILE, ON A SOAP CALLED "TOMORROW'S DAWN." MAKING A SUPERHERO FLIP AND TUMBLE RIGHT ON A TV BUDGET.
ONCE THEY DROPPED THE CHARACTER FROM THE SHOW, I MOVED ON, AND MOST OF MY WORK THESE DAYS COMES FROM L.A. --
-- BUT I LIKED BEING BACK HOME. SO I STAYED, WHEN I COULD.
I HAD A GOOD JOB. I WAS USING MY POWERS, AND I DIDN'T HAVE TO GET INTO ANY FIGHTS. IT FELT GOOD, IT FELT SETTLED.
AND BY THEN, THERE WERE THE OTHERS, TOO...

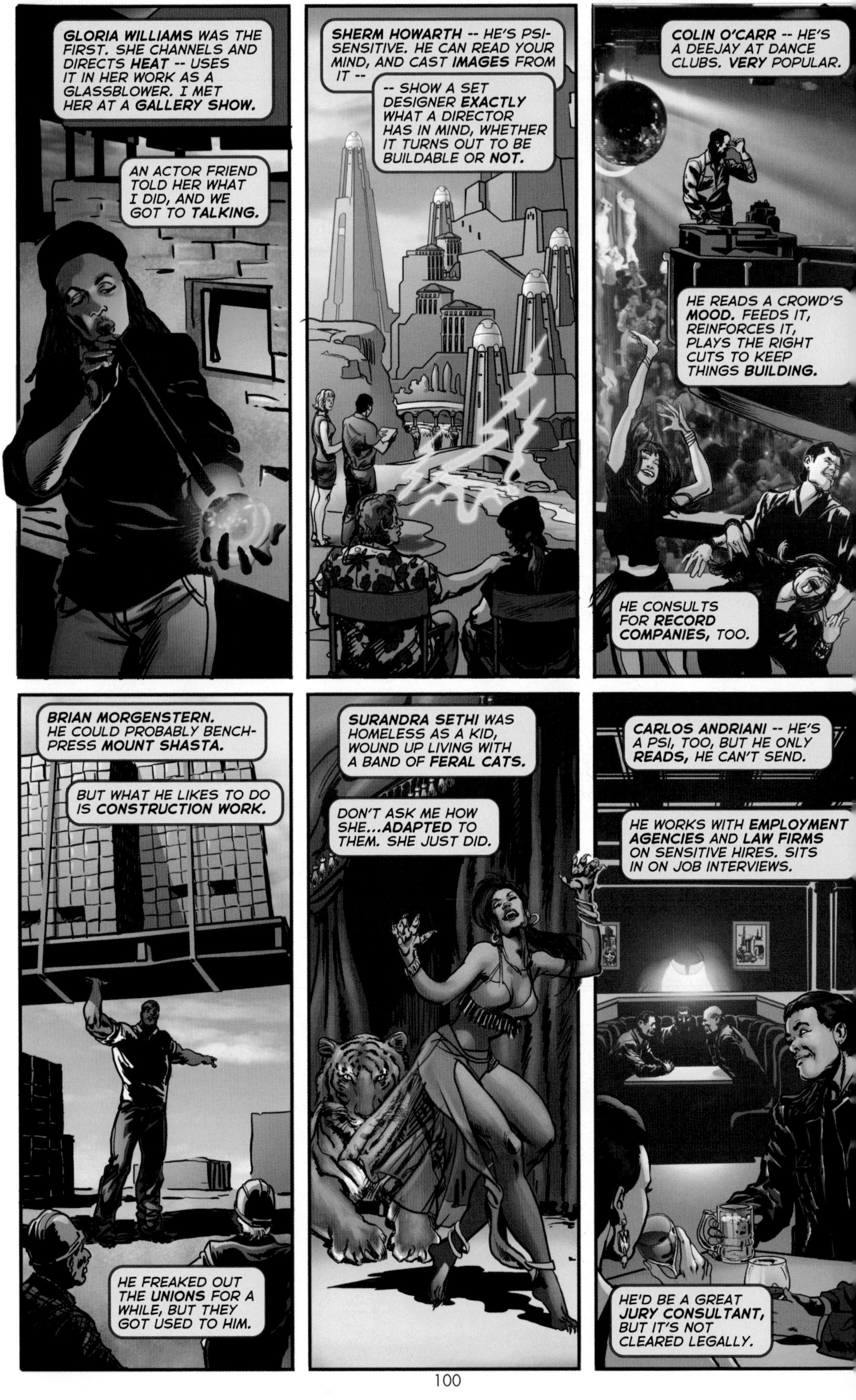
GLORIA WILLIAMS WAS THE FIRST. SHE CHANNELS AND DIRECTS HEAT -- USES IT IN HER WORK AS A GLASSBLOWER. I MET HER AT A GALLERY SHOW.
AN ACTOR FRIEND TOLD HER WHAT I DID, AND WE GOT TO TALKING.
SHERM HOWARTH -- HE'S PSI-SENSITIVE. HE CAN READ YOUR MIND, AND CAST IMAGES FROM IT --
-- SHOW A SET DESIGNER EXACTLY WHAT A DIRECTOR HAS IN MIND, WHETHER IT TURNS OUT TO BE BUILDABLE OR NOT.
COLIN O'CARR -- HE'S A DEEJAY AT DANCE CLUBS. VERY POPULAR.
HE READS A CROWD'S MOOD. FEEDS IT, REINFORCES IT, PLAYS THE RIGHT CUTS TO KEEP THINGS BUILDING.
HE CONSULTS FOR RECORD COMPANIES, TOO.
BRIAN MORGENSTERN. HE COULD PROBABLY BENCH-PRESS MOUNT SHASTA.
BUT WHAT HE LIKES TO DO IS CONSTRUCTION WORK.
HE FREAKED OUT THE UNIONS FOR A WHILE, BUT THEY GOT USED TO HIM.
SURANDRA SETHI WAS HOMELESS AS A KID, WOUND UP LIVING WITH A BAND OF FERAL CATS.
DON'T ASK ME HOW SHE...ADAPTED TO THEM. SHE JUST DID.
CARLOS ANDRIANI -- HE'S A PSI, TOO, BUT HE ONLY READS, HE CAN'T SEND.
HE WORKS WITH EMPLOYMENT AGENCIES AND LAW FIRMS ON SENSITIVE HIRES. SITS IN ON JOB INTERVIEWS.
HE'D BE A GREAT JURY CONSULTANT, BUT IT'S NOT CLEARED LEGALLY.

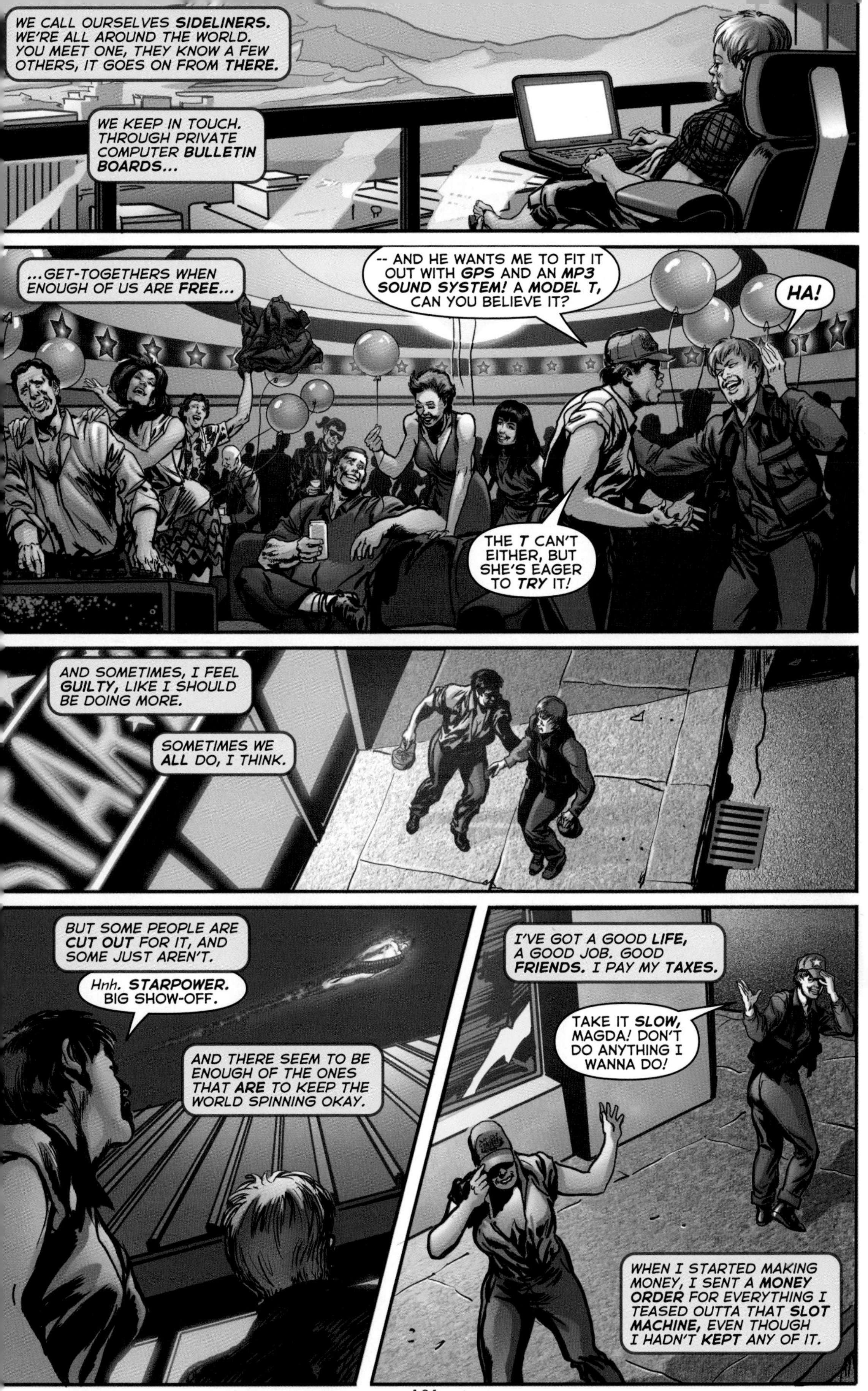
WE CALL OURSELVES SIDELINERS. WE'RE ALL AROUND THE WORLD. YOU MEET ONE, THEY KNOW A FEW OTHERS, IT GOES ON FROM THERE.
WE KEEP IN TOUCH. THROUGH PRIVATE COMPUTER BULLETIN BOARDS...
...GET-TOGETHERS WHEN ENOUGH OF US ARE FREE...
-- AND HE WANTS ME TO FIT IT OUT WITH GPS AND AN MP3 SOUND SYSTEM! A MODEL T, CAN YOU BELIEVE IT?
HA!
THE T CAN'T EITHER, BUT SHE'S EAGER TO TRY IT!
AND SOMETIMES, I FEEL GUILTY, LIKE I SHOULD BE DOING MORE.
SOMETIMES WE ALL DO, I THINK.
BUT SOME PEOPLE ARE CUT OUT FOR IT, AND SOME JUST AREN'T.
Hnh. STARPOWER. BIG SHOW-OFF.
AND THERE SEEM TO BE ENOUGH OF THE ONES THAT ARE TO KEEP THE WORLD SPINNING OKAY.
I'VE GOT A GOOD LIFE, A GOOD JOB. GOOD FRIENDS. I PAY MY TAXES.
TAKE IT SLOW, MAGDA! DON'T DO ANYTHING I WANNA DO!
WHEN I STARTED MAKING MONEY, I SENT A MONEY ORDER FOR EVERYTHING I TEASED OUTTA THAT SLOT MACHINE, EVEN THOUGH I HADN'T KEPT ANY OF IT.

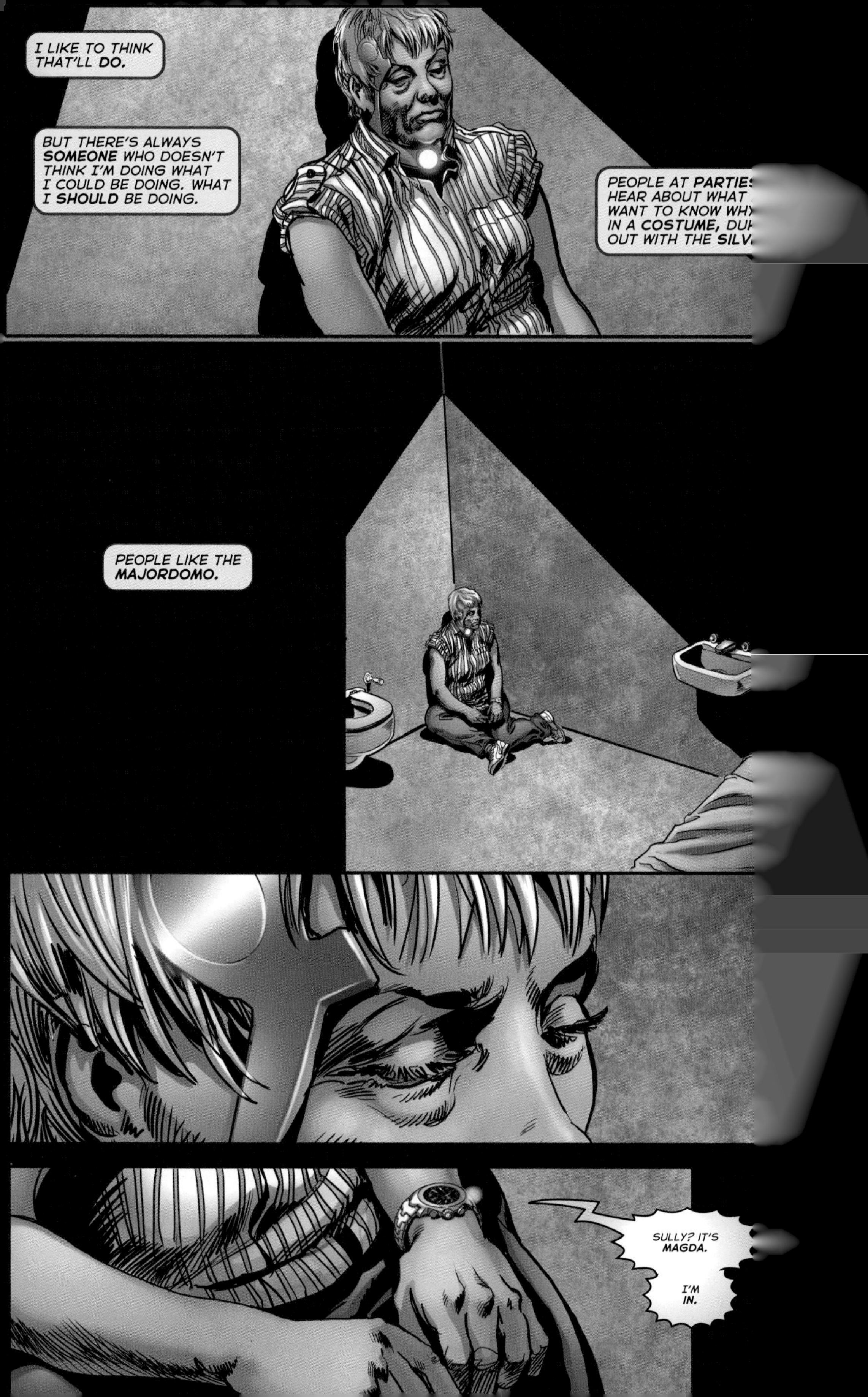
I LIKE TO THINK THAT'LL DO.
BUT THERE'S ALWAYS SOMEONE WHO DOESN'T THINK I'M DOING WHAT I COULD BE DOING. WHAT I SHOULD BE DOING.
PEOPLE AT PARTIES HEAR ABOUT WHAT WANT TO KNOW WHY IN A COSTUME, DU OUT WITH THE SILV
PEOPLE LIKE THE MAJORDOMO.
SULLY? IT'S MAGDA.
I'M IN.

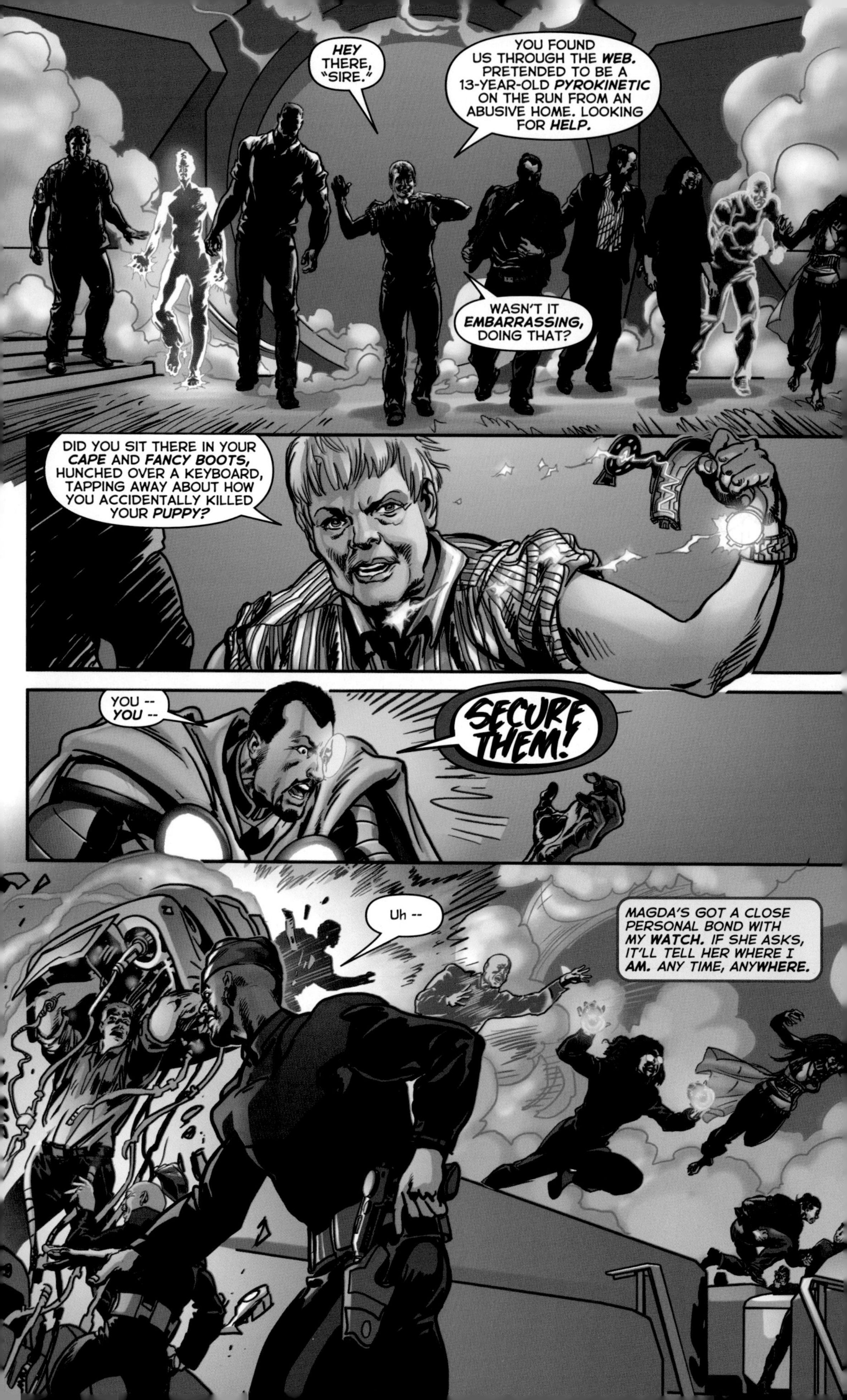
HEY THERE, "SIRE."
YOU FOUND US THROUGH THE WEB. PRETENDED TO BE A 13-YEAR-OLD PYROKINETIC ON THE RUN FROM AN ABUSIVE HOME. LOOKING FOR HELP.
WASN'T IT EMBARRASSING, DOING THAT?
DID YOU SIT THERE IN YOUR CAPE AND FANCY BOOTS, HUNCHED OVER A KEYBOARD, TAPPING AWAY ABOUT HOW YOU ACCIDENTALLY KILLED YOUR PUPPY?
YOU -- YOU --
SECURE THEM!
Uh --
MAGDA'S GOT A CLOSE PERSONAL BOND WITH MY WATCH. IF SHE ASKS, IT'LL TELL HER WHERE I AM. ANY TIME, ANYWHERE.

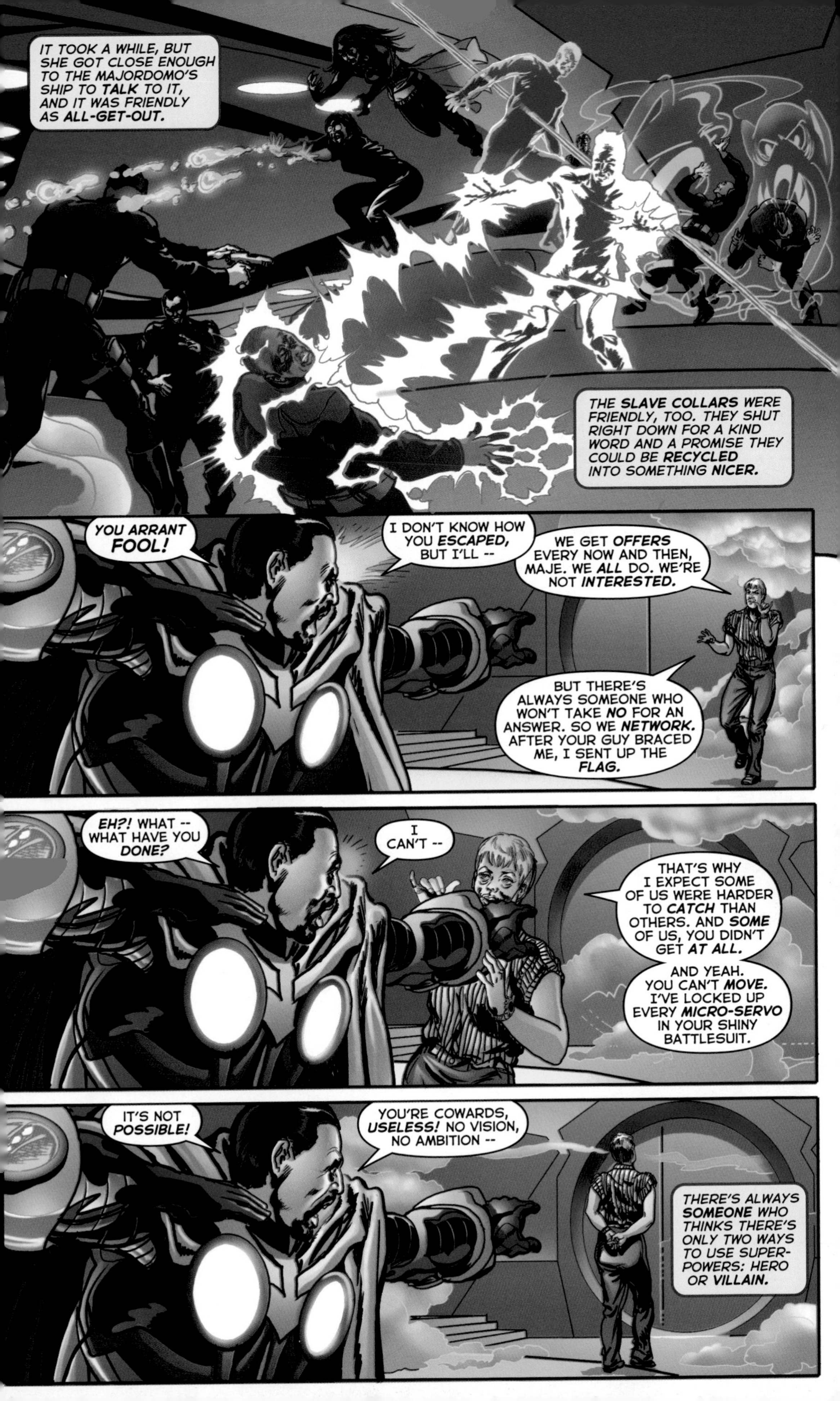

IT TOOK A WHILE, BUT SHE GOT CLOSE ENOUGH TO THE MAJORDOMO'S SHIP TO **TALK** TO IT, AND IT WAS FRIENDLY AS **ALL-GET-OUT.**
THE **SLAVE COLLARS** WERE FRIENDLY, TOO. THEY SHUT RIGHT DOWN FOR A KIND WORD AND A PROMISE THEY COULD BE **RECYCLED** INTO SOMETHING **NICER.**
YOU ARRANT **FOOL!**
I DON'T KNOW HOW YOU **ESCAPED,** BUT I'LL --
WE GET **OFFERS** EVERY NOW AND THEN, MAJE. WE **ALL** DO. WE'RE NOT **INTERESTED.**
BUT THERE'S ALWAYS SOMEONE WHO WON'T TAKE **NO** FOR AN ANSWER. SO WE **NETWORK.** AFTER YOUR GUY BRACED ME, I SENT UP THE **FLAG.**
EH?! WHAT -- WHAT HAVE YOU **DONE?**
I CAN'T --
THAT'S WHY I EXPECT SOME OF US WERE HARDER TO **CATCH** THAN OTHERS. AND **SOME** OF US, YOU DIDN'T GET **AT ALL.**
AND YEAH. YOU CAN'T **MOVE.** I'VE LOCKED UP EVERY **MICRO-SERVO** IN YOUR SHINY BATTLESUIT.
IT'S NOT **POSSIBLE!**
YOU'RE COWARDS, **USELESS!** NO VISION, NO AMBITION --
THERE'S ALWAYS **SOMEONE** WHO THINKS THERE'S ONLY TWO WAYS TO USE SUPER-POWERS: HERO OR **VILLAIN.**

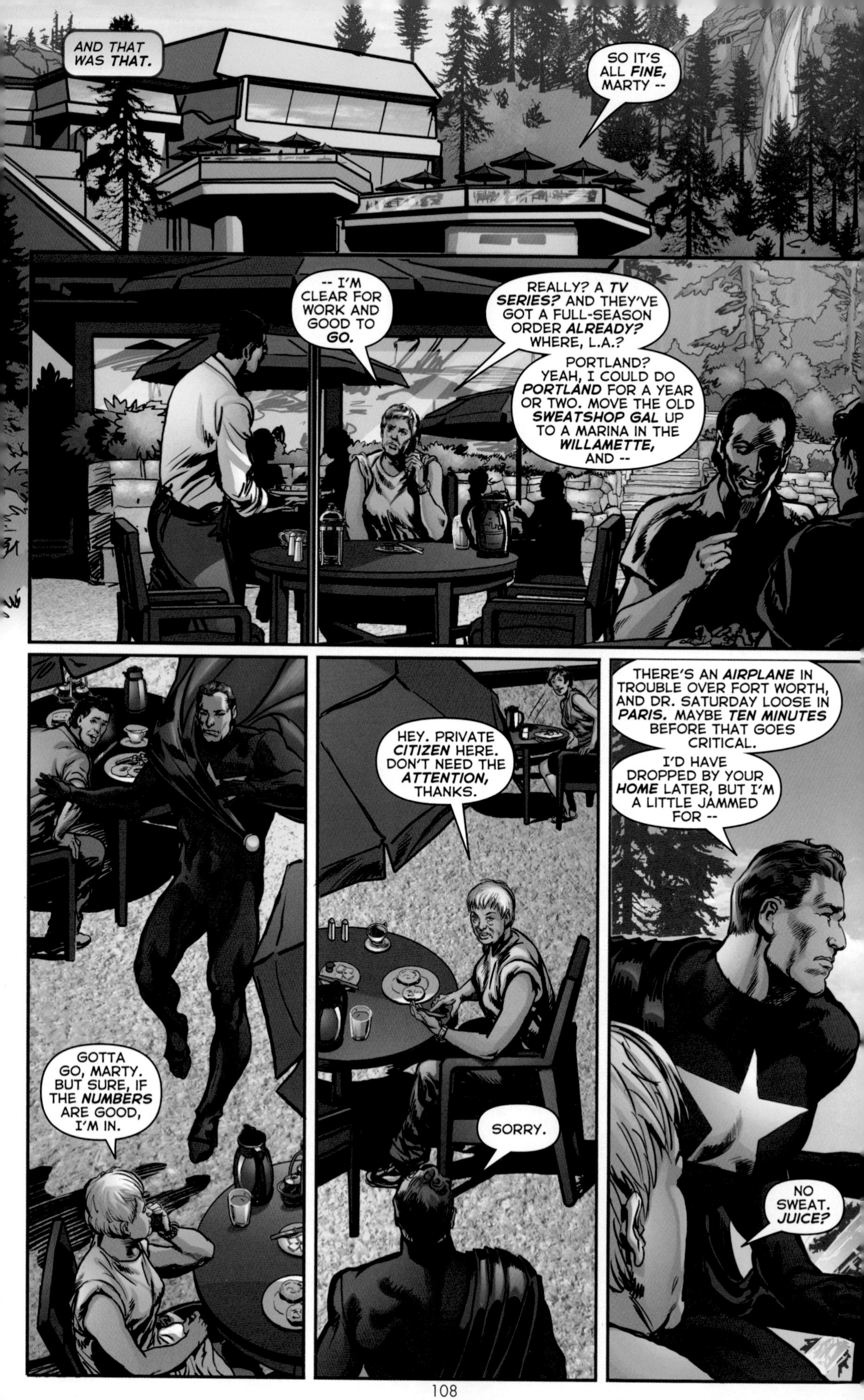
AND THAT WAS THAT.
SO IT'S ALL FINE, MARTY --
-- I'M CLEAR FOR WORK AND GOOD TO GO.
REALLY? A TV SERIES? AND THEY'VE GOT A FULL-SEASON ORDER ALREADY? WHERE, L.A.?
PORTLAND? YEAH, I COULD DO PORTLAND FOR A YEAR OR TWO. MOVE THE OLD SWEATSHOP GAL UP TO A MARINA IN THE WILLAMETTE, AND --
GOTTA GO, MARTY. BUT SURE, IF THE NUMBERS ARE GOOD, I'M IN.
HEY. PRIVATE CITIZEN HERE. DON'T NEED THE ATTENTION, THANKS.
SORRY.
THERE'S AN AIRPLANE IN TROUBLE OVER FORT WORTH, AND DR. SATURDAY LOOSE IN PARIS. MAYBE TEN MINUTES BEFORE THAT GOES CRITICAL.
I'D HAVE DROPPED BY YOUR HOME LATER, BUT I'M A LITTLE JAMMED FOR --
NO SWEAT. JUICE?

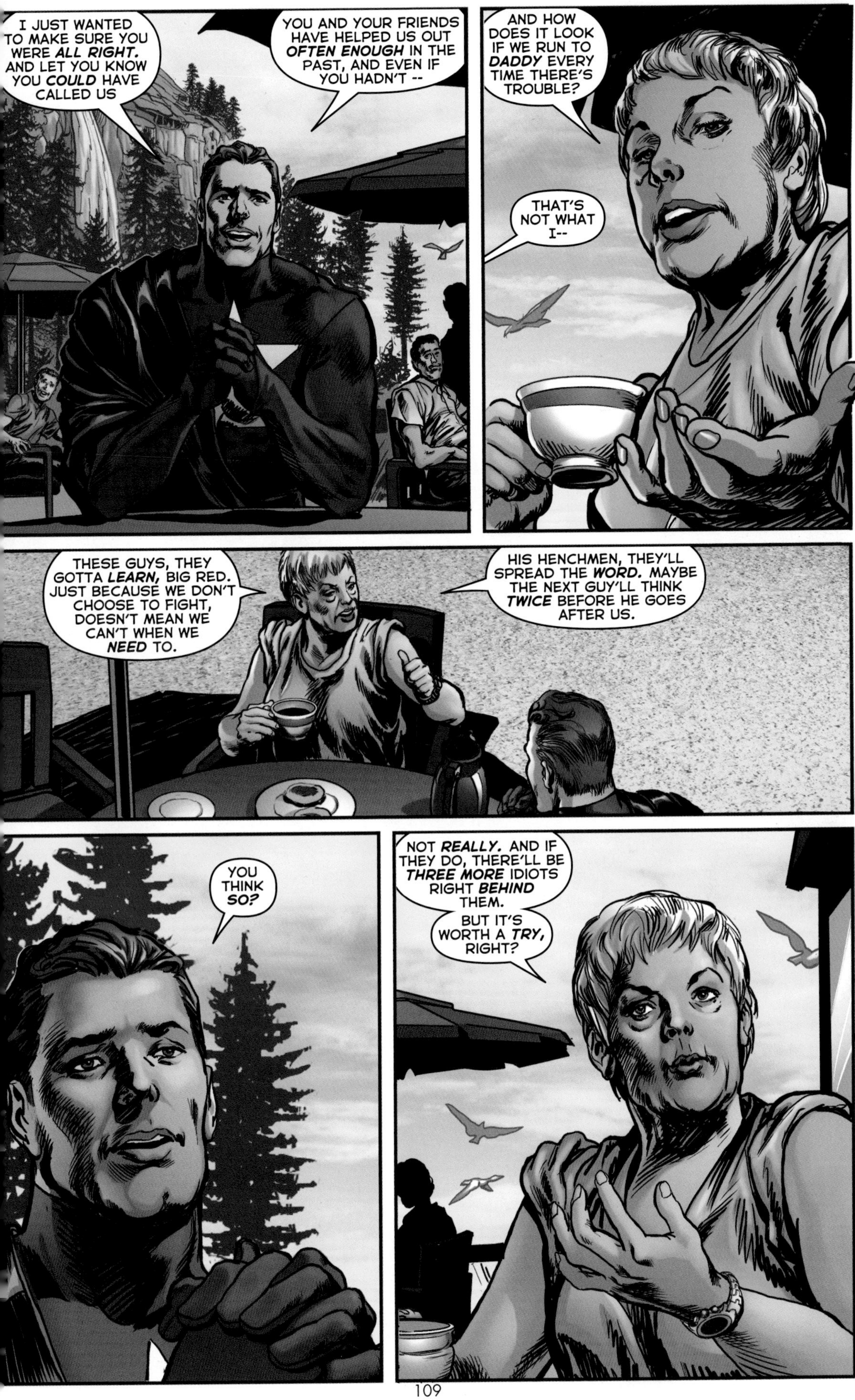

I JUST WANTED TO MAKE SURE YOU WERE **ALL RIGHT.** AND LET YOU KNOW YOU **COULD** HAVE CALLED US
YOU AND YOUR FRIENDS HAVE HELPED US OUT **OFTEN ENOUGH** IN THE PAST, AND EVEN IF YOU HADN'T --
AND HOW DOES IT LOOK IF WE RUN TO **DADDY** EVERY TIME THERE'S TROUBLE?
THAT'S NOT WHAT I--
THESE GUYS, THEY GOTTA **LEARN,** BIG RED. JUST BECAUSE WE DON'T CHOOSE TO FIGHT, DOESN'T MEAN WE CAN'T WHEN WE **NEED** TO.
HIS HENCHMEN, THEY'LL SPREAD THE **WORD.** MAYBE THE NEXT GUY'LL THINK **TWICE** BEFORE HE GOES AFTER US.
YOU THINK **SO?**
NOT **REALLY.** AND IF THEY DO, THERE'LL BE **THREE MORE** IDIOTS RIGHT **BEHIND** THEM.
BUT IT'S WORTH A **TRY,** RIGHT?

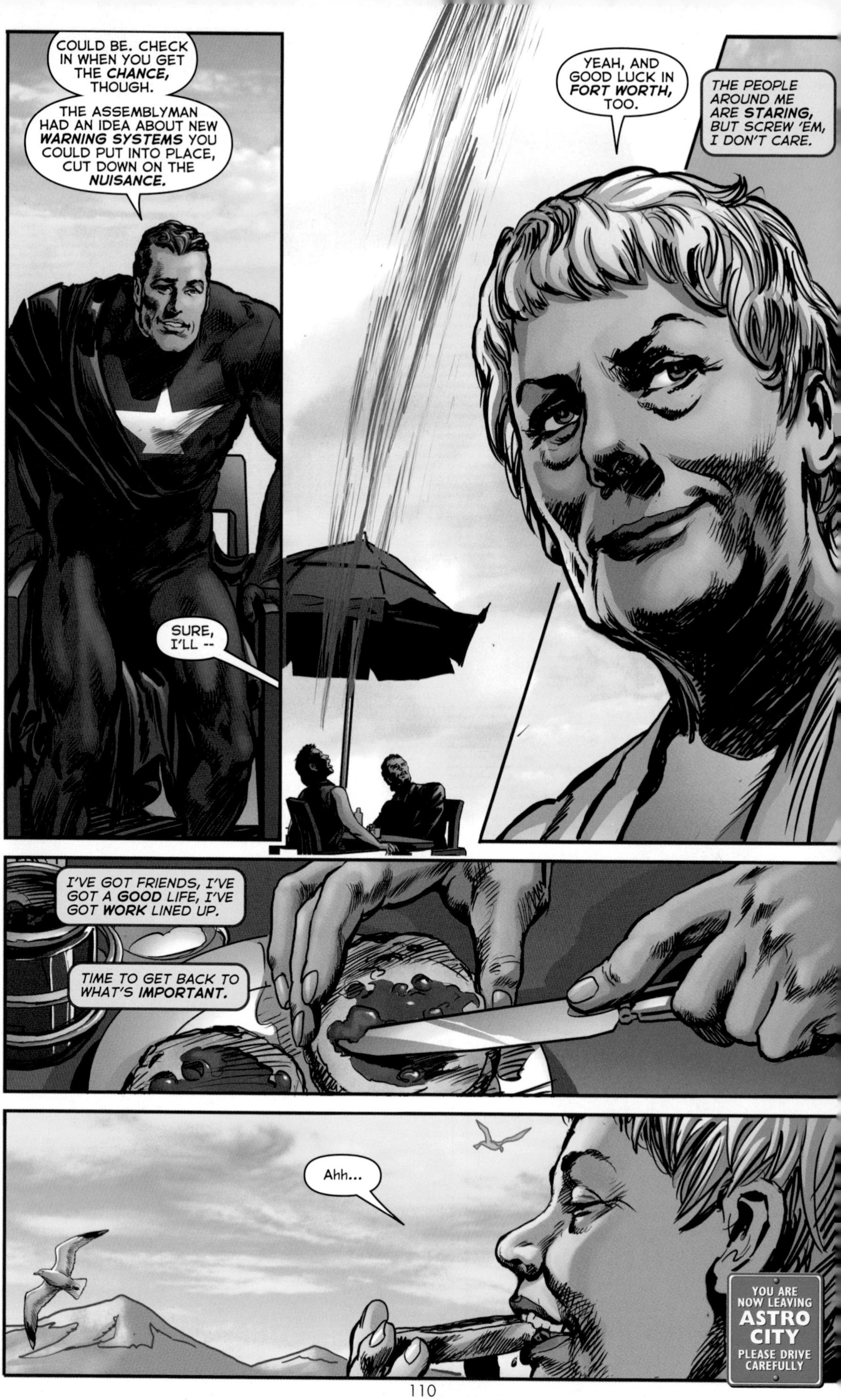
COULD BE. CHECK IN WHEN YOU GET THE *CHANCE,* THOUGH.
THE ASSEMBLYMAN HAD AN IDEA ABOUT NEW *WARNING SYSTEMS* YOU COULD PUT INTO PLACE, CUT DOWN ON THE *NUISANCE.*
SURE, I'LL --
YEAH, AND GOOD LUCK IN *FORT WORTH,* TOO.
THE PEOPLE AROUND ME ARE **STARING,** BUT SCREW 'EM, I DON'T CARE.
I'VE GOT FRIENDS, I'VE GOT A **GOOD** LIFE, I'VE GOT **WORK** LINED UP.
TIME TO GET BACK TO WHAT'S **IMPORTANT.**
Ahh...
YOU ARE NOW LEAVING
ASTRO CITY
PLEASE DRIVE CAREFULLY

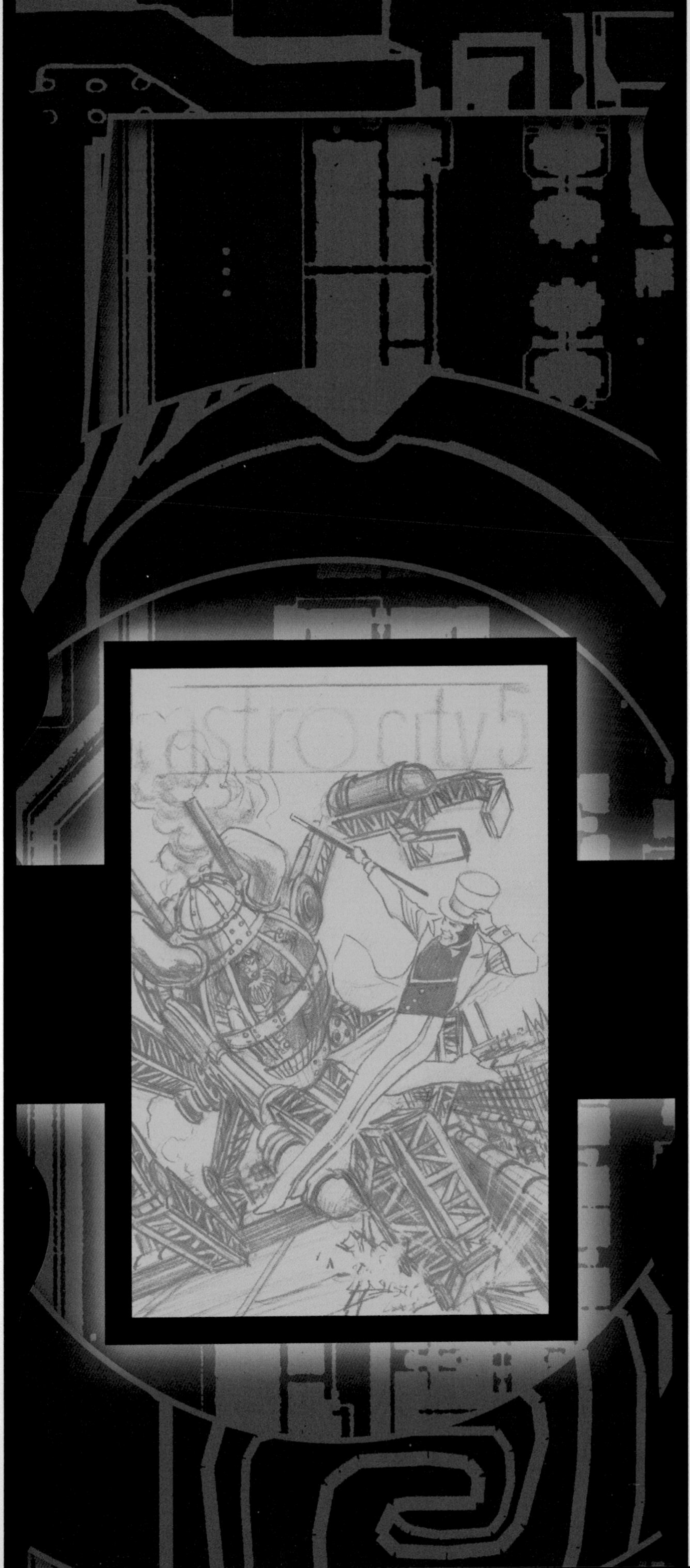
astro city 5

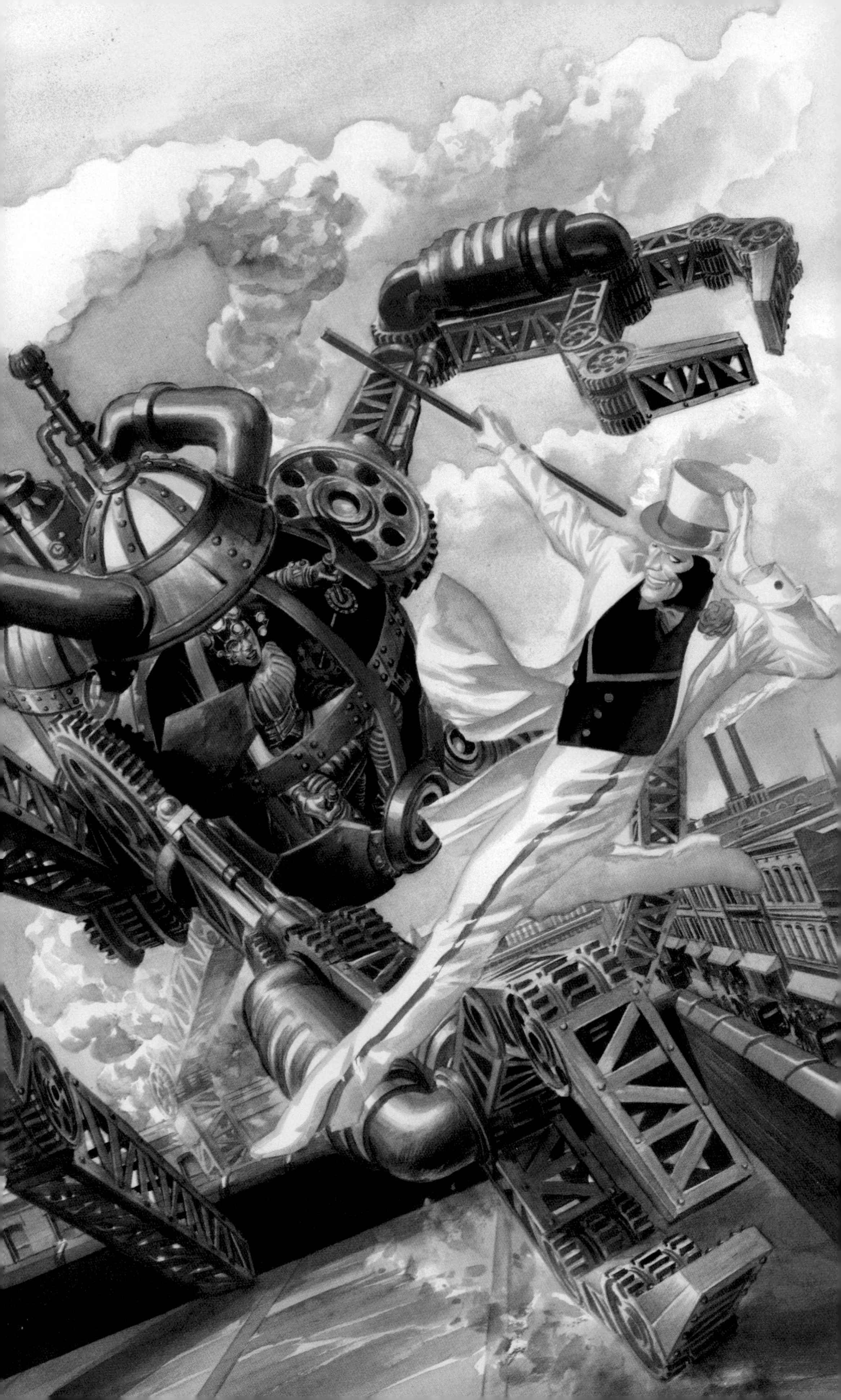

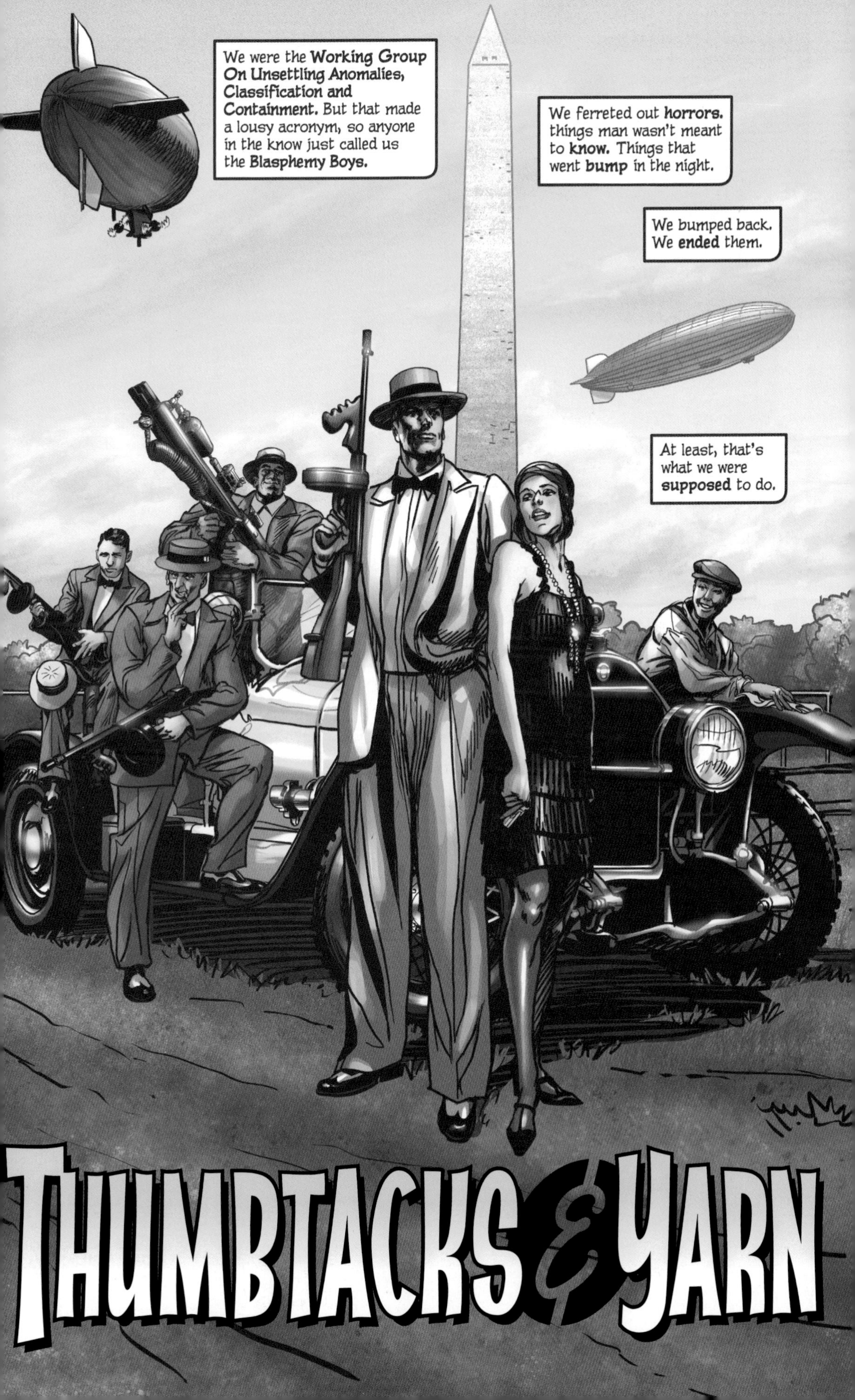
We were the Working Group On Unsettling Anomalies, Classification and Containment. But that made a lousy acronym, so anyone in the know just called us the Blasphemy Boys.
We ferreted out horrors. things man wasn't meant to know. Things that went bump in the night.
We bumped back. We ended them.
At least, that's what we were supposed to do.
THUMBTACKS & YARN

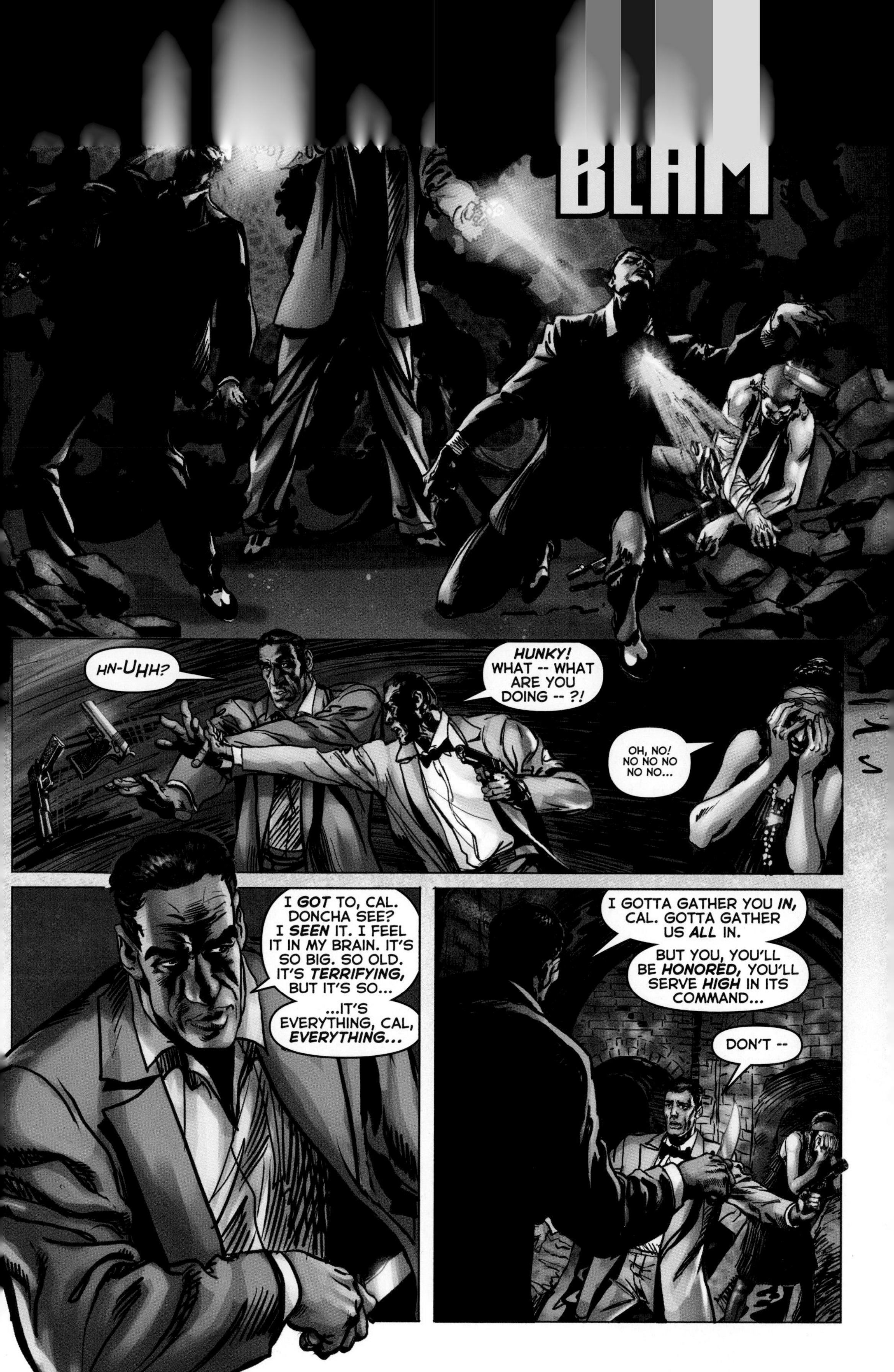

BLAM
HN-UHH?
HUNKY! WHAT -- WHAT ARE YOU DOING -- ?!
OH, NO! NO NO NO NO NO...
I GOT TO, CAL. DONCHA SEE? I SEEN IT. I FEEL IT IN MY BRAIN. IT'S SO BIG. SO OLD. IT'S TERRIFYING, BUT IT'S SO...
...IT'S EVERYTHING, CAL, EVERYTHING...
I GOTTA GATHER YOU IN, CAL. GOTTA GATHER US ALL IN.
BUT YOU, YOU'LL BE HONORED, YOU'LL SERVE HIGH IN ITS COMMAND...
DON'T --

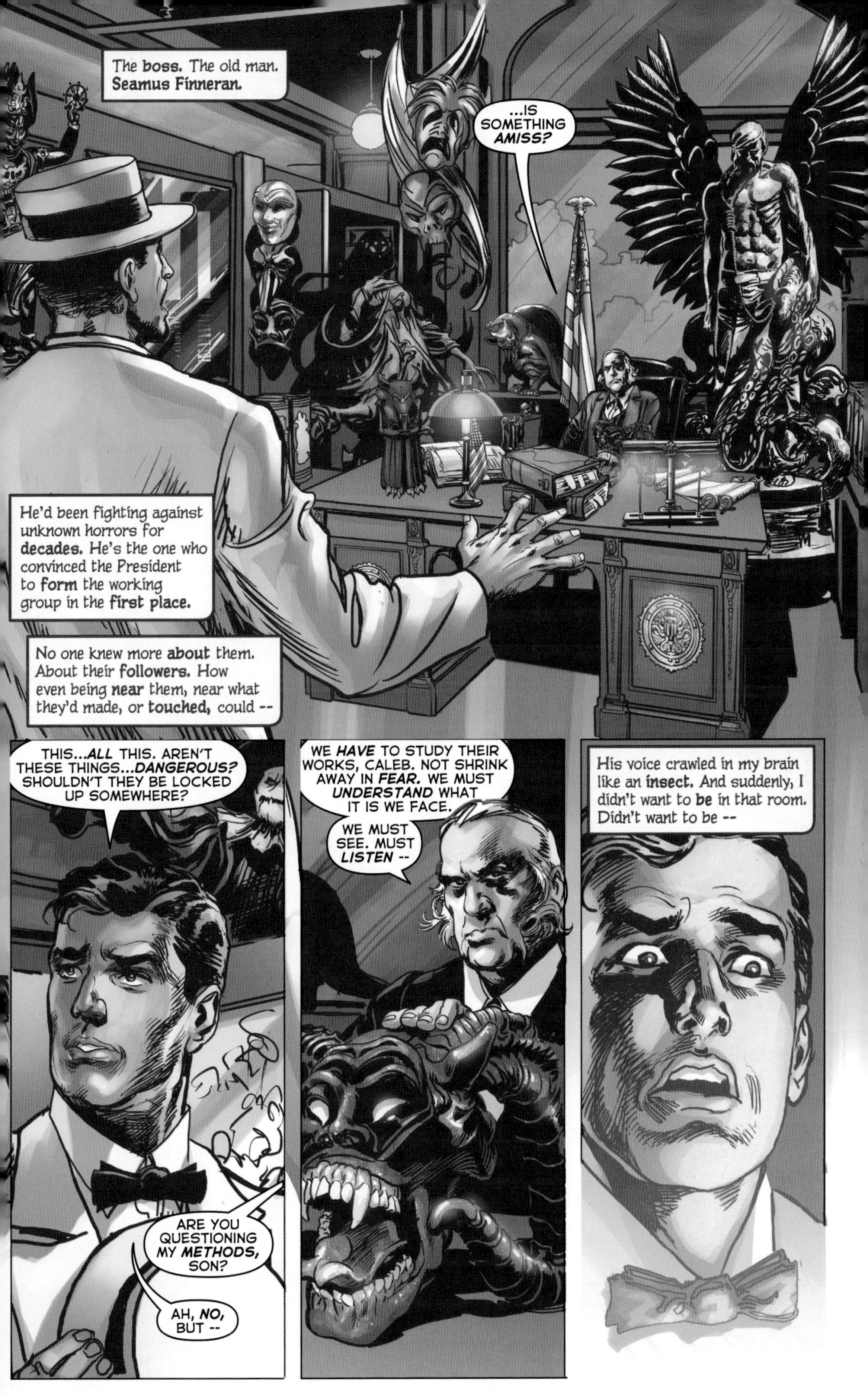

The boss. The old man. Seamus Finneran.
...IS SOMETHING AMISS?
He'd been fighting against unknown horrors for decades. He's the one who convinced the President to form the working group in the first place.
No one knew more about them. About their followers. How even being near them, near what they'd made, or touched, could --
THIS...ALL THIS. AREN'T THESE THINGS...DANGEROUS? SHOULDN'T THEY BE LOCKED UP SOMEWHERE?
ARE YOU QUESTIONING MY METHODS, SON?
AH, NO, BUT --
WE HAVE TO STUDY THEIR WORKS, CALEB. NOT SHRINK AWAY IN FEAR. WE MUST UNDERSTAND WHAT IT IS WE FACE.
WE MUST SEE. MUST LISTEN --
His voice crawled in my brain like an insect. And suddenly, I didn't want to be in that room. Didn't want to be --

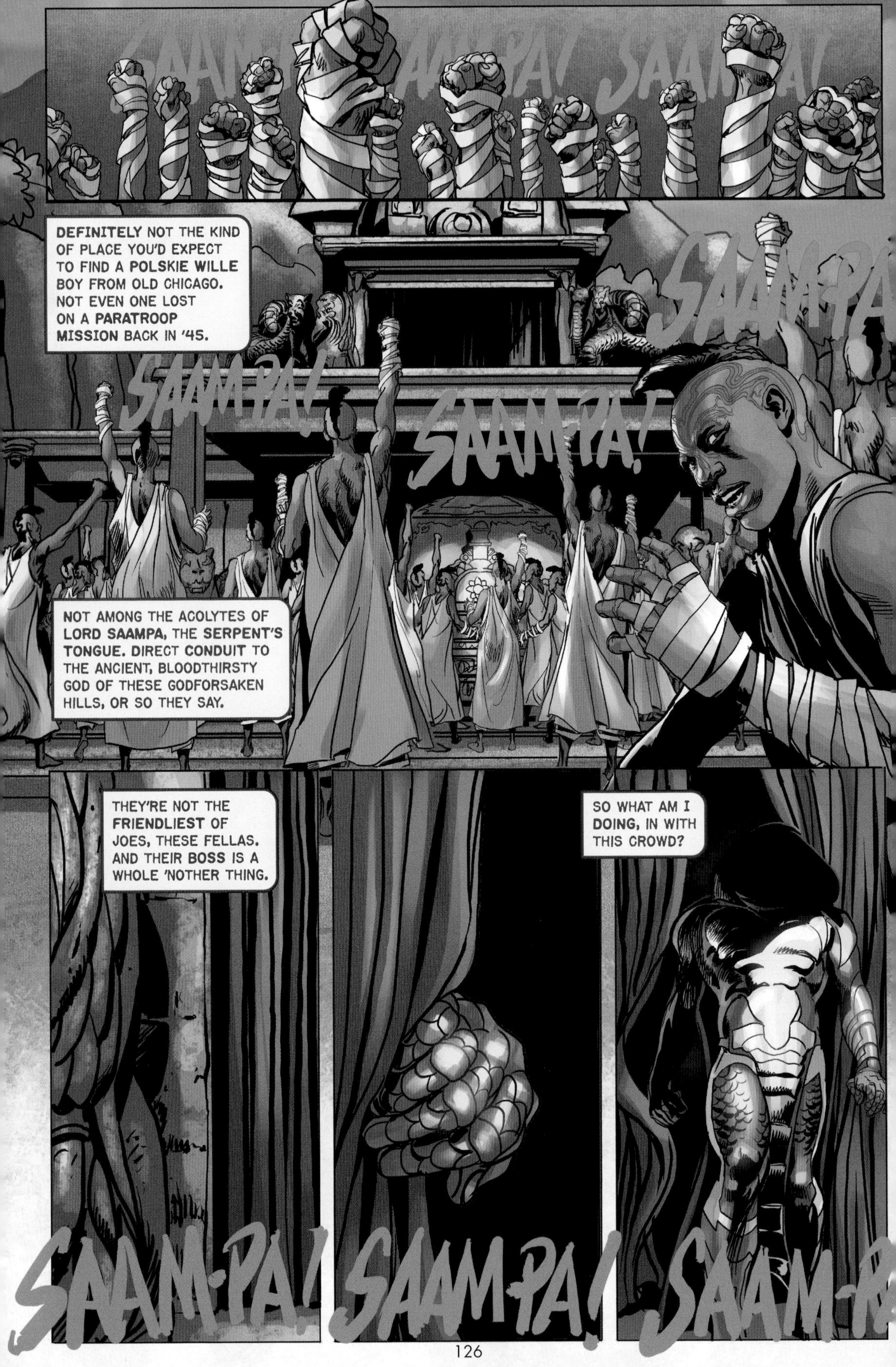

SAAMPA! SAAMPA! SAAMPA!
DEFINITELY NOT THE KIND OF PLACE YOU'D EXPECT TO FIND A POLSKIE WILLE BOY FROM OLD CHICAGO. NOT EVEN ONE LOST ON A PARATROOP MISSION BACK IN '45.
SAAMPA!
SAAMPA!
SAAMPA!
NOT AMONG THE ACOLYTES OF LORD SAAMPA, THE SERPENT'S TONGUE. DIRECT CONDUIT TO THE ANCIENT, BLOODTHIRSTY GOD OF THESE GODFORSAKEN HILLS, OR SO THEY SAY.
THEY'RE NOT THE FRIENDLIEST OF JOES, THESE FELLAS. AND THEIR BOSS IS A WHOLE 'NOTHER THING.
SO WHAT AM I DOING, IN WITH THIS CROWD?
SAAM-PA! SAAM-PA!

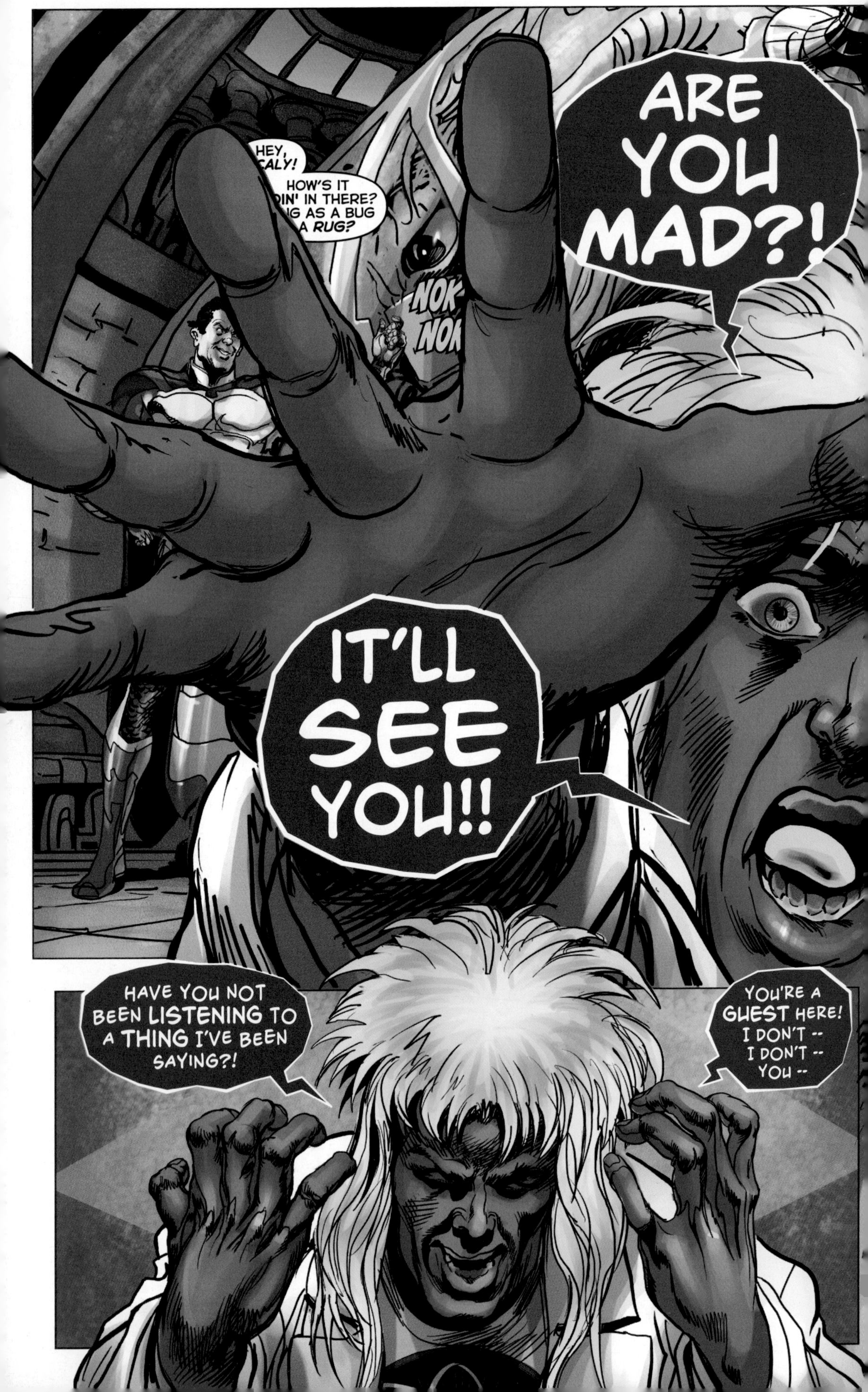
HEY, CALY!
HOW'S IT DIN' IN THERE? IG AS A BUG A RUG?
NOK NOK
ARE YOU MAD?!
IT'LL SEE YOU!!
HAVE YOU NOT BEEN LISTENING TO A THING I'VE BEEN SAYING?!
YOU'RE A GUEST HERE! I DON'T -- I DON'T -- YOU --

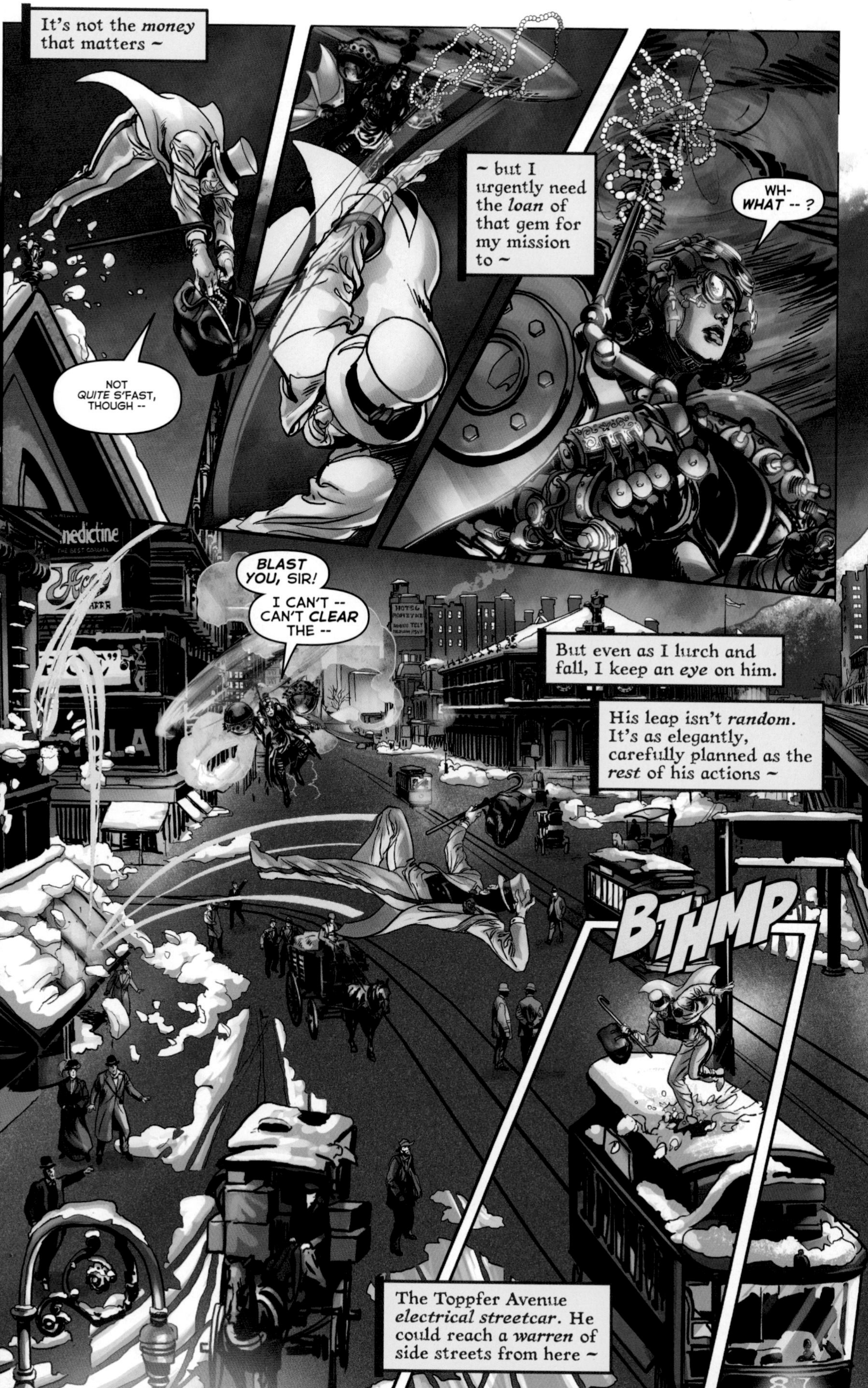

It's not the *money* that matters ~
NOT *QUITE* S'FAST, THOUGH --
~ but I urgently need the *loan* of that gem for my mission to ~
WH- *WHAT* -- ?
BLAST YOU, SIR!
I CAN'T -- CAN'T *CLEAR* THE --
But even as I lurch and fall, I keep an *eye* on him.
His leap isn't *random*. It's as elegantly, carefully planned as the *rest* of his actions ~
BTHMP
The Toppfer Avenue *electrical streetcar*. He could reach a *warren* of side streets from here ~

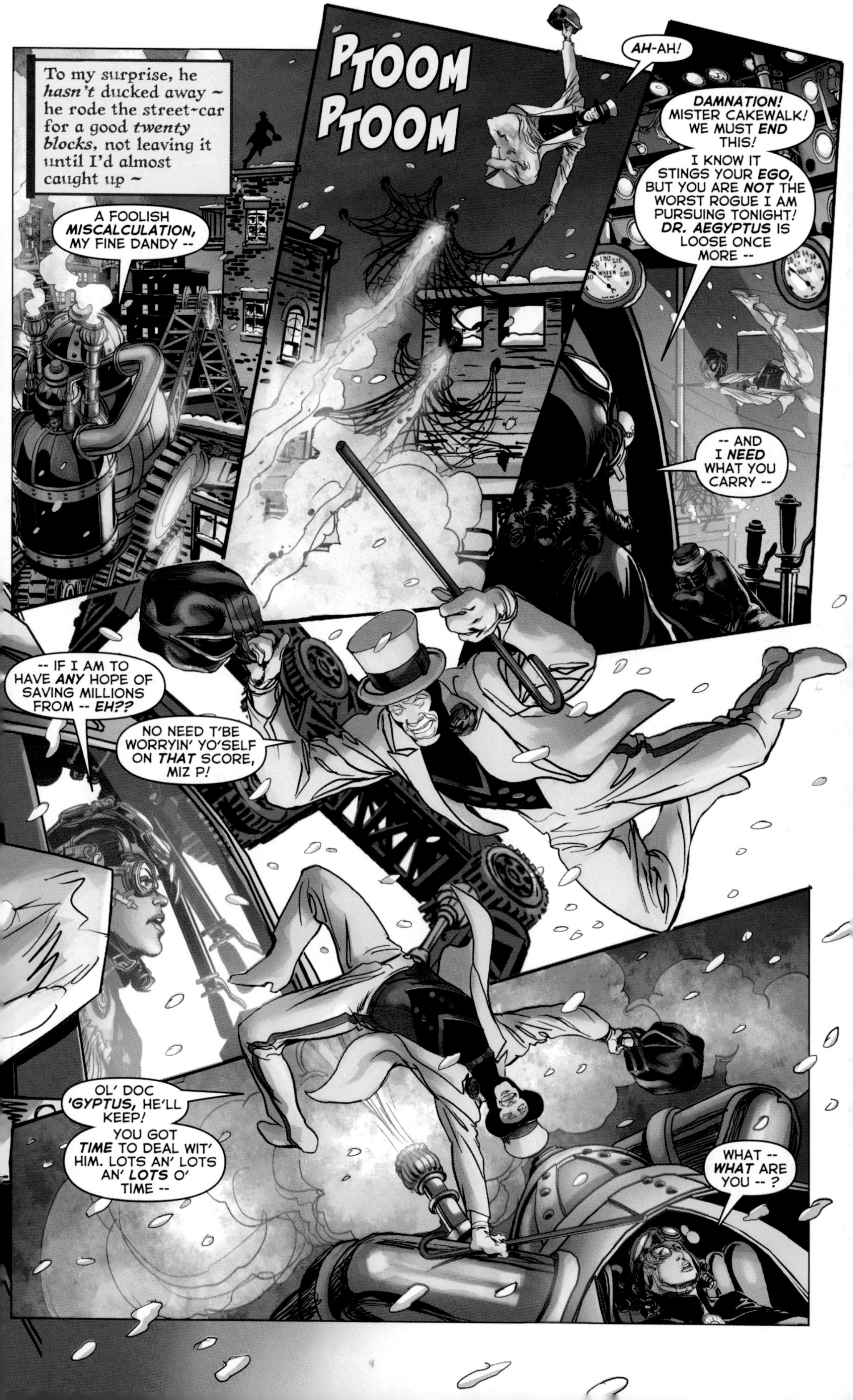
To my surprise, he *hasn't* ducked away ~ he rode the street~car for a good *twenty blocks*, not leaving it until I'd almost caught up ~
A FOOLISH **MISCALCULATION,** MY FINE DANDY --
PTOOM PTOOM
AH-AH!
DAMNATION! MISTER CAKEWALK! WE MUST END THIS!
I KNOW IT STINGS YOUR EGO, BUT YOU ARE NOT THE WORST ROGUE I AM PURSUING TONIGHT! DR. AEGYPTUS IS LOOSE ONCE MORE --
-- AND I NEED WHAT YOU CARRY --
-- IF I AM TO HAVE ANY HOPE OF SAVING MILLIONS FROM -- EH??
NO NEED T'BE WORRYIN' YO'SELF ON THAT SCORE, MIZ P!
OL' DOC 'GYPTUS, HE'LL KEEP! YOU GOT TIME TO DEAL WIT' HIM. LOTS AN' LOTS AN' LOTS O' TIME --
WHAT -- WHAT ARE YOU -- ?

US *PUBLIC NUISANCES* -- WE JUST GOT NO SENSE O' *BOUNDARIES*, DO WE?

I was able to *stop* Aegyptus ~ rescue hundreds he'd have condemned to a *lifetime* of horror.

Perhaps Mister Cakewalk was not *truly* the menace he was made out to be. This would bear some *thought*...

THERE! *HAPPY* NOW? YOU GOT A *STORY*. GOT AN *ADVENTURE*! THAT'S WHAT YOU *CAME* FOR, ISN'T IT? NOT TO HELP.

I HADN'T BEEN PLANNING ON *SHOWING* YOU THAT FOR A WHILE -- YOU CAN'T *POSSIBLY* UNDERSTAND ALL ITS IMPLICATIONS, NOT YET --

BUT PERHAPS IT'LL *HOLD* YOU. STOP YOU MEDDLING FURTHER INTO DANGEROUS AREAS.

≶SIGH≷ PERHAPS... PERHAPS I'VE MADE AN *ERROR*. PERHAPS I SHOULDN'T *ALLOW* YOU HERE AT ALL. *SHOCKING* LACK OF DISCIPLINE.

NOW GO, GO. BACK TO YOUR WORLD. *MAYBE* I'LL LET YOU BACK IN. MAYBE *NOT*. IN THE MEANTIME, SOME OF US HAVE WORK TO --

≶HMPH!≷ OF ALL THE BRASS! GO, I SAID!

MENAGERIE GANG MEMBERS ON TRIAL

E-MASTER THREATENS ANADIAN REFINERY

SILVER ADEPT AIDS HONOR GUARD

ASTRO CITY - The Silver Adept, the sorcerous heroine who has apparently recently relocated to Astro City, joined Honor Guard Monday night in a battle against Mister Mystoro, career criminal and self-proclaimed "heir to the secrets of Rasputin." Mystoro had abduc-

somehow drawing on the life forces in a way that granted him the power to summon extra-dimensional forces. His ultimate goal appears to be immortality and the permanent

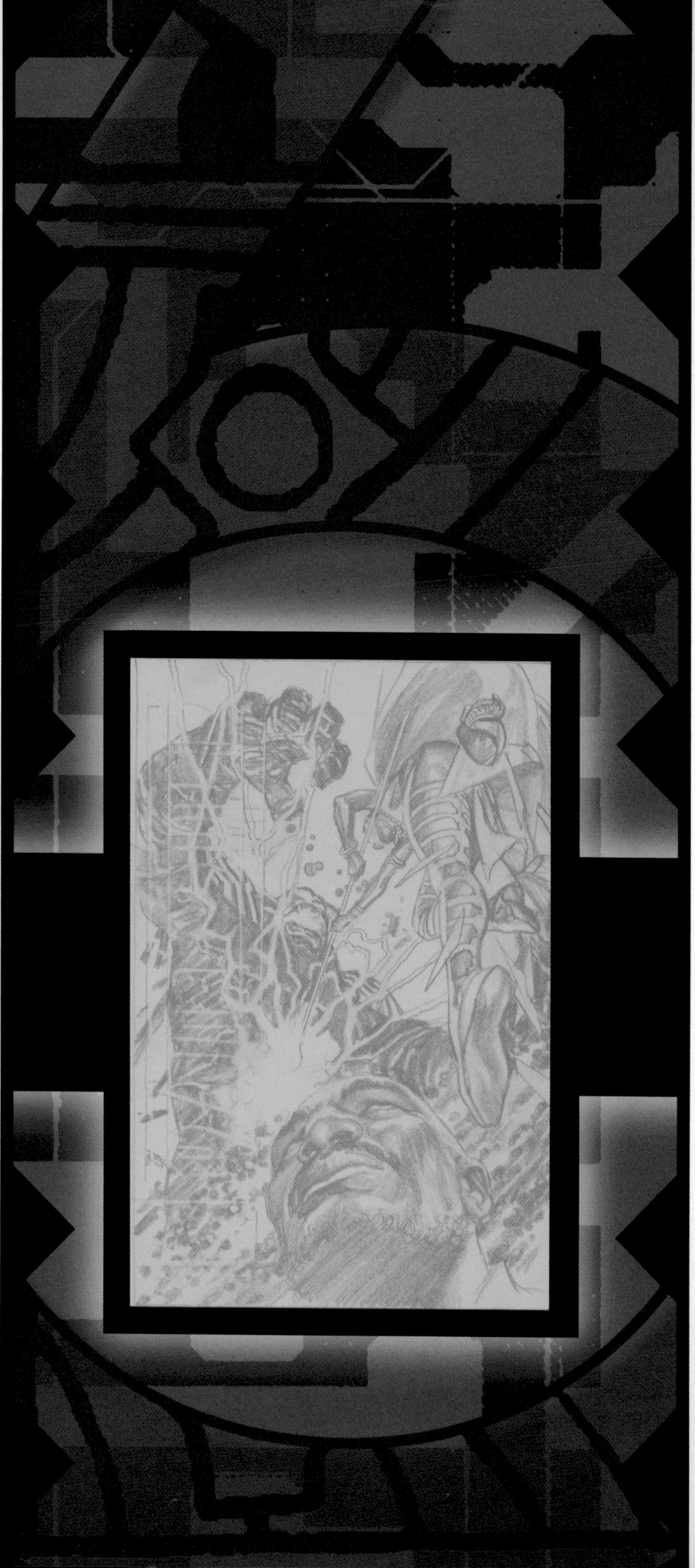

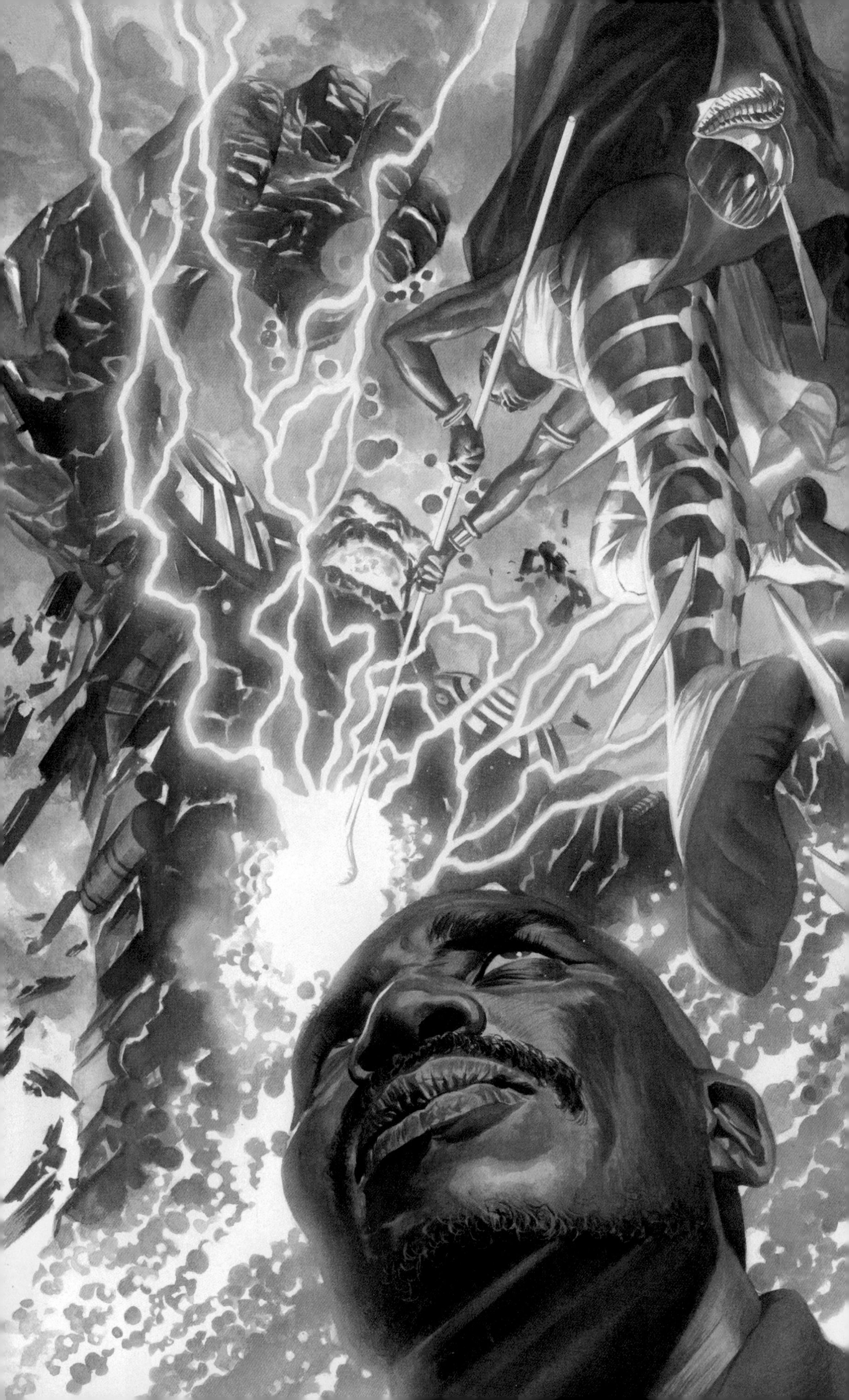

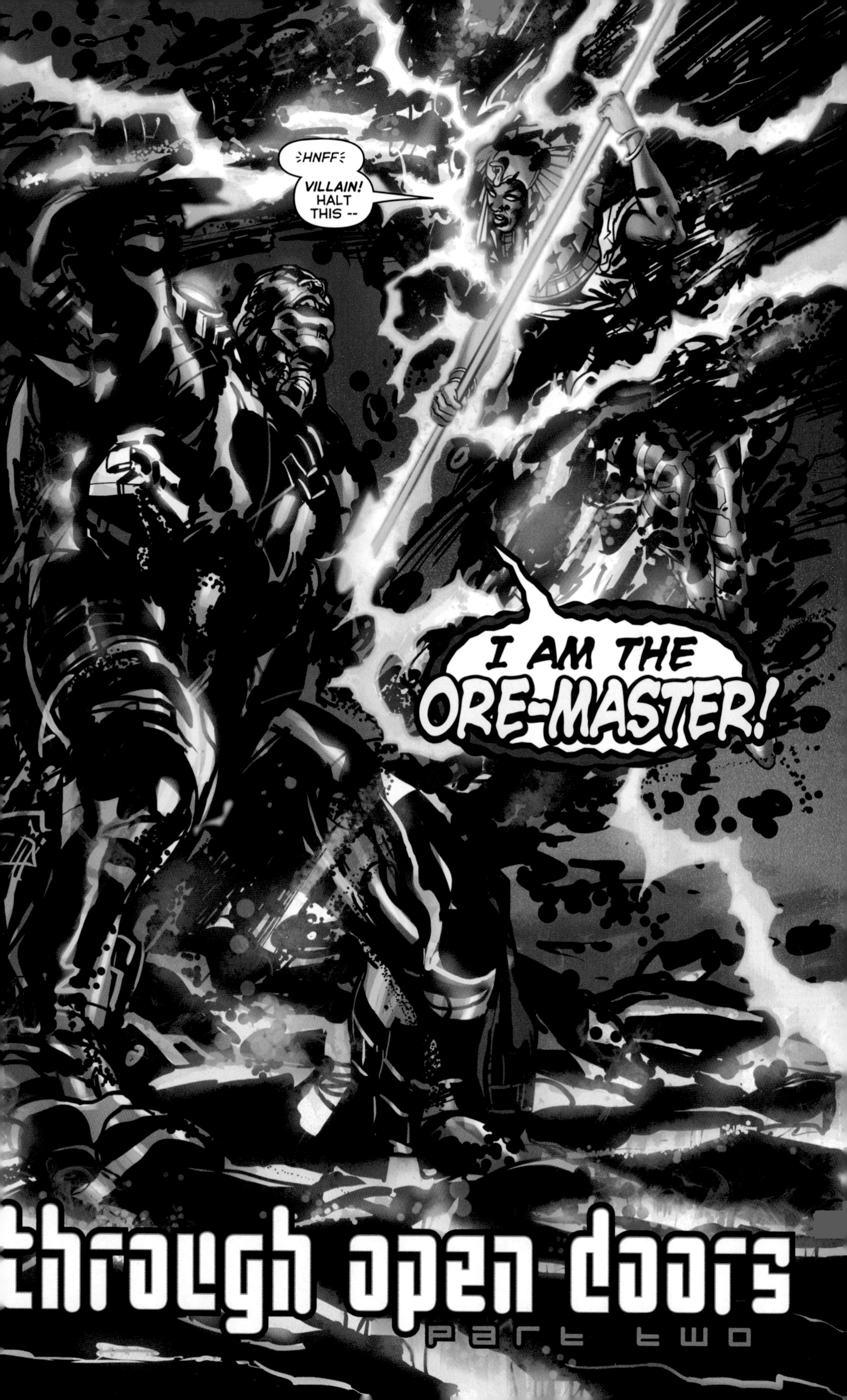

HNFF
VILLAIN! HALT THIS --
I AM THE ORE-MASTER!
through open doors
part two

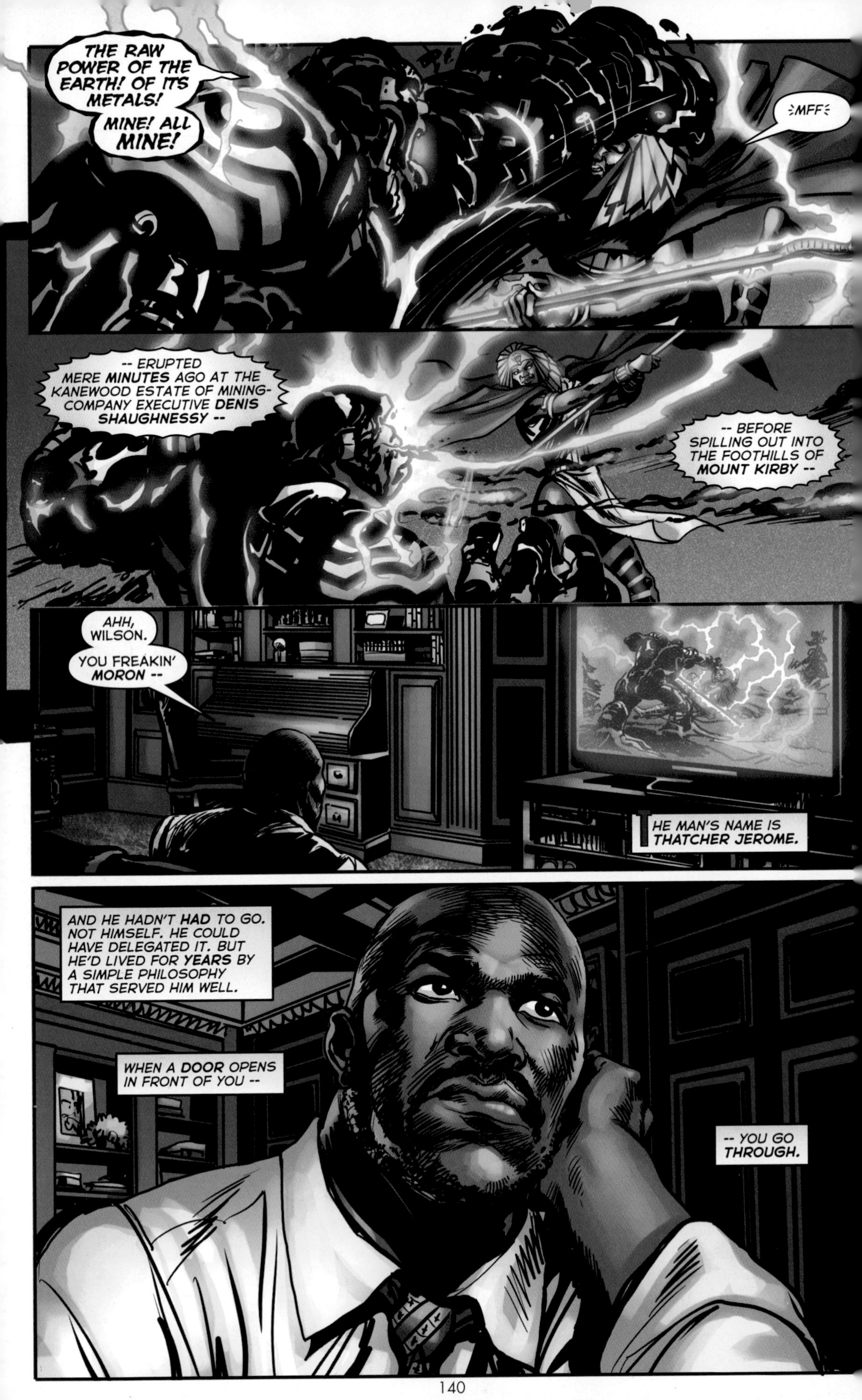
THE RAW POWER OF THE EARTH! OF ITS METALS!
MINE! ALL MINE!
MFF
-- ERUPTED MERE MINUTES AGO AT THE KANEWOOD ESTATE OF MINING-COMPANY EXECUTIVE DENIS SHAUGHNESSY --
-- BEFORE SPILLING OUT INTO THE FOOTHILLS OF MOUNT KIRBY --
AHH, WILSON.
YOU FREAKIN' MORON --
THE MAN'S NAME IS THATCHER JEROME.
AND HE HADN'T HAD TO GO. NOT HIMSELF. HE COULD HAVE DELEGATED IT. BUT HE'D LIVED FOR YEARS BY A SIMPLE PHILOSOPHY THAT SERVED HIM WELL.
WHEN A DOOR OPENS IN FRONT OF YOU --
-- YOU GO THROUGH.

143

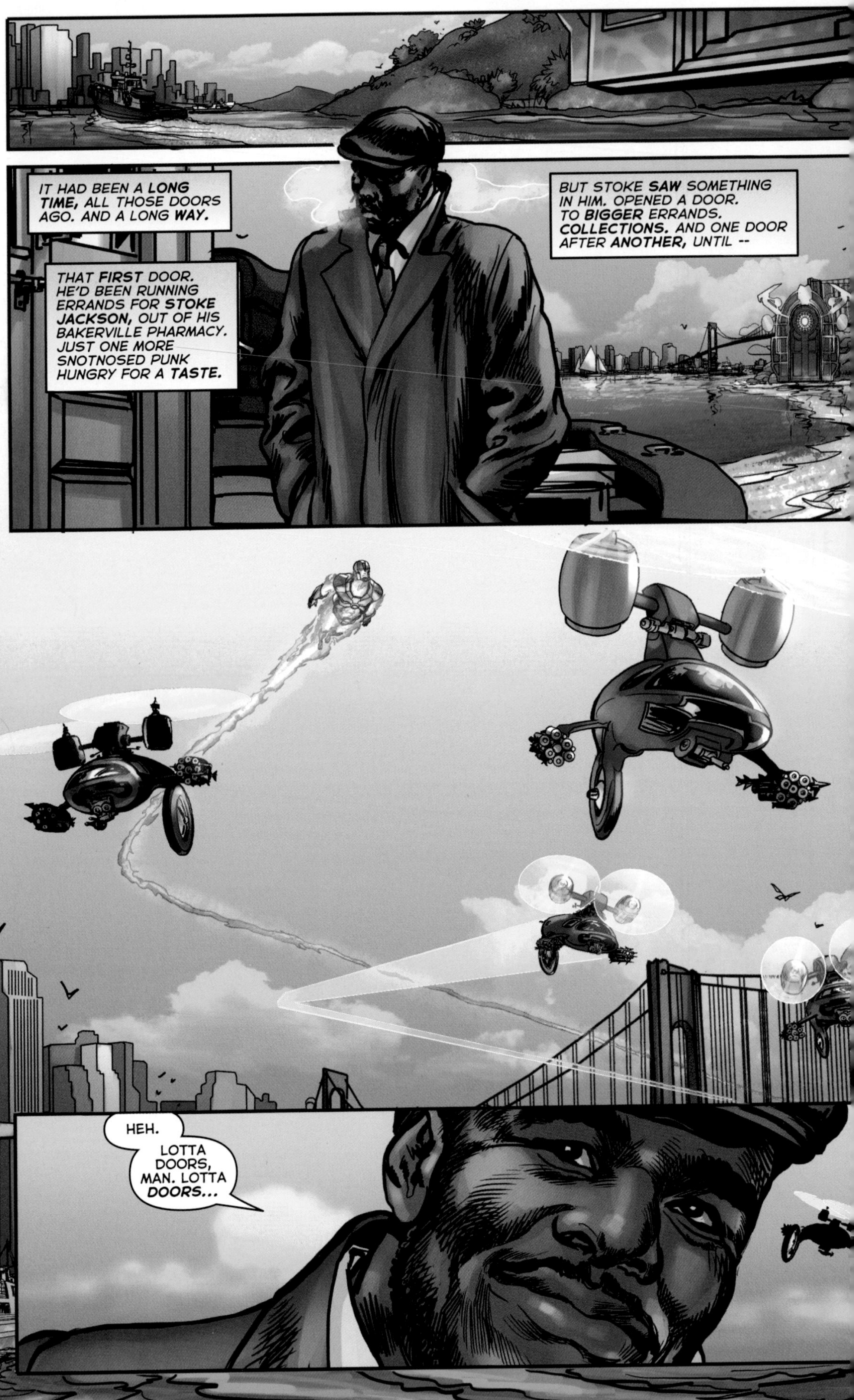
IT HAD BEEN A LONG TIME, ALL THOSE DOORS AGO. AND A LONG WAY.
THAT FIRST DOOR. HE'D BEEN RUNNING ERRANDS FOR STOKE JACKSON, OUT OF HIS BAKERVILLE PHARMACY. JUST ONE MORE SNOTNOSED PUNK HUNGRY FOR A TASTE.
BUT STOKE SAW SOMETHING IN HIM. OPENED A DOOR. TO BIGGER ERRANDS. COLLECTIONS. AND ONE DOOR AFTER ANOTHER, UNTIL --
HEH.
LOTTA DOORS, MAN. LOTTA DOORS...

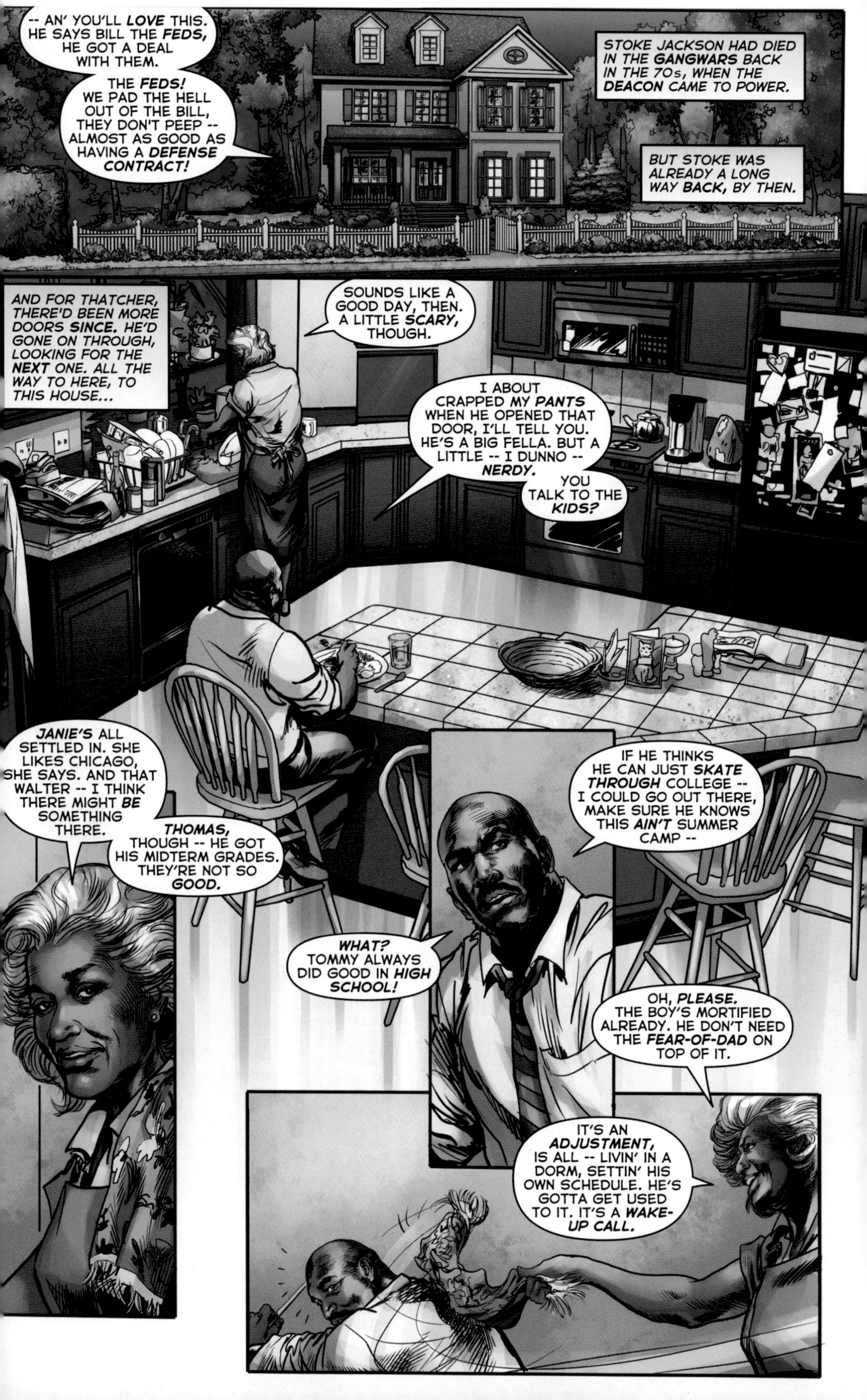

-- AN' YOU'LL LOVE THIS. HE SAYS BILL THE FEDS, HE GOT A DEAL WITH THEM.
THE FEDS! WE PAD THE HELL OUT OF THE BILL, THEY DON'T PEEP -- ALMOST AS GOOD AS HAVING A DEFENSE CONTRACT!
STOKE JACKSON HAD DIED IN THE GANGWARS BACK IN THE 70s, WHEN THE DEACON CAME TO POWER.
BUT STOKE WAS ALREADY A LONG WAY BACK, BY THEN.
AND FOR THATCHER, THERE'D BEEN MORE DOORS SINCE. HE'D GONE ON THROUGH, LOOKING FOR THE NEXT ONE. ALL THE WAY TO HERE, TO THIS HOUSE...
SOUNDS LIKE A GOOD DAY, THEN. A LITTLE SCARY, THOUGH.
I ABOUT CRAPPED MY PANTS WHEN HE OPENED THAT DOOR, I'LL TELL YOU. HE'S A BIG FELLA. BUT A LITTLE -- I DUNNO -- NERDY.
YOU TALK TO THE KIDS?
JANIE'S ALL SETTLED IN. SHE LIKES CHICAGO, SHE SAYS. AND THAT WALTER -- I THINK THERE MIGHT BE SOMETHING THERE.
THOMAS, THOUGH -- HE GOT HIS MIDTERM GRADES. THEY'RE NOT SO GOOD.
IF HE THINKS HE CAN JUST SKATE THROUGH COLLEGE -- I COULD GO OUT THERE, MAKE SURE HE KNOWS THIS AIN'T SUMMER CAMP --
WHAT? TOMMY ALWAYS DID GOOD IN HIGH SCHOOL!
OH, PLEASE. THE BOY'S MORTIFIED ALREADY. HE DON'T NEED THE FEAR-OF-DAD ON TOP OF IT.
IT'S AN ADJUSTMENT, IS ALL -- LIVIN' IN A DORM, SETTIN' HIS OWN SCHEDULE. HE'S GOTTA GET USED TO IT. IT'S A WAKE-UP CALL.

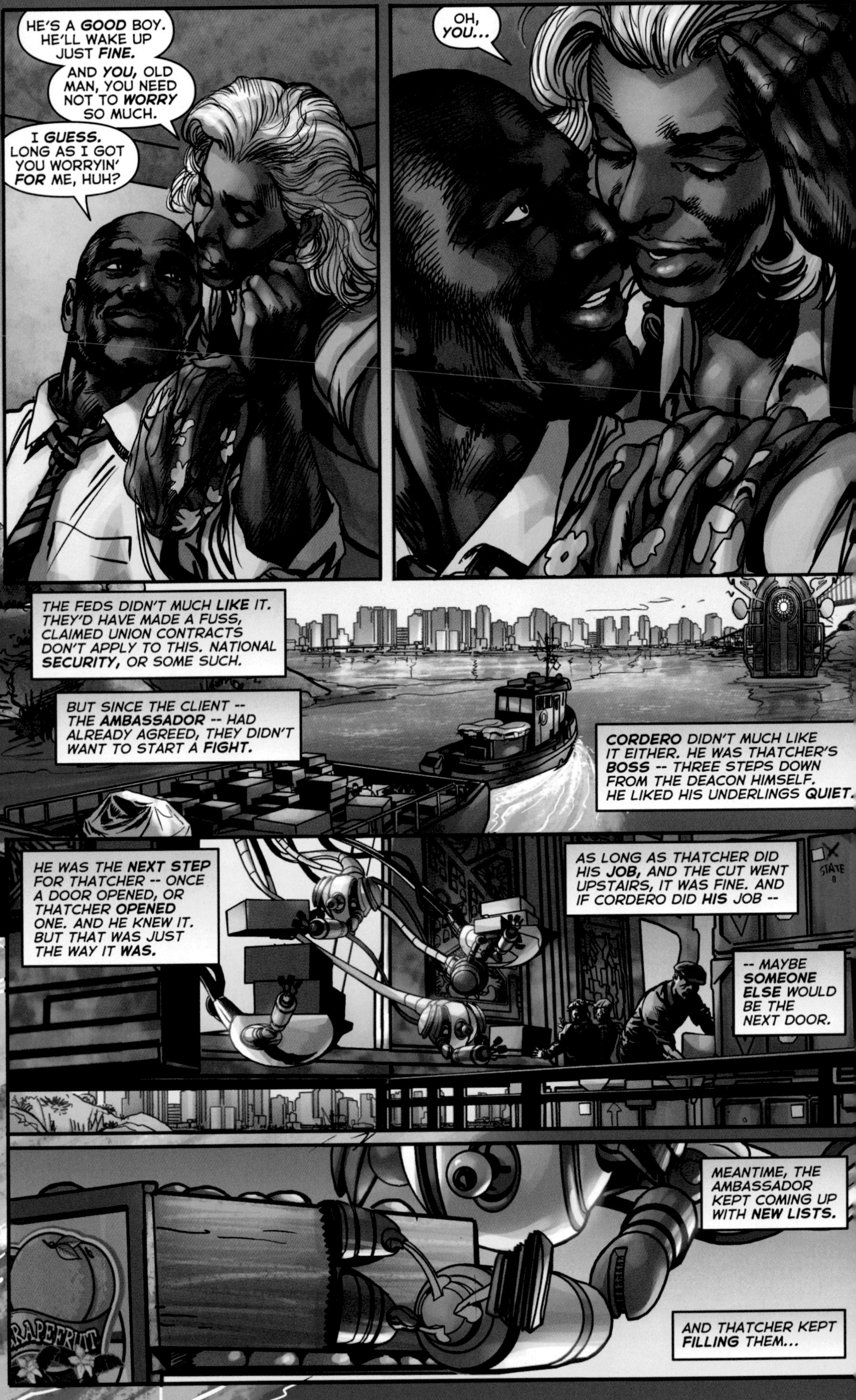
HE'S A GOOD BOY. HE'LL WAKE UP JUST FINE.
AND YOU, OLD MAN, YOU NEED NOT TO WORRY SO MUCH.
I GUESS. LONG AS I GOT YOU WORRYIN' FOR ME, HUH?
OH, YOU...
THE FEDS DIDN'T MUCH LIKE IT. THEY'D HAVE MADE A FUSS, CLAIMED UNION CONTRACTS DON'T APPLY TO THIS. NATIONAL SECURITY, OR SOME SUCH.
BUT SINCE THE CLIENT -- THE AMBASSADOR -- HAD ALREADY AGREED, THEY DIDN'T WANT TO START A FIGHT.
CORDERO DIDN'T MUCH LIKE IT EITHER. HE WAS THATCHER'S BOSS -- THREE STEPS DOWN FROM THE DEACON HIMSELF. HE LIKED HIS UNDERLINGS QUIET.
HE WAS THE NEXT STEP FOR THATCHER -- ONCE A DOOR OPENED, OR THATCHER OPENED ONE. AND HE KNEW IT. BUT THAT WAS JUST THE WAY IT WAS.
AS LONG AS THATCHER DID HIS JOB, AND THE CUT WENT UPSTAIRS, IT WAS FINE. AND IF CORDERO DID HIS JOB --
-- MAYBE SOMEONE ELSE WOULD BE THE NEXT DOOR.
MEANTIME, THE AMBASSADOR KEPT COMING UP WITH NEW LISTS.
AND THATCHER KEPT FILLING THEM...

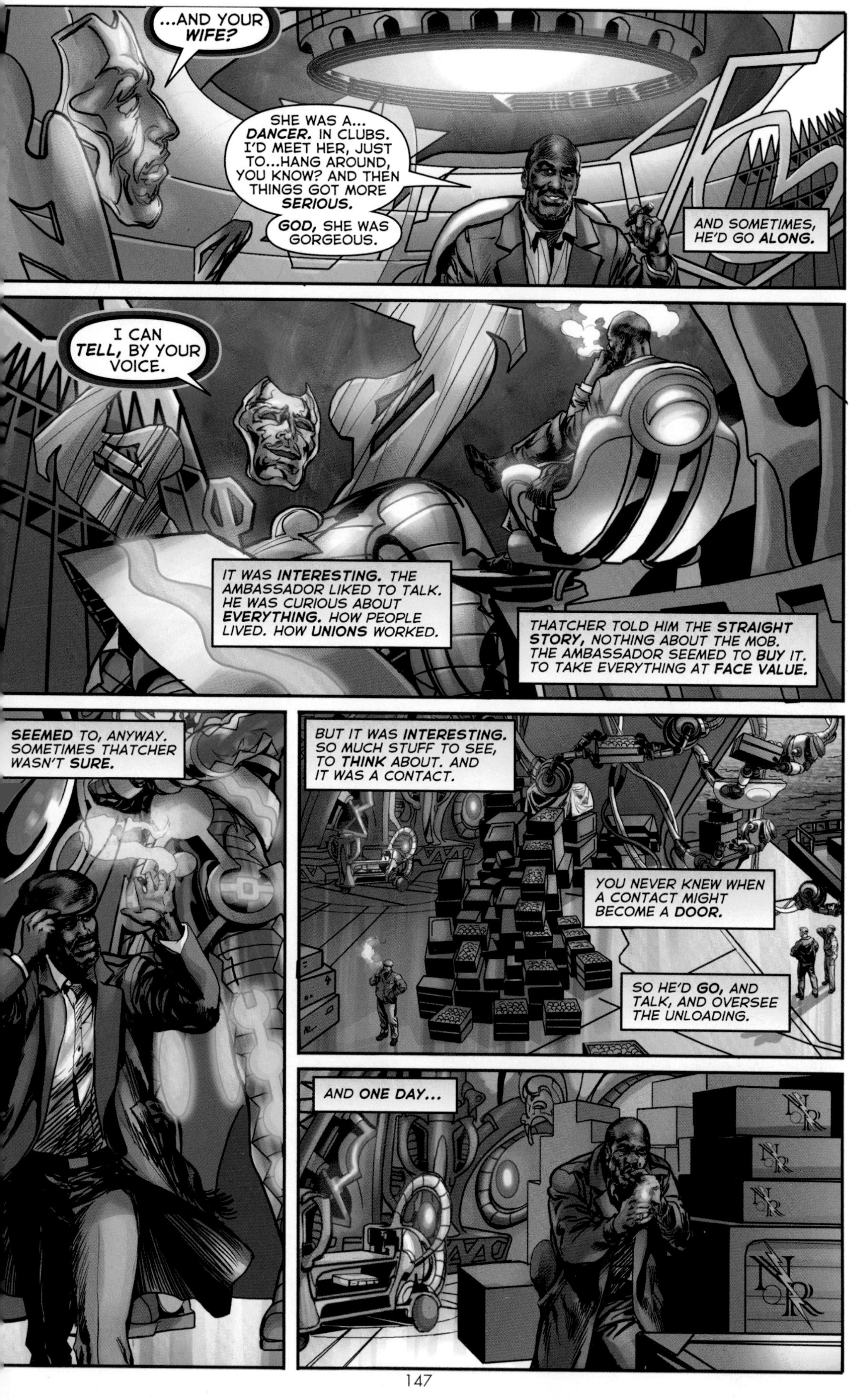
...AND YOUR WIFE?
SHE WAS A... DANCER. IN CLUBS. I'D MEET HER, JUST TO...HANG AROUND, YOU KNOW? AND THEN THINGS GOT MORE SERIOUS.
GOD, SHE WAS GORGEOUS.
AND SOMETIMES, HE'D GO ALONG.
I CAN TELL, BY YOUR VOICE.
IT WAS INTERESTING. THE AMBASSADOR LIKED TO TALK. HE WAS CURIOUS ABOUT EVERYTHING. HOW PEOPLE LIVED. HOW UNIONS WORKED.
THATCHER TOLD HIM THE STRAIGHT STORY, NOTHING ABOUT THE MOB. THE AMBASSADOR SEEMED TO BUY IT. TO TAKE EVERYTHING AT FACE VALUE.
SEEMED TO, ANYWAY. SOMETIMES THATCHER WASN'T SURE.
BUT IT WAS INTERESTING. SO MUCH STUFF TO SEE, TO THINK ABOUT. AND IT WAS A CONTACT.
YOU NEVER KNEW WHEN A CONTACT MIGHT BECOME A DOOR.
SO HE'D GO, AND TALK, AND OVERSEE THE UNLOADING.
AND ONE DAY...

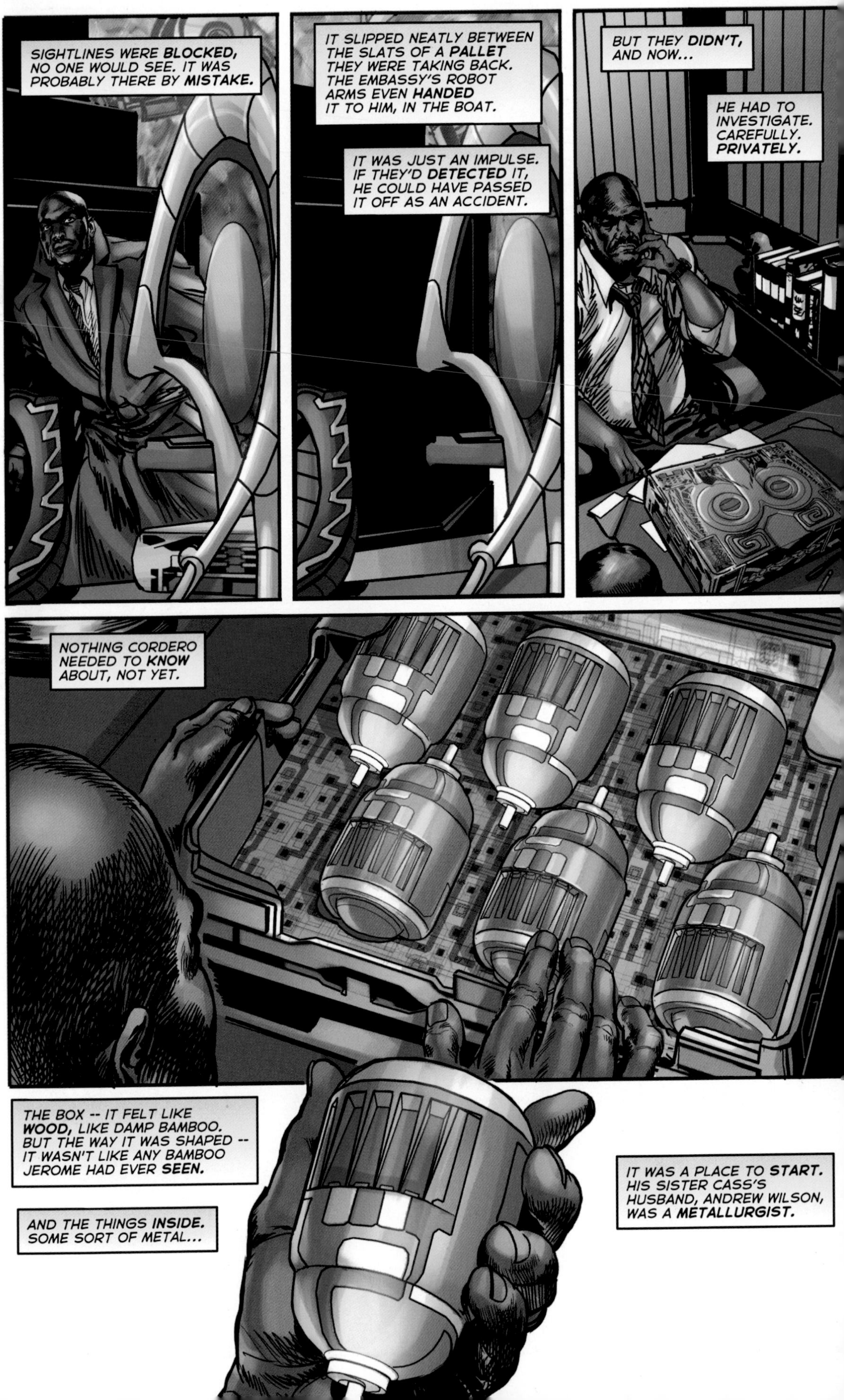
SIGHTLINES WERE BLOCKED, NO ONE WOULD SEE. IT WAS PROBABLY THERE BY MISTAKE.
IT SLIPPED NEATLY BETWEEN THE SLATS OF A PALLET THEY WERE TAKING BACK. THE EMBASSY'S ROBOT ARMS EVEN HANDED IT TO HIM, IN THE BOAT.
IT WAS JUST AN IMPULSE. IF THEY'D DETECTED IT, HE COULD HAVE PASSED IT OFF AS AN ACCIDENT.
BUT THEY DIDN'T, AND NOW...
HE HAD TO INVESTIGATE. CAREFULLY. PRIVATELY.
NOTHING CORDERO NEEDED TO KNOW ABOUT, NOT YET.
THE BOX -- IT FELT LIKE WOOD, LIKE DAMP BAMBOO. BUT THE WAY IT WAS SHAPED -- IT WASN'T LIKE ANY BAMBOO JEROME HAD EVER SEEN.
AND THE THINGS INSIDE. SOME SORT OF METAL...
IT WAS A PLACE TO START. HIS SISTER CASS'S HUSBAND, ANDREW WILSON, WAS A METALLURGIST.

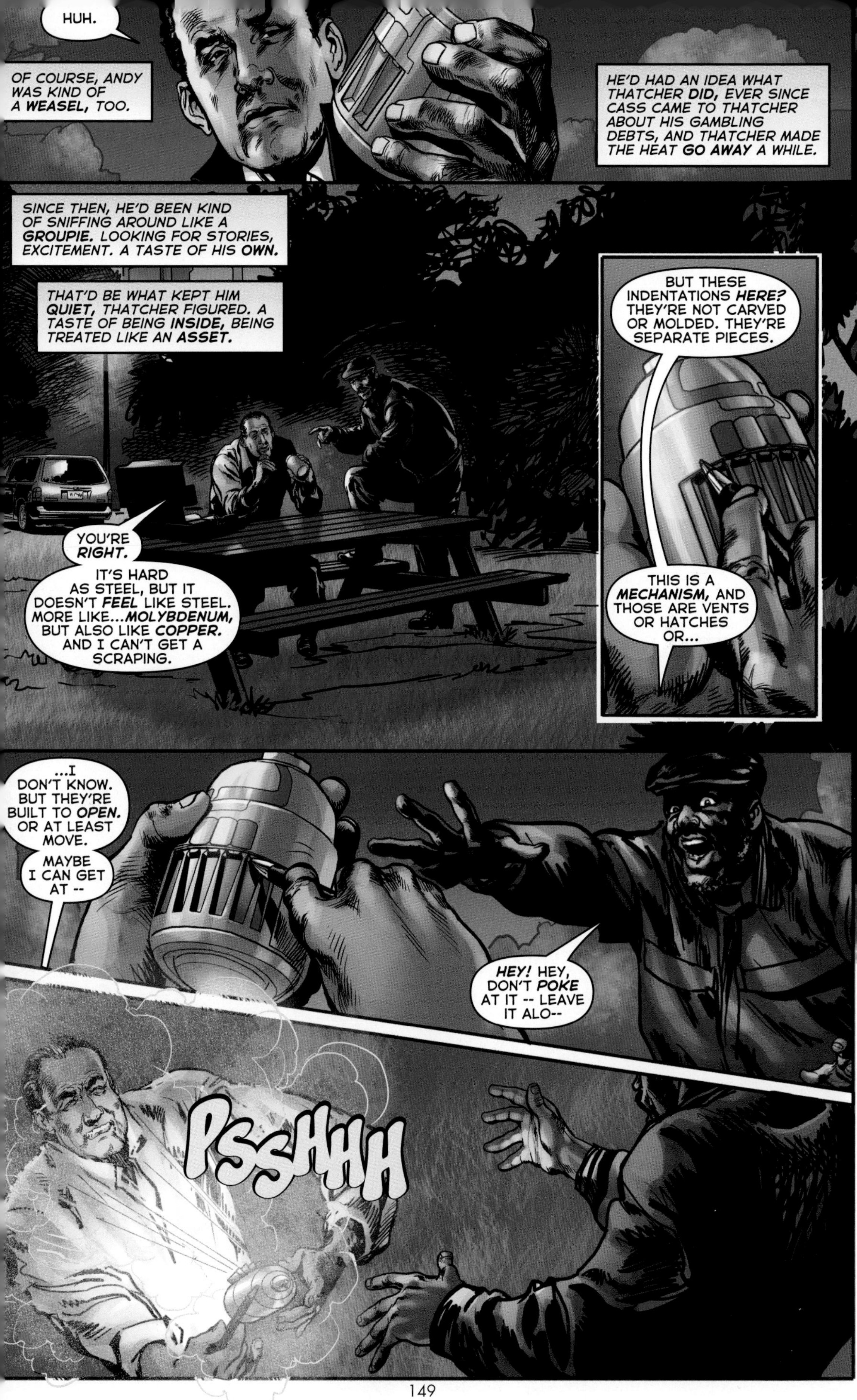
HUH.
OF COURSE, ANDY WAS KIND OF A WEASEL, TOO.
HE'D HAD AN IDEA WHAT THATCHER DID, EVER SINCE CASS CAME TO THATCHER ABOUT HIS GAMBLING DEBTS, AND THATCHER MADE THE HEAT GO AWAY A WHILE.
SINCE THEN, HE'D BEEN KIND OF SNIFFING AROUND LIKE A GROUPIE. LOOKING FOR STORIES, EXCITEMENT. A TASTE OF HIS OWN.
THAT'D BE WHAT KEPT HIM QUIET, THATCHER FIGURED. A TASTE OF BEING INSIDE, BEING TREATED LIKE AN ASSET.
YOU'RE RIGHT.
IT'S HARD AS STEEL, BUT IT DOESN'T FEEL LIKE STEEL. MORE LIKE...MOLYBDENUM, BUT ALSO LIKE COPPER. AND I CAN'T GET A SCRAPING.
BUT THESE INDENTATIONS HERE? THEY'RE NOT CARVED OR MOLDED. THEY'RE SEPARATE PIECES.
THIS IS A MECHANISM, AND THOSE ARE VENTS OR HATCHES OR...
...I DON'T KNOW. BUT THEY'RE BUILT TO OPEN. OR AT LEAST MOVE.
MAYBE I CAN GET AT --
HEY! HEY, DON'T POKE AT IT -- LEAVE IT ALO--
PSSHHH

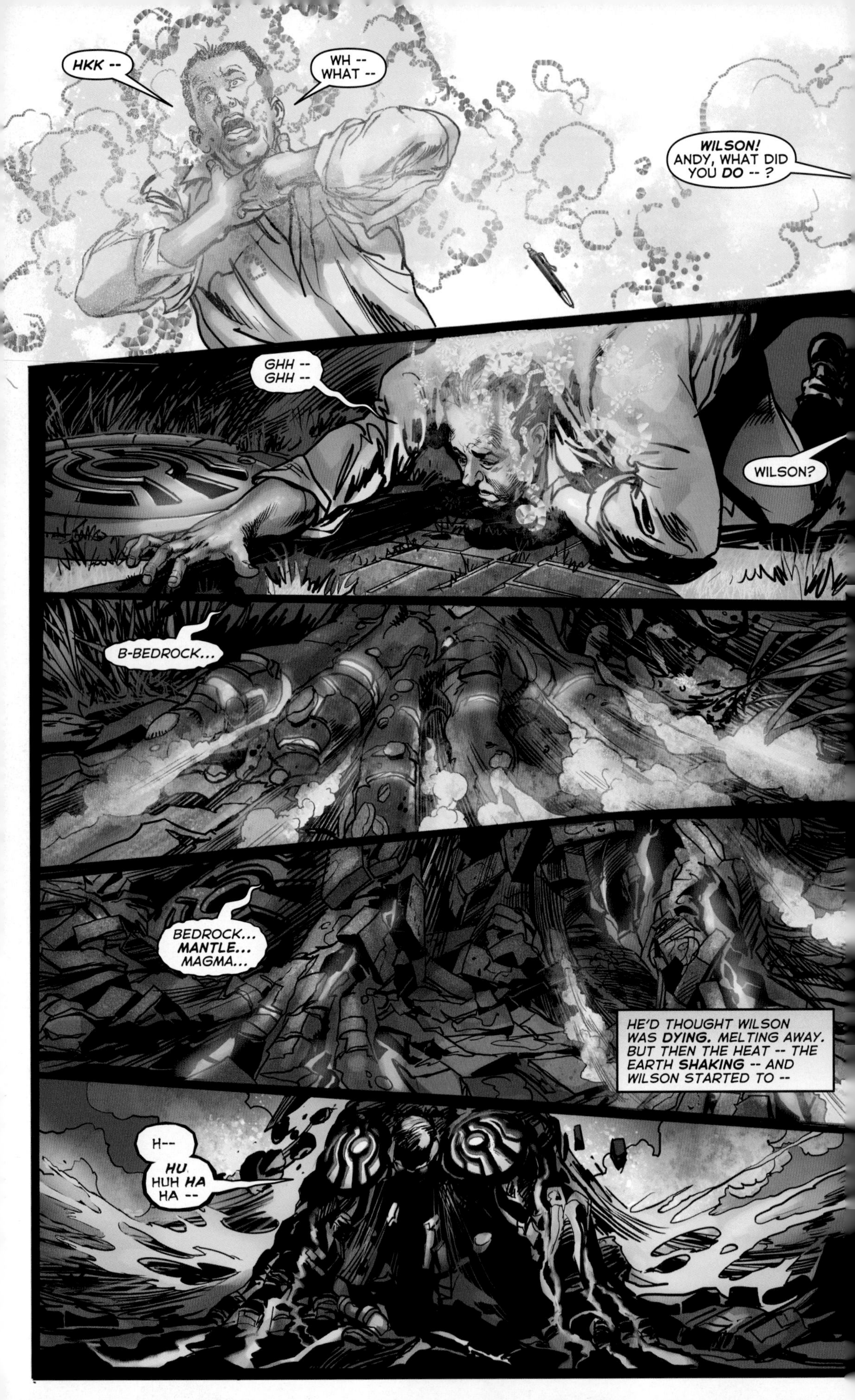
HKK --
WH -- WHAT --
WILSON! ANDY, WHAT DID YOU DO -- ?
GHH -- GHH --
WILSON?
B-BEDROCK...
BEDROCK... MANTLE... MAGMA...
HE'D THOUGHT WILSON WAS DYING. MELTING AWAY. BUT THEN THE HEAT -- THE EARTH SHAKING -- AND WILSON STARTED TO --
H--
HU HUH HA HA --

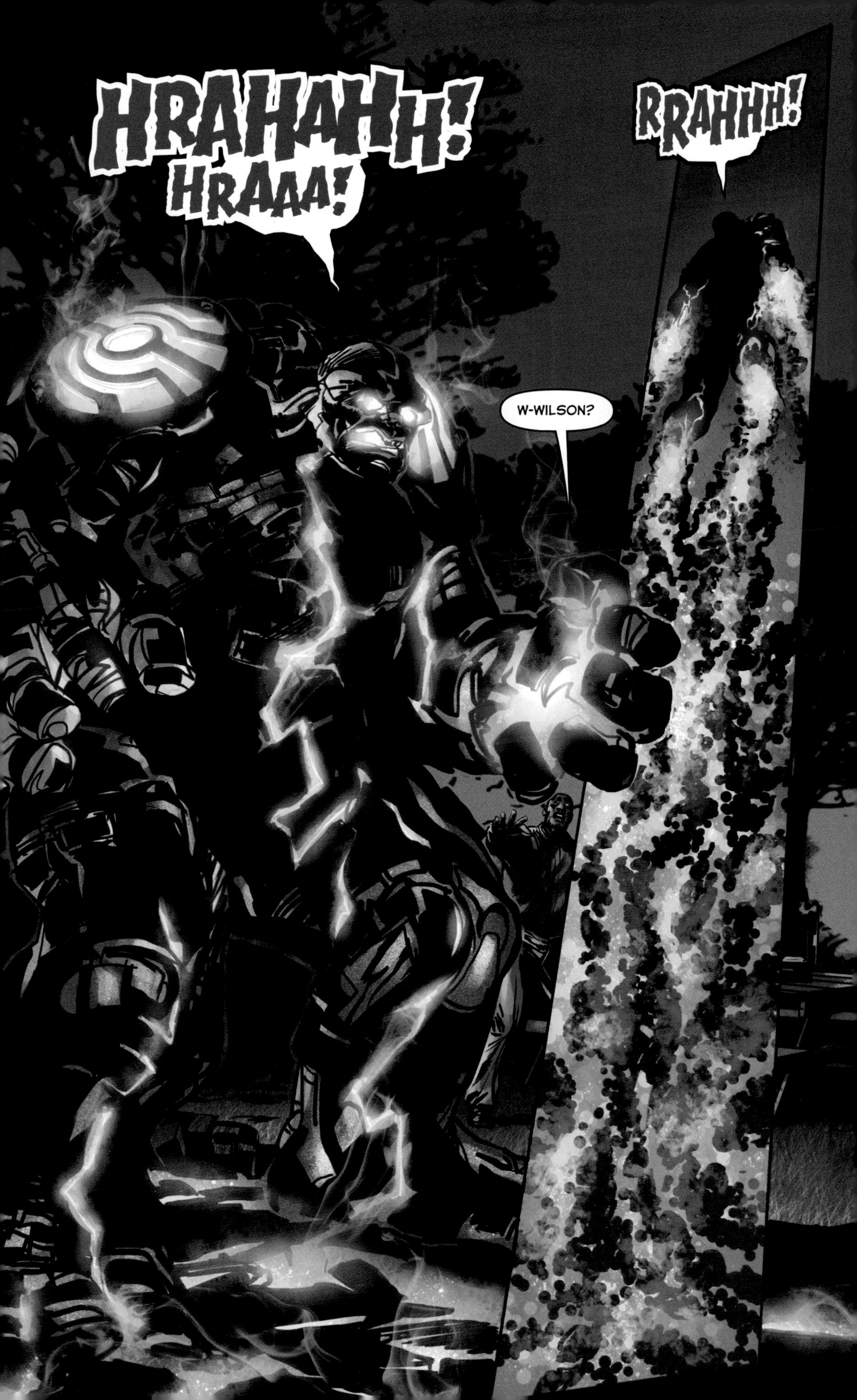
HRAHAHH! HRAAA!
RRAHHH!
W-WILSON?

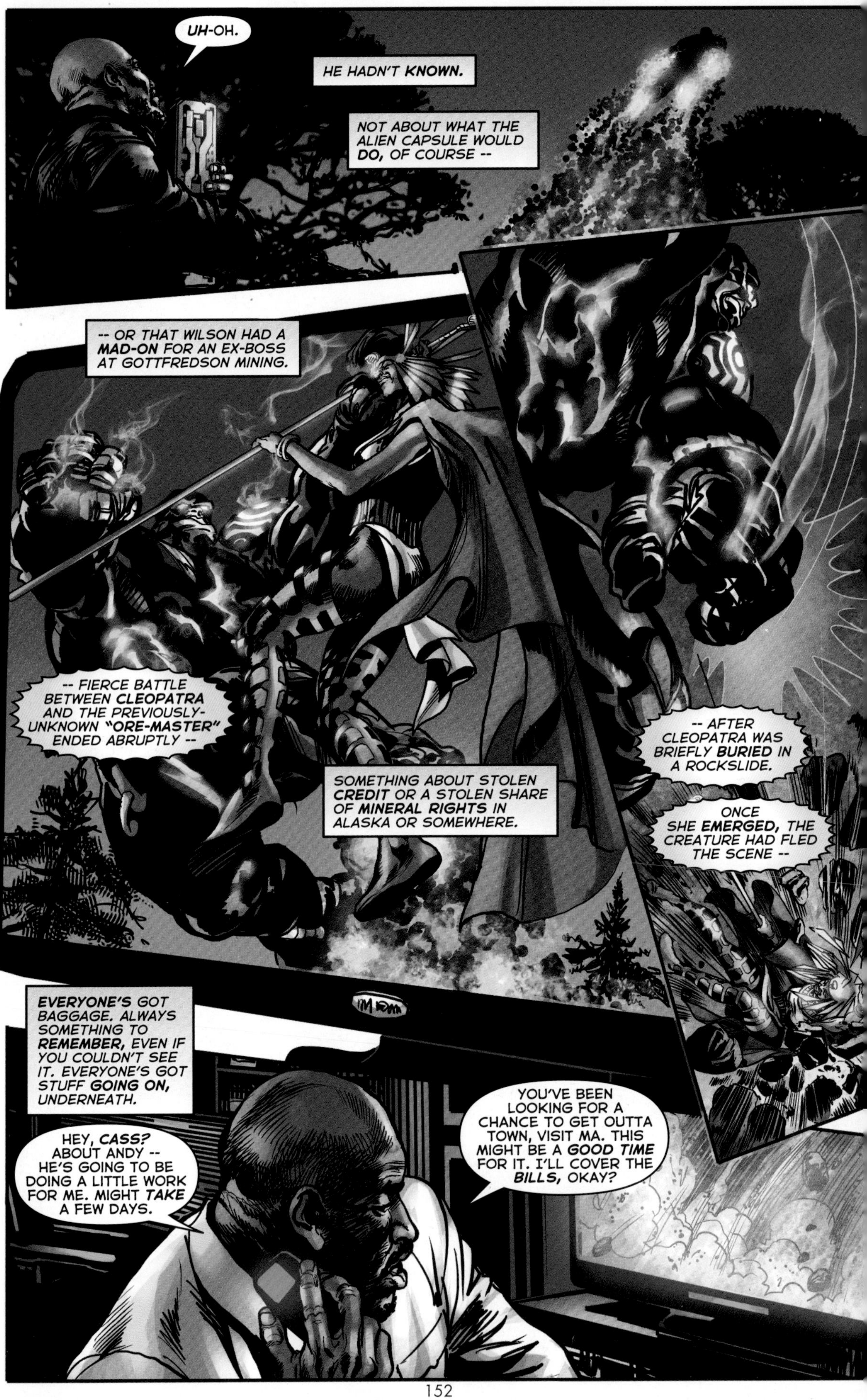
UH-OH.
HE HADN'T KNOWN.
NOT ABOUT WHAT THE ALIEN CAPSULE WOULD DO, OF COURSE --
-- OR THAT WILSON HAD A MAD-ON FOR AN EX-BOSS AT GOTTFREDSON MINING.
-- FIERCE BATTLE BETWEEN CLEOPATRA AND THE PREVIOUSLY-UNKNOWN "ORE-MASTER" ENDED ABRUPTLY --
SOMETHING ABOUT STOLEN CREDIT OR A STOLEN SHARE OF MINERAL RIGHTS IN ALASKA OR SOMEWHERE.
-- AFTER CLEOPATRA WAS BRIEFLY BURIED IN A ROCKSLIDE.
ONCE SHE EMERGED, THE CREATURE HAD FLED THE SCENE --
EVERYONE'S GOT BAGGAGE. ALWAYS SOMETHING TO REMEMBER, EVEN IF YOU COULDN'T SEE IT. EVERYONE'S GOT STUFF GOING ON, UNDERNEATH.
HEY, CASS? ABOUT ANDY -- HE'S GOING TO BE DOING A LITTLE WORK FOR ME. MIGHT TAKE A FEW DAYS.
YOU'VE BEEN LOOKING FOR A CHANCE TO GET OUTTA TOWN, VISIT MA. THIS MIGHT BE A GOOD TIME FOR IT. I'LL COVER THE BILLS, OKAY?

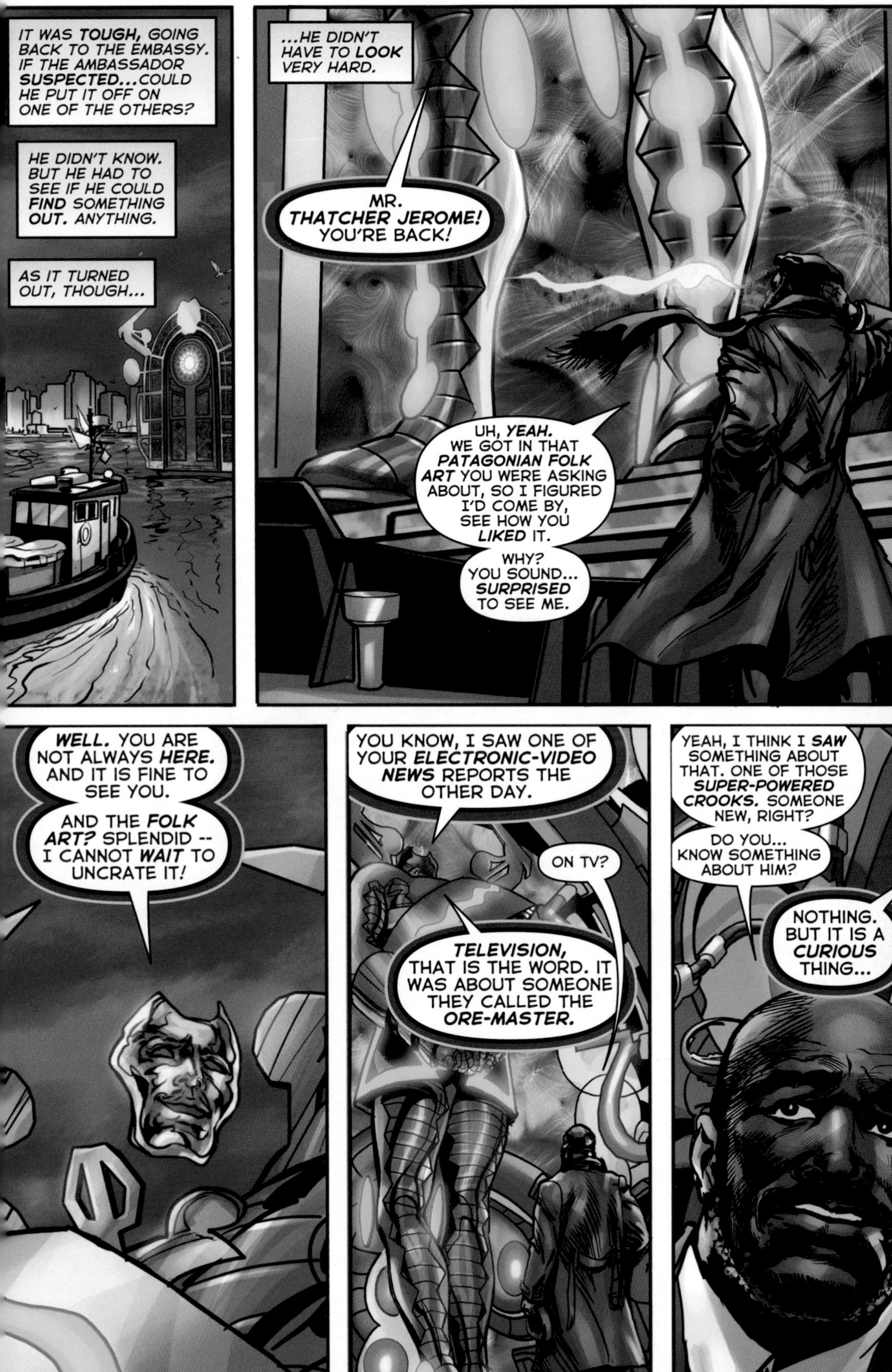

IT WAS TOUGH, GOING BACK TO THE EMBASSY. IF THE AMBASSADOR SUSPECTED...COULD HE PUT IT OFF ON ONE OF THE OTHERS?
HE DIDN'T KNOW. BUT HE HAD TO SEE IF HE COULD FIND SOMETHING OUT. ANYTHING.
AS IT TURNED OUT, THOUGH...
...HE DIDN'T HAVE TO LOOK VERY HARD.
MR. THATCHER JEROME! YOU'RE BACK!
UH, YEAH. WE GOT IN THAT PATAGONIAN FOLK ART YOU WERE ASKING ABOUT, SO I FIGURED I'D COME BY, SEE HOW YOU LIKED IT.
WHY? YOU SOUND... SURPRISED TO SEE ME.
WELL. YOU ARE NOT ALWAYS HERE. AND IT IS FINE TO SEE YOU.
AND THE FOLK ART? SPLENDID -- I CANNOT WAIT TO UNCRATE IT!
YOU KNOW, I SAW ONE OF YOUR ELECTRONIC-VIDEO NEWS REPORTS THE OTHER DAY.
ON TV?
TELEVISION, THAT IS THE WORD. IT WAS ABOUT SOMEONE THEY CALLED THE ORE-MASTER.
YEAH, I THINK I SAW SOMETHING ABOUT THAT. ONE OF THOSE SUPER-POWERED CROOKS. SOMEONE NEW, RIGHT?
DO YOU... KNOW SOMETHING ABOUT HIM?
NOTHING. BUT IT IS A CURIOUS THING...

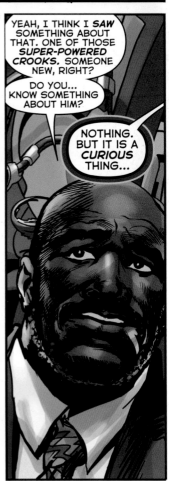

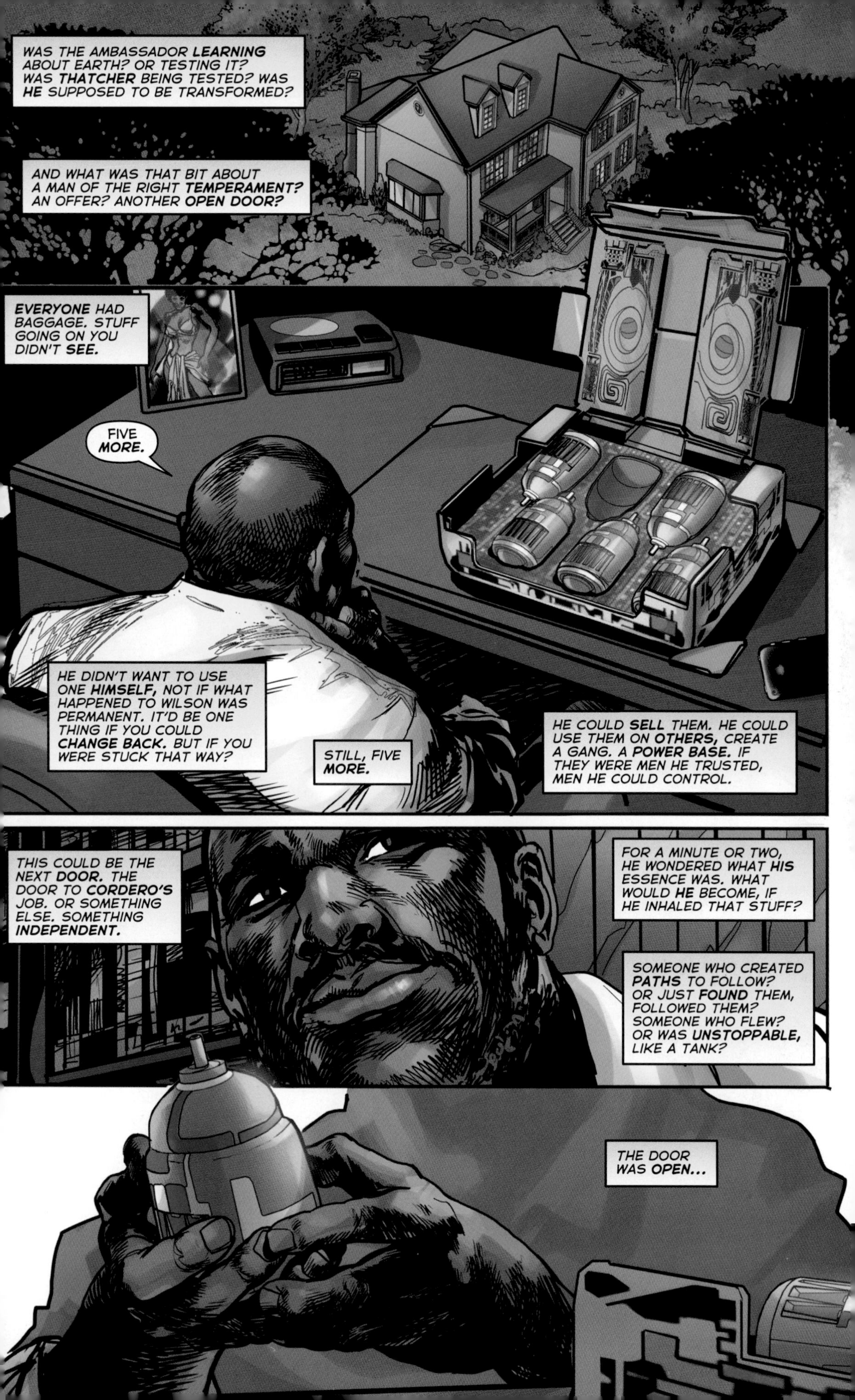
WAS THE AMBASSADOR LEARNING ABOUT EARTH? OR TESTING IT? WAS THATCHER BEING TESTED? WAS HE SUPPOSED TO BE TRANSFORMED?
AND WHAT WAS THAT BIT ABOUT A MAN OF THE RIGHT TEMPERAMENT? AN OFFER? ANOTHER OPEN DOOR?
EVERYONE HAD BAGGAGE. STUFF GOING ON YOU DIDN'T SEE.
FIVE MORE.
HE DIDN'T WANT TO USE ONE HIMSELF, NOT IF WHAT HAPPENED TO WILSON WAS PERMANENT. IT'D BE ONE THING IF YOU COULD CHANGE BACK. BUT IF YOU WERE STUCK THAT WAY?
STILL, FIVE MORE.
HE COULD SELL THEM. HE COULD USE THEM ON OTHERS, CREATE A GANG. A POWER BASE. IF THEY WERE MEN HE TRUSTED, MEN HE COULD CONTROL.
THIS COULD BE THE NEXT DOOR. THE DOOR TO CORDERO'S JOB. OR SOMETHING ELSE. SOMETHING INDEPENDENT.
FOR A MINUTE OR TWO, HE WONDERED WHAT HIS ESSENCE WAS. WHAT WOULD HE BECOME, IF HE INHALED THAT STUFF?
SOMEONE WHO CREATED PATHS TO FOLLOW? OR JUST FOUND THEM, FOLLOWED THEM? SOMEONE WHO FLEW? OR WAS UNSTOPPABLE, LIKE A TANK?
THE DOOR WAS OPEN...

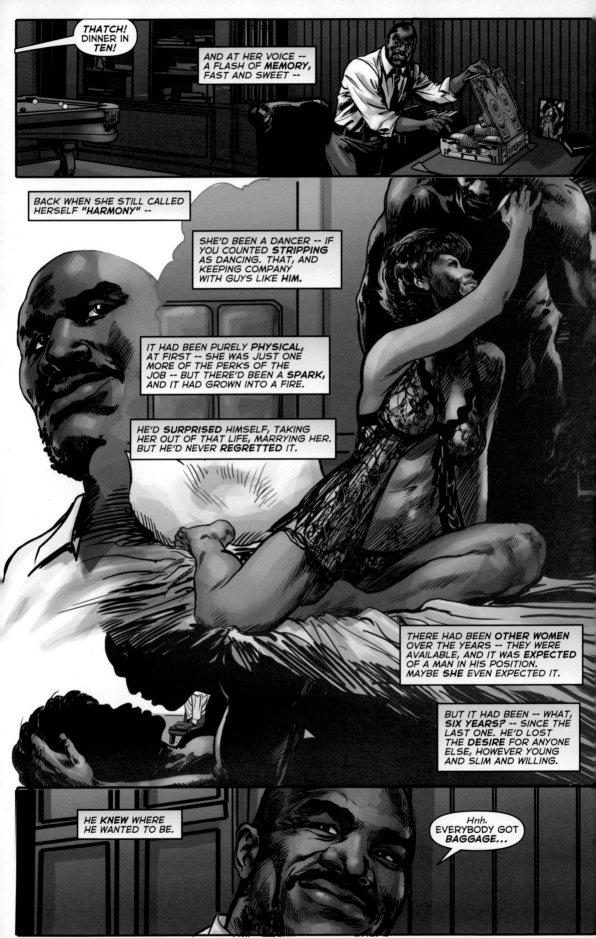

THATCH! DINNER IN TEN!

AND AT HER VOICE -- A FLASH OF MEMORY, FAST AND SWEET --

BACK WHEN SHE STILL CALLED HERSELF "HARMONY" --

SHE'D BEEN A DANCER -- IF YOU COUNTED STRIPPING AS DANCING. THAT, AND KEEPING COMPANY WITH GUYS LIKE HIM.

IT HAD BEEN PURELY PHYSICAL, AT FIRST -- SHE WAS JUST ONE MORE OF THE PERKS OF THE JOB -- BUT THERE'D BEEN A SPARK, AND IT HAD GROWN INTO A FIRE.

HE'D SURPRISED HIMSELF, TAKING HER OUT OF THAT LIFE, MARRYING HER. BUT HE'D NEVER REGRETTED IT.

THERE HAD BEEN OTHER WOMEN OVER THE YEARS -- THEY WERE AVAILABLE, AND IT WAS EXPECTED OF A MAN IN HIS POSITION. MAYBE SHE EVEN EXPECTED IT.

BUT IT HAD BEEN -- WHAT, SIX YEARS? -- SINCE THE LAST ONE. HE'D LOST THE DESIRE FOR ANYONE ELSE, HOWEVER YOUNG AND SLIM AND WILLING.

HE KNEW WHERE HE WANTED TO BE.

Hnh. EVERYBODY GOT BAGGAGE...

HE COULD **CHANGE BACK.**
HE WASN'T STUCK IN
THAT FORM. **THAT** WAS
INTERESTING TO KNOW.

THE **COPS** CAME AROUND, OF
COURSE. THEY SNIFFED AROUND
EVEN AT THE **BEST** OF TIMES.

AND WITH THE LATEST
"SUPER-VILLAIN" BEING
HIS BROTHER-IN-LAW,
THEY'D COME EVEN IF HE
HAD A STRAIGHT JOB.
BUT HE DIDN'T **GIVE** THEM
ANYTHING, AND APPARENTLY
NEITHER DID **WILSON.**

NO, CORDERO. AS BIG
A SURPRISE TO **ME**
AS TO YOU.

WE CAN **REACH**
OUT TO HIM, THOUGH.
SEE IF HE'D BE UP FOR
MAKING SOME **SERIOUS**
CASH WITH THOSE POWERS,
ONCE HE'S COOLED
A LITTLE.

CORDERO **TOO.** HE COULD
HEAR IT IN THE MAN'S VOICE,
HE WAS NERVOUS ABOUT
JEROME HAVING A **CONNECTION**
TO THAT KIND OF POWERHOUSE.

LET HIM **SWEAT.** IT ONLY MADE
THATCHER MORE VALUABLE
TO THE DEACON, SO CORDERO
WOULDN'T **DO** ANYTHING.

AND THEN THERE
WAS **CASS.**

SHE WAS PRETTY **SHOOK**
UP, AND IT WAS A GOOD
THING SHE HADN'T BEEN
HOME WHEN WILSON HAD
RETURNED. BUT THERE
WERE NO KIDS, AND THE
MARRIAGE -- IT HAD BEEN
ON **SHAKY GROUND** ANYWAY.

HE'D FIND HER A **JOB,** FUNNEL
HER SOME STEADY MONEY.
SHE WAS HIS **SISTER** -- HE'D
TAKE CARE OF HER EVEN IF
HE WASN'T RESPONSIBLE.

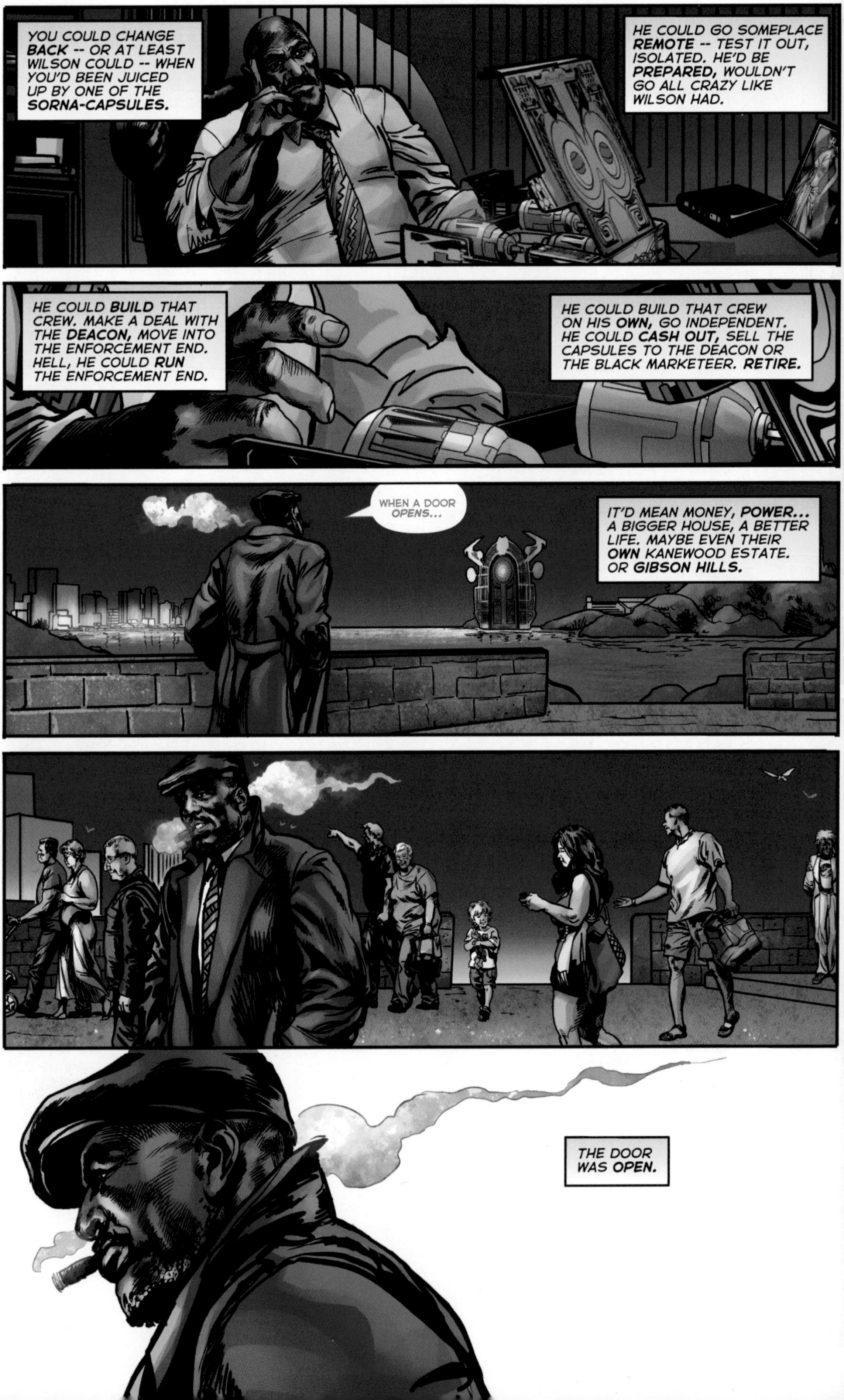
YOU COULD CHANGE BACK -- OR AT LEAST WILSON COULD -- WHEN YOU'D BEEN JUICED UP BY ONE OF THE SORNA-CAPSULES.
HE COULD GO SOMEPLACE REMOTE -- TEST IT OUT, ISOLATED. HE'D BE PREPARED, WOULDN'T GO ALL CRAZY LIKE WILSON HAD.
HE COULD BUILD THAT CREW. MAKE A DEAL WITH THE DEACON, MOVE INTO THE ENFORCEMENT END. HELL, HE COULD RUN THE ENFORCEMENT END.
HE COULD BUILD THAT CREW ON HIS OWN, GO INDEPENDENT. HE COULD CASH OUT, SELL THE CAPSULES TO THE DEACON OR THE BLACK MARKETEER. RETIRE.
WHEN A DOOR OPENS...
IT'D MEAN MONEY, POWER... A BIGGER HOUSE, A BETTER LIFE. MAYBE EVEN THEIR OWN KANEWOOD ESTATE. OR GIBSON HILLS.
THE DOOR WAS OPEN.

THATCH! YOU'RE BACK!

YOU WANT PANCAKES?

HEY, RACHEL. PANCAKES SOUND GREAT, BUT NOT IF IT'S ANY TROUBLE.

OF COURSE, THE DOOR TO EVERY CATHOUSE AND STRIP JOINT IN THE CITY WAS OPEN TO HIM, TOO. BUT HE DIDN'T GO THROUGH THEM ANY MORE.

OH, YOU KNOW I JUST MAKE 'EM BECAUSE I WANT SOME MYSELF. NOW LET GO OF ME, OR THE BACON'S GONNA BURN. PAPER'S ON THE TABLE.

WAS IT BECAUSE HE'D ALREADY BEEN THROUGH? OR...

LET ME ASK YOU SOMETHING, RACHEL.

IS WHAT WE'VE GOT ENOUGH? ARE YOU HAPPY?

I'M FROM THE SWEATSHOP, THATCH. THIS IS MORE THAN I EVER DREAMED.

WE GOT OUR KIDS, WE GOT OUR HOME. AND AS LONG AS YOU'RE WITH ME, I'M HAPPY, YOU?

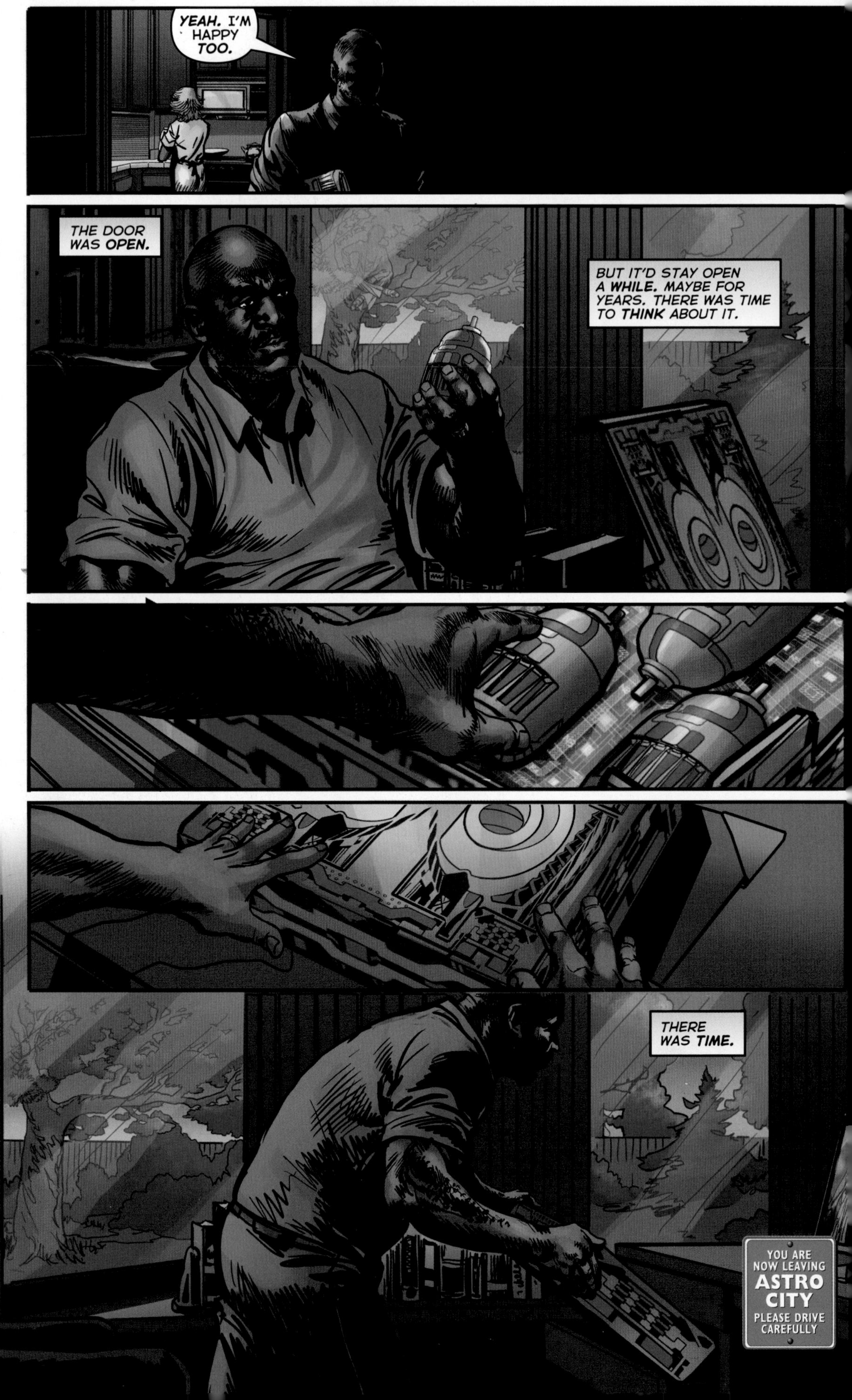
YEAH. I'M HAPPY TOO.
THE DOOR WAS OPEN.
BUT IT'D STAY OPEN A WHILE. MAYBE FOR YEARS. THERE WAS TIME TO THINK ABOUT IT.
THERE WAS TIME.
YOU ARE NOW LEAVING ASTRO CITY PLEASE DRIVE CAREFULLY

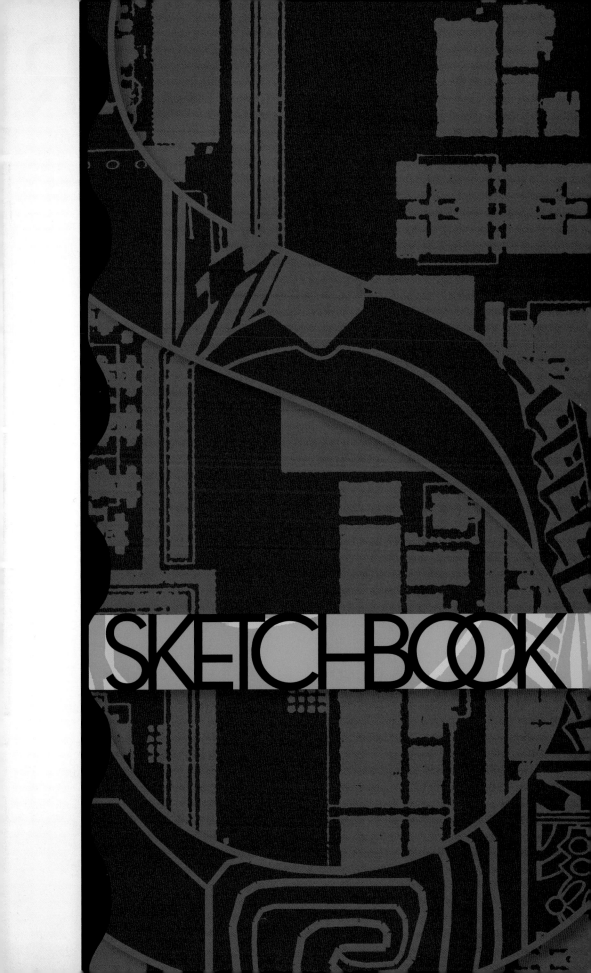

SKETCHBOOK

AMBASSADOR

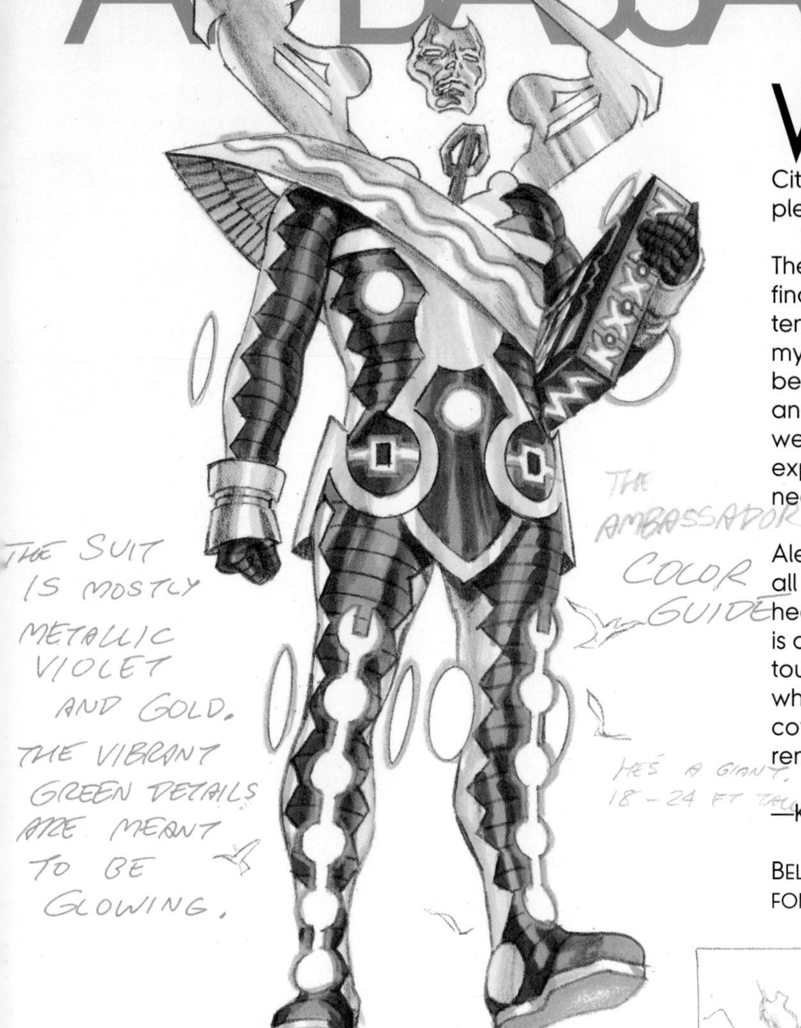
THE SUIT IS MOSTLY METALLIC VIOLET AND GOLD. THE VIBRANT GREEN DETAILS ARE MEANT TO BE GLOWING.
THE AMBASSADOR COLOR GUIDE
HE'S A GIANT. 18 - 24 FT TALL

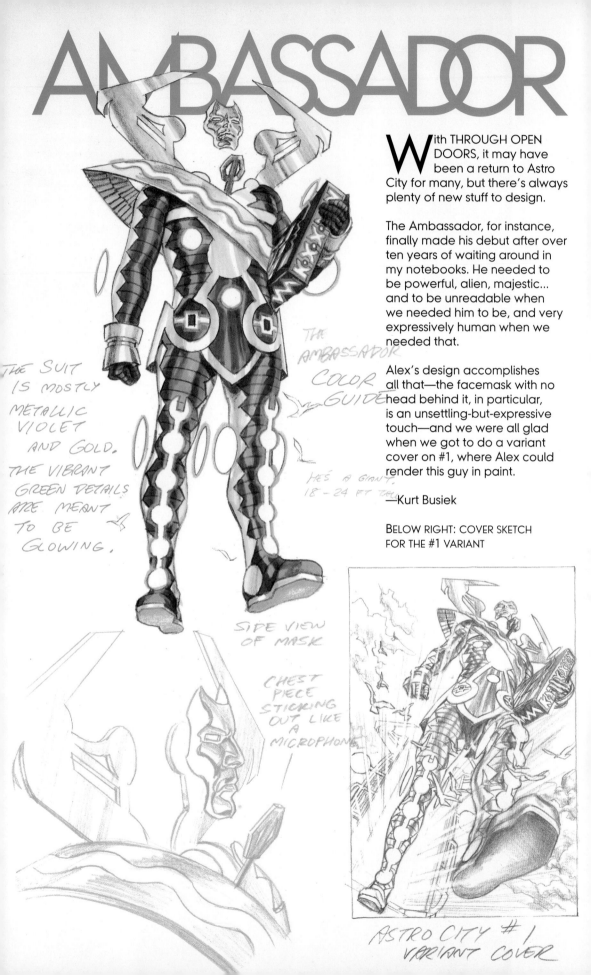

With THROUGH OPEN DOORS, it may have been a return to Astro City for many, but there's always plenty of new stuff to design.

The Ambassador, for instance, finally made his debut after over ten years of waiting around in my notebooks. He needed to be powerful, alien, majestic... and to be unreadable when we needed him to be, and very expressively human when we needed that.

Alex's design accomplishes all that—the facemask with no head behind it, in particular, is an unsettling-but-expressive touch—and we were all glad when we got to do a variant cover on #1, where Alex could render this guy in paint.

—Kurt Busiek

BELOW RIGHT: COVER SKETCH FOR THE #1 VARIANT

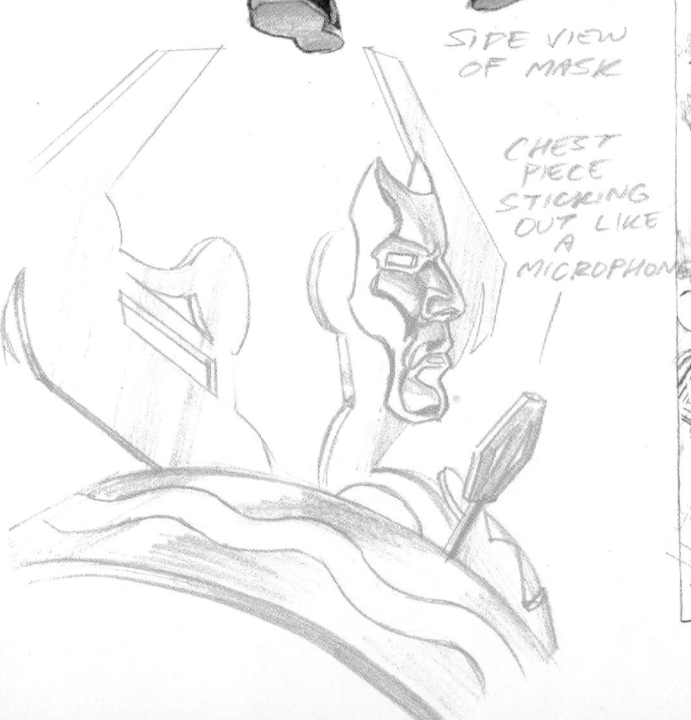
SIDE VIEW OF MASK
CHEST PIECE STICKING OUT LIKE A MICROPHONE

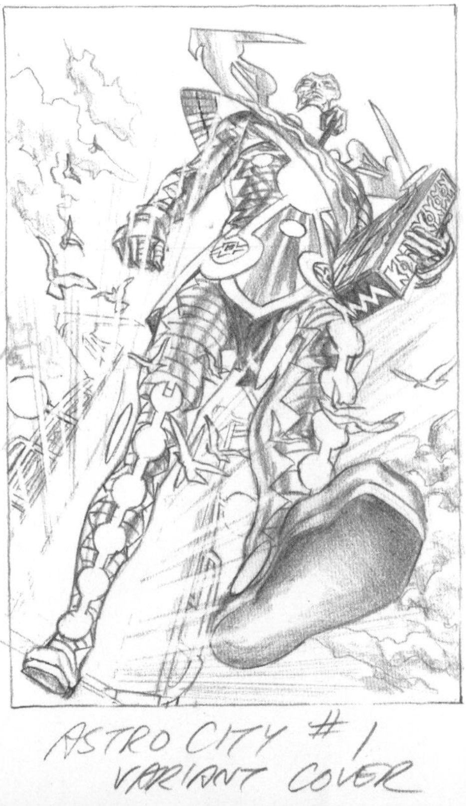
ASTRO CITY #1 VARIANT COVER

AMERICAN CHIBI

PIGTAILS INSTEAD OF PONY TAIL

SQUARER HEAD SHAPE WITH LARGER EYES

SASH BELT INSTEAD OF CAPE

O riginally inspired by my old friend Scott McCloud drawing a chibi version of himself on a napkin, which led to us discussing the term "American chibi" and me deciding there had to be an Astro City hero of that name…

Designing her was a lot of work, figuring out the right head shape, hairstyle, eye size and more, and a lot of scans went back and forth between us. We'd better get her back on stage soon, after all that!

TOP LEFT: BRENT'S INITIAL DESIGN.
MIDDLE: ALEX'S REVISION.
TOP RIGHT AND BOTTOM:
BRENT TRYING OUT HAIRSTYLES
AND COLORS.

THE BROKEN MAN

A lot of people assume he was added as a nod to our becoming a Vertigo series, but #1 was written and drawn two years before the book joined Vertigo. And as you can see from Brent's notes, we were inspired by the Englehart/Rogers take on the Joker from DETECTIVE COMICS in the 1970s, as much or more than anything else.

Plus, the Broken Man's (secret) history goes almost all the way back to our very first issue, as you'll eventually discover...

More cartoony attitude!

M. Rogers' Joker attitude Theatrical + ring master

less insistent — more cool

white color

OUTSIDE DESIGNS

The 13 circles theater

"The Broken Man" AC #23 8-12-10

NEGATIVE STYLE

BASIC COLOR STYLE

THE IRON LEGION

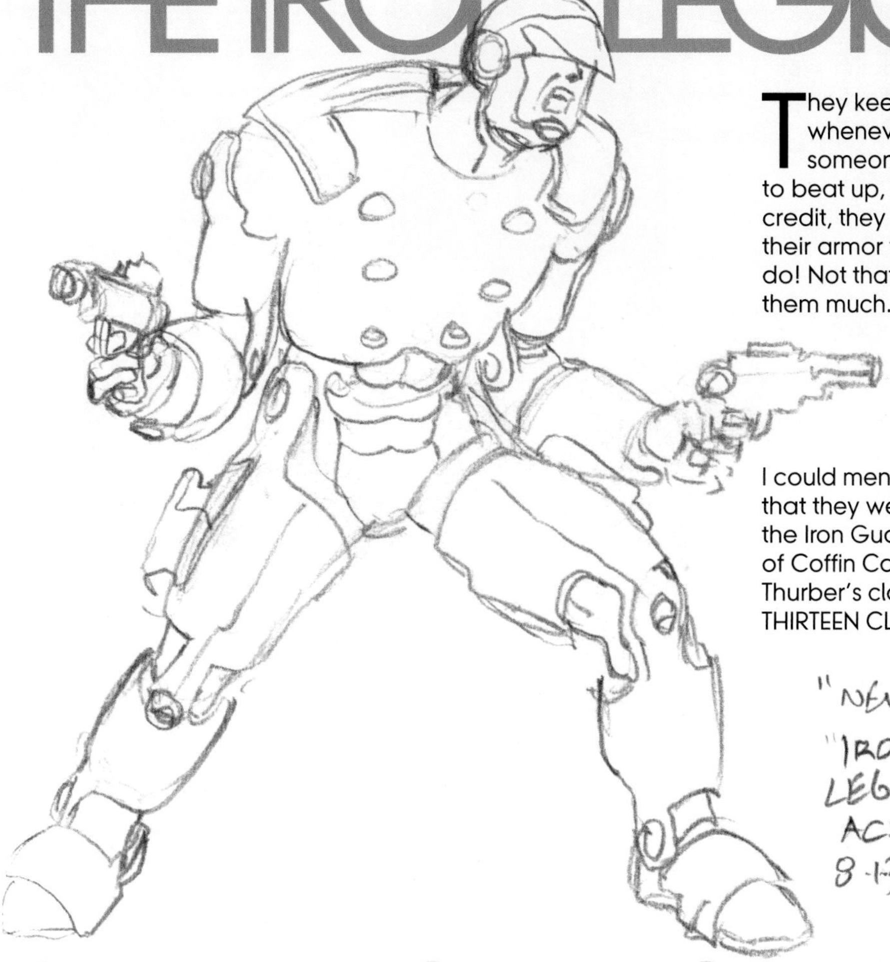
"NEW
"IRON
LEGION"
AC#23
8-13-10

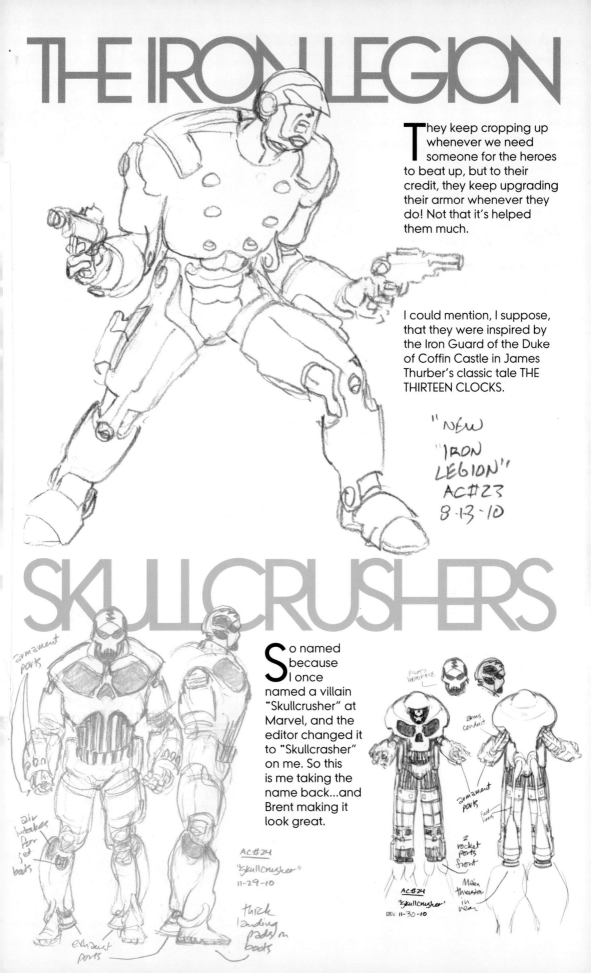

They keep cropping up whenever we need someone for the heroes to beat up, but to their credit, they keep upgrading their armor whenever they do! Not that it's helped them much.

I could mention, I suppose, that they were inspired by the Iron Guard of the Duke of Coffin Castle in James Thurber's classic tale THE THIRTEEN CLOCKS.

SKULLCRUSHERS

So named because I once named a villain "Skullcrusher" at Marvel, and the editor changed it to "Skullcrasher" on me. So this is me taking the name back...and Brent making it look great.

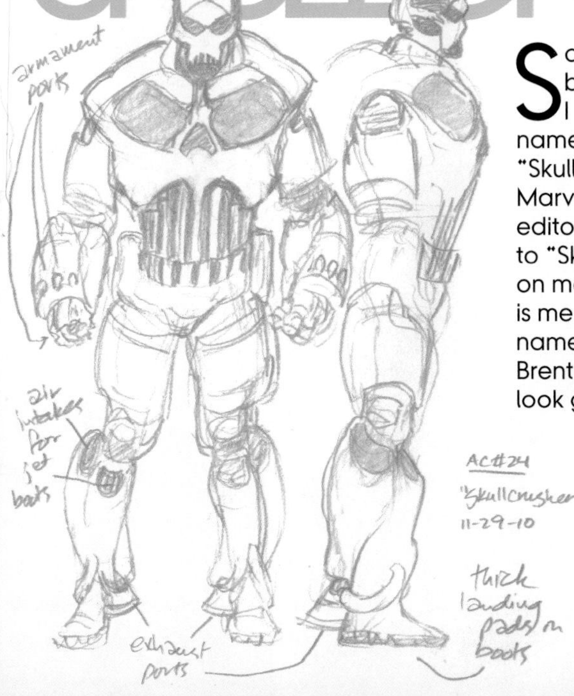
armament ports
air intakes for jet boots
AC#24
"Skullcrusher"
11-29-10
thick landing pads on boots
exhaust ports

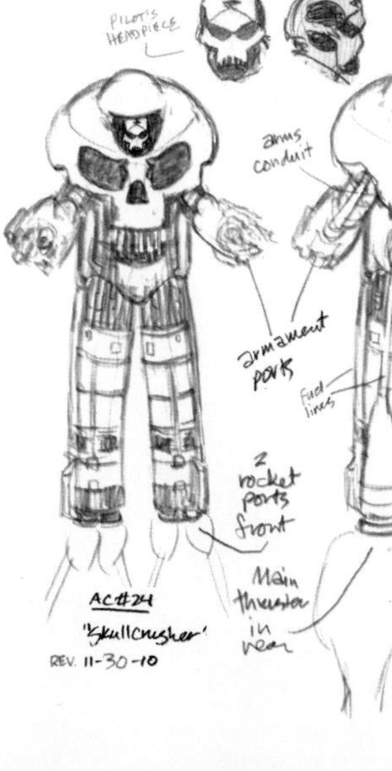
PILOT'S HEADPIECE
arms conduit
armament ports
fuel lines
2 rocket ports front
Main thruster in rear
AC#24
"Skullcrusher"
REV. 11-30-10

A lot of design work for a guy who's appeared in three whole panels so far!

We started with actual wolf spiders, and tried to figure out how to incorporate those tufts of hair and extra eyes. My first stabs at a mask and chest emblem built around them can be seen to the right, whereupon Alex wisely ignored me and went in other directions...

WOLFSPIDER

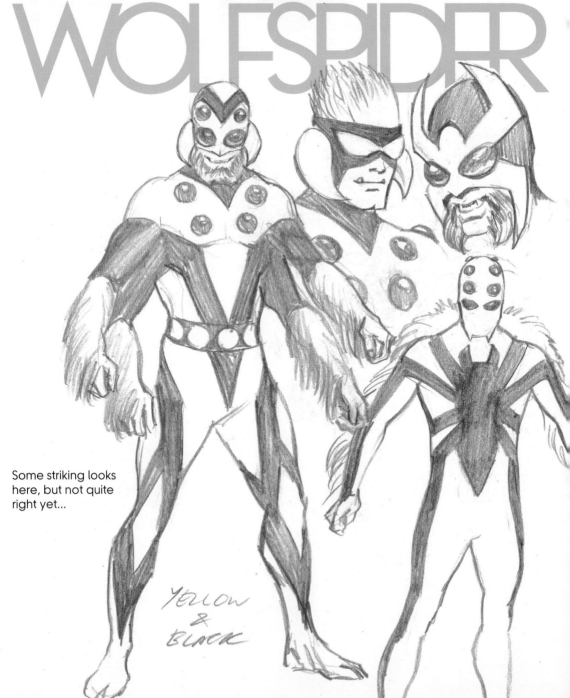

Some striking looks here, but not quite right yet...

YELLOW & BLACK

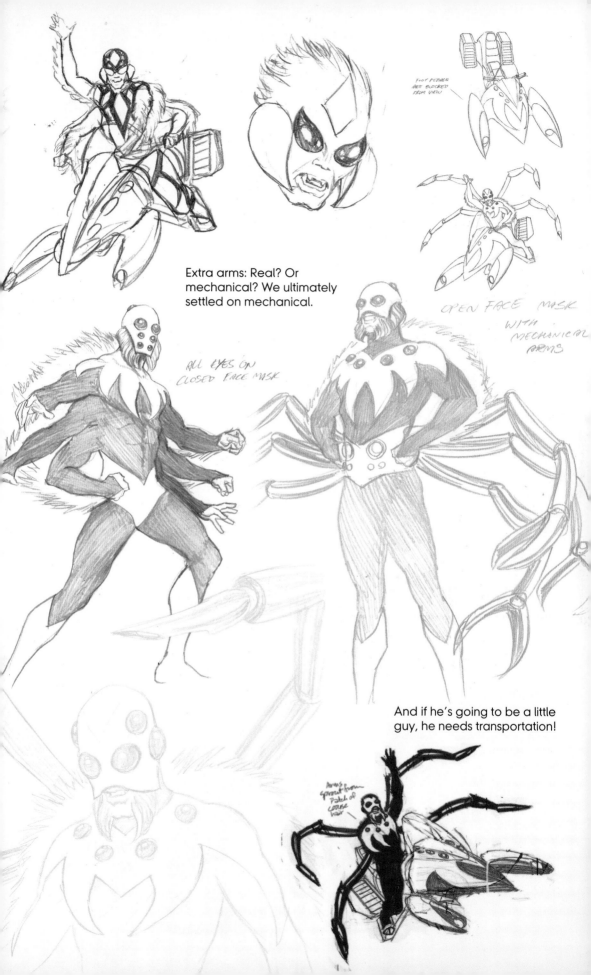

Extra arms: Real? Or mechanical? We ultimately settled on mechanical.

ALL EYES ON CLOSED FACE MASK

OPEN FACE MASK WITH MECHANICAL ARMS

FOOT PEDALS ARE BLOCKED FROM VIEW

And if he's going to be a little guy, he needs transportation!

Arms sprout from patch of coarse hair

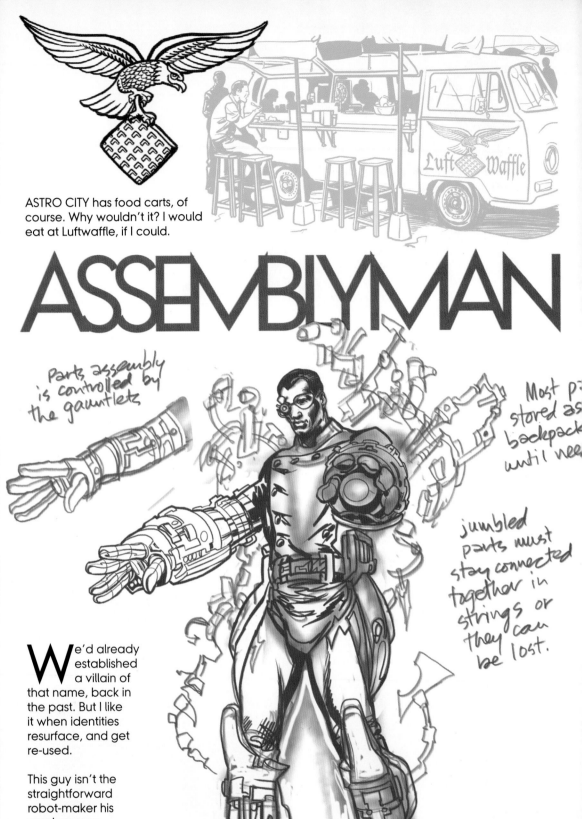

ASTRO CITY has food carts, of course. Why wouldn't it? I would eat at Luftwaffle, if I could.

ASSEMBLYMAN

Parts assembly is controlled by the gauntlets

Most p= stored as backpack until nee=

jumbled parts must stay connected together in strings or they can be lost.

We'd already established a villain of that name, back in the past. But I like it when identities resurface, and get re-used.

This guy isn't the straightforward robot-maker his predecessor was, but he still "assembles" things.

"ASSEMBLYMAN"
AC vol 3 #3
4-5-11

How do you design a character who's got attitude and bluster, but who really doesn't have the chops to make it in the super-villain world?

He had to look good enough to be perceived as a threat when he first showed up, but when the tables get turned on him, the comedy has to work, too. So he needs to be, essentially, an imitation villain—looks good on the surface, but nothing beneath it.

Brent did a great job assembling a collection of "master-villain" clichés— the armor, the cloak, the goatee, the boots—that project the right flavor but don't really add up to anything specific. And the crowning touch, the oversized, glowing monocle, is both dramatic and slightly foolish, a nice sign that this guy is perhaps playing dress-up. Serving the outfit rather than the outfit serving him.

Blaze of white widow's peak in dark grey blue hair

Floating power monocle yellow-green energy, also seen in elbow lenses

'Major Domo'
AC v3_4
7-30-13

MAJORDOMO

time piece

valence in front under skirt

Dame Progress 'Gyrocopter Pack' 6-24-13 ACV3_S

Hang skirt from 'ischium' — hip blast protection

No bare leg.

"DAME PROGRESS. 4-22-10 (ACSP:SA

↑ Rocket Ball

Electricity Ball

DAME PROGRESS

We saw the above sketch last volume, but here it is with Brent's additions, as we refined our approach.

She's not a superhero—she predates the concept, really—so we tried to emphasize her as a steampunk "scientific adventurer."

Gotta have the gadgetry and the vehicles, and they need to feel like it's 1903…

MISTER CAKEWALK

We pulled a lot of "cakewalk" imagery from the right time period, and Alex set out to abstract them down into something simple and bold, something that would look a bit more than human. Not a man dressed to cakewalk, but a man who embodied it.

THE CAKEWALKER

Complicating this was that we wanted him to look dapper but not minstrel-y— the cakewalk was an African-American thing, co-opted into racist imagery by minstrel shows, and we wanted to stay on the right side of it.

Plus, Mr. Cakewalk has secrets we can't reveal yet, that nonetheless had to be designed in…

Mobster Thatcher Jerome and wife Rachel...

THE ORE MASTER

Some characters are nice and blunt and simple. He's made of raw metal and he's violent! Boom, done. But Brent still had to bring that through on the page, combining metal and raw ore and a molten core...

...creating an arresting and powerful visual.

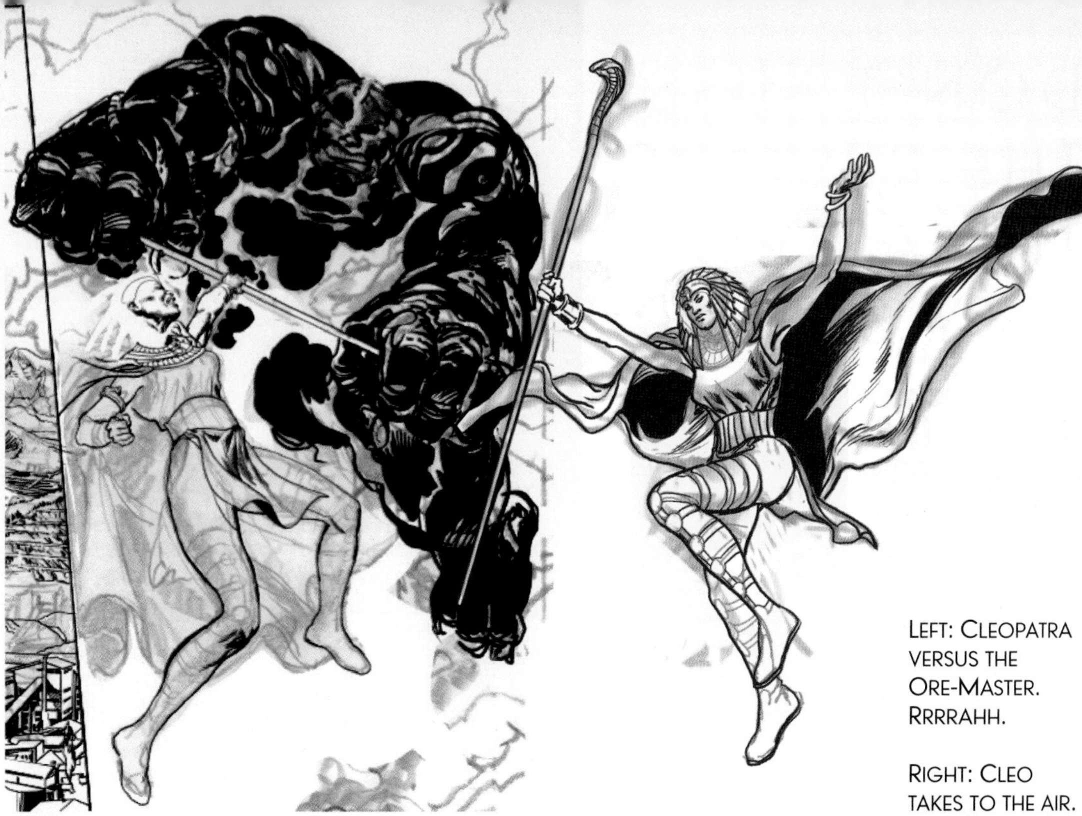

LEFT: CLEOPATRA VERSUS THE ORE-MASTER. RRRRAHH.

RIGHT: CLEO TAKES TO THE AIR.

BOX O' SORNA

Easy enough to describe a hi-tech alien carrying case, but making sure it looks right sometimes requires making a model.

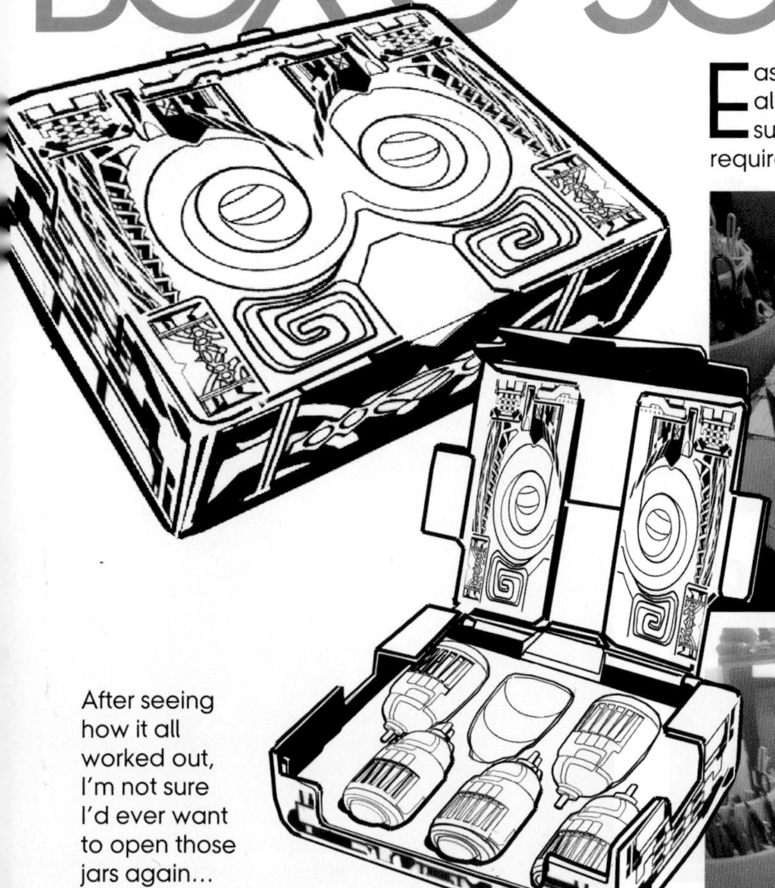

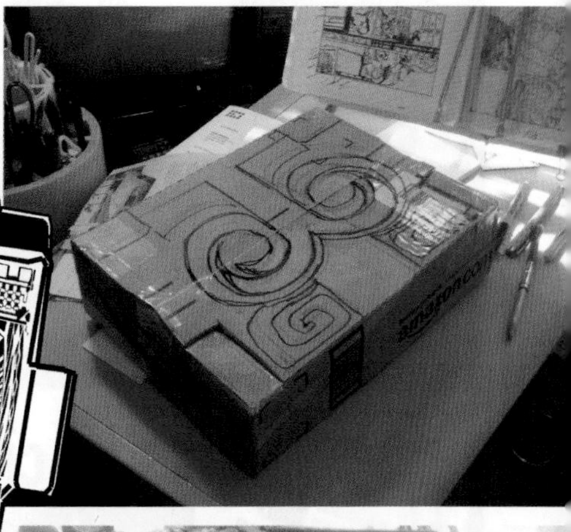

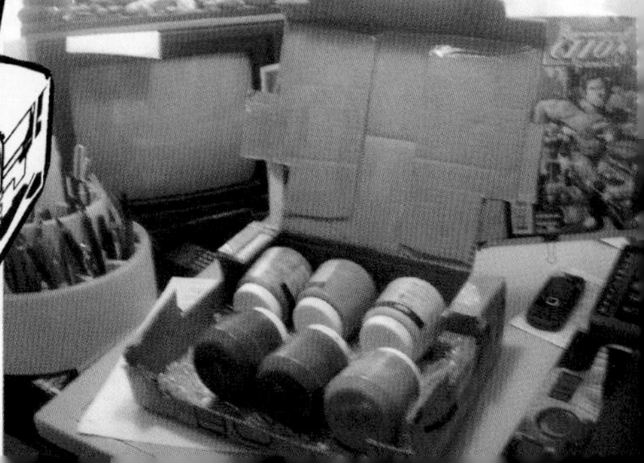

After seeing how it all worked out, I'm not sure I'd ever want to open those jars again...

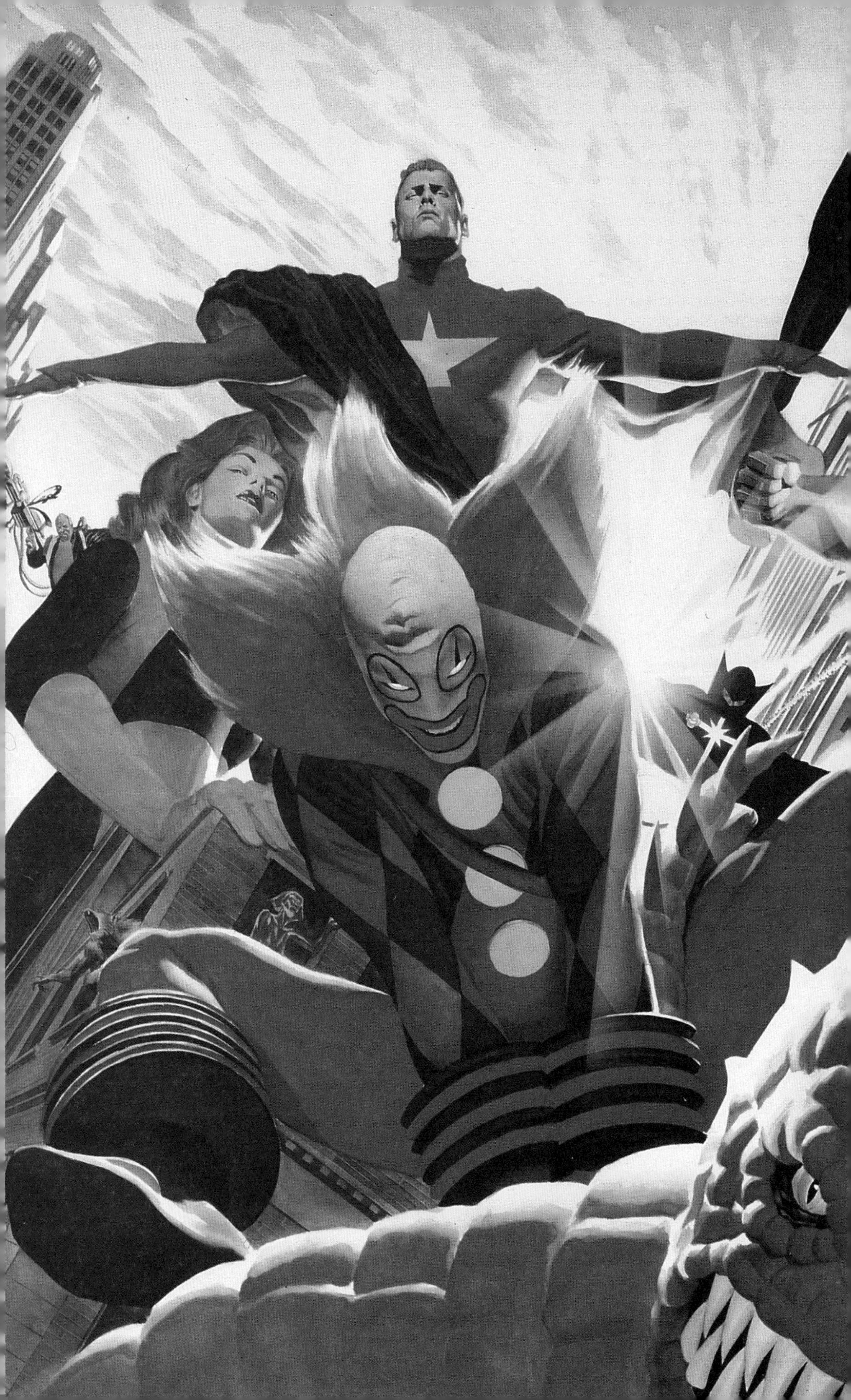